Cognitive Confusions
Dreams, Delusions and Illusions in
Early Modern European Culture

LEGENDA

LEGENDA is the Modern Humanities Research Association's book imprint for new research in the Humanities. Founded in 1995 by Malcolm Bowie and others within the University of Oxford, Legenda has always been a collaborative publishing enterprise, directly governed by scholars. The Modern Humanities Research Association (MHRA) joined this collaboration in 1998, became half-owner in 2004, in partnership with Maney Publishing and then Routledge, and has since 2016 been sole owner. Titles range from medieval texts to contemporary cinema and form a widely comparative view of the modern humanities, including works on Arabic, Catalan, English, French, German, Greek, Italian, Portuguese, Russian, Spanish, and Yiddish literature. Editorial boards and committees of more than 60 leading academic specialists work in collaboration with bodies such as the Society for French Studies, the British Comparative Literature Association and the Association of Hispanists of Great Britain & Ireland.

The MHRA encourages and promotes advanced study and research in the field of the modern humanities, especially modern European languages and literature, including English, and also cinema. It aims to break down the barriers between scholars working in different disciplines and to maintain the unity of humanistic scholarship. The Association fulfils this purpose through the publication of journals, bibliographies, monographs, critical editions, and the MHRA Style Guide, and by making grants in support of research. Membership is open to all who work in the Humanities, whether independent or in a University post, and the participation of younger colleagues entering the field is especially welcomed.

ALSO PUBLISHED BY THE ASSOCIATION

Critical Texts
Tudor and Stuart Translations • *New Translations* • *European Translations*
MHRA Library of Medieval Welsh Literature

MHRA Bibliographies
Publications of the Modern Humanities Research Association

The Annual Bibliography of English Language & Literature
Austrian Studies
Modern Language Review
Portuguese Studies
The Slavonic and East European Review
Working Papers in the Humanities
The Yearbook of English Studies

www.mhra.org.uk
www.legendabooks.com

EDITORIAL BOARD

Chair: Professor Colin Davis, Royal Holloway, University of London
For *Germanic Literatures*: Ritchie Robertson (University of Oxford)
For *Italian Perspectives*: Simon Gilson (University of Warwick)
For *Moving Image*: Emma Wilson (University of Cambridge)
For *Research Monographs in French Studies*:
Diana Knight (University of Nottingham)
For *Selected Essays*: Susan Harrow (University of Bristol)
For *Studies in Comparative Literature*: Duncan Large
(British Centre for Literary Translation, University of East Anglia)
For *Studies in Hispanic and Lusophone Cultures*:
Trevor Dadson (Queen Mary, University of London)
For *Studies in Yiddish*: Gennady Estraikh (New York University)
For *Transcript*: Matthew Reynolds (University of Oxford)

Managing Editor
Dr Graham Nelson
41 Wellington Square, Oxford OX1 2JF, UK

www.legendabooks.com

Cognitive Confusions

*Dreams, Delusions and Illusions in
Early Modern European Culture*

Edited by
Ita Mac Carthy, Kirsti Sellevold and Olivia Smith

Modern Humanities Research Association
2016

Published by Legenda
an imprint of the Modern Humanities Research Association
Salisbury House, Station Road, Cambridge CB1 2LA

ISBN 978-1-909662-99-5 (HB)
ISBN 978-1-78188-342-6 (PB)

First published 2016

All rights reserved. No part of this publication may be reproduced or disseminated or transmitted in any form or by any means, electronic, mechanical, photocopying, recording or otherwise, or stored in any retrieval system, or otherwise used in any manner whatsoever without written permission of the copyright owner, except in accordance with the provisions of the Copyright, Designs and Patents Act 1988, or under the terms of a licence permitting restricted copying issued in the UK by the Copyright Licensing Agency Ltd, Saffron House, 6–10 Kirby Street, London EC1N 8TS, England, or in the USA by the Copyright Clearance Center, 222 Rosewood Drive, Danvers MA 01923. Application for the written permission of the copyright owner to reproduce any part of this publication must be made by email to legenda@mhra.org.uk.

Disclaimer: Statements of fact and opinion contained in this book are those of the author and not of the editors or the Modern Humanities Research Association. The publisher makes no representation, express or implied, in respect of the accuracy of the material in this book and cannot accept any legal responsibility or liability for any errors or omissions that may be made.

Trademark notice: Product or corporate names may be trademarks or registered trademarks, and are used only for identification and explanation without intent to infringe.

© Modern Humanities Research Association 2016

Copy-Editor: Dr Anna J. Davies

CONTENTS

❖

	Preface	ix
	Introduction TERENCE CAVE	1
1	Reverse Othello Syndrome by Another Name: Ariosto's Deluded Hero ITA MAC CARTHY	15
2	What Makes a Belief Delusional? LISA BORTOLOTTI, RACHEL GUNN, EMA SULLIVAN-BISSETT	37
3	Cognition, Relevance and Early Modern Ghosts TIMOTHY CHESTERS	53
4	A World Within: The Devil, Delusions and Early Modern Cognition THIBAUT MAUS DE ROLLEY	71
5	Delusion, Drowsiness and Discernment: Degrees of Awareness in Renaissance Dream Activity GUIDO GIGLIONI	89
6	Others' Dreams, Others' Minds in Descartes's *Meditations* JAMES HELGESON	111
7	Fiction, Vision, Dream, Revelation: D'Aubigné's *Tragiques* and the Ocean episode KATHRYN BANKS	125
8	'Imagine this Place': Doni's Utopian Dream KIRSTI SELLEVOLD	147
9	Unstill Life: the Uses of Illusion in Hans Holbein's *The Ambassadors* OLIVIA SMITH	163
	Index	180

PREFACE

How do humans distinguish between factual and counterfactual scenarios? When do rational thoughts and beliefs become delusions and illusions and why do we often fail to monitor the boundaries between different forms of cognitive activity? Where do dreams fit into our lived experience of the world and what role do they have, if any, in our strategies and procedures for thinking about it? These are pressing questions for the twenty-first century, but they troubled early modern Europeans no less. Like the twenty-first century, the early modern period was a time of rapid cultural transformation, accompanied by a marked degree of turbulence. Powerful new technologies were developed, fissures opened up in long-established forms of thought and social organization, demographic expansion and territorial displacement brought both conflict and fresh openings. New ways of living brought new ways of thinking about and with the world.

Cognitive Confusions: Dreams, Delusions and Illusions in Early Modern European Culture is one of the first studies to bring the enriched understandings of cognition afforded by present-day research to bear on an exploration of how writers, thinkers and artists thought about and with the world in early modern Europe. From a cognitively inflected perspective, it investigates afresh the early modern fascination with the imagination and its potentially supernatural scope; its reflections on the uncertain boundary between wisdom and folly or madness; its preoccupation with prophetic and apocalyptic dreams and visions; its engagement with magic (especially diabolic illusion and delusion); and its inventive appropriation of new technologies of vision, together with an enhanced understanding of optical illusion.

Our book is a product of the project 'Literature as an Object of Knowledge' which was established and directed by Professor Terence Cave after he won the International Balzan Foundation Prize for 'Literature since 1500' in 2009. Based at St John's College, Oxford, the project was organized along two complementary lines, a historical and a cognitive one, and involved three intensive years of collaboration between literary scholars and an interdisciplinary group of experts from cognitive science, psychology, philosophy, communication theory, and the creative arts. As a group, we read and evaluated new cognitive methodologies, but we also worked separately on early modern texts, staying faithful to the questions that they generate. Key questions were 'how does literature function as a vehicle for thought?' and 'how do we think with literature?' This book represents a response to those questions.[1]

Most of the essays published here began as presentations at two Balzan project workshops, the first at St John's College, Oxford, on 7 June 2013 (organized by Kirsti Sellevold and Olivia Smith) and the second at Birmingham on 3–4 April 2014 (organized by Ita Mac Carthy). A preliminary discussion of delusions at Oxford was developed into a broader theme a year later in Birmingham, all the while supplemented and nourished by a rich programme of regular seminars, reading groups and meetings of the Balzan work group. The editors would like to take this opportunity to thank the Balzan work group in general and the contributors to the Oxford 2013 and Birmingham 2014 workshops in particular. The project was characterized by an open-minded collegiality, which we hope is reflected in the chapters that follow, and for which we are very grateful.

From 2010–13 Ita Mac Carthy was Balzan Research Lecturer, Kirsti Sellevold was Associate Researcher, and Olivia Smith was Postdoctoral Research Fellow within the project. Kathryn Banks, Tim Chesters, and James Helgeson were also Balzan Research Lecturers. We are grateful to the Balzan Foundation and St John's College, Oxford, for generous funding and support, and the University of Birmingham for hosting the 2014 workshop. We would also like to extend our thanks to Terence Cave, whose vision and expertise sets an example for the kind of productive literary engagement that we have endeavoured to undertake here.

★ ★ ★ ★ ★

The sequence in which the contributions are arranged follows neither a necessary nor a strictly logical order. However, it is by no means arbitrary. The book opens (Mac Carthy) with a celebrated literary example of what we would call a delusion in Ariosto's *Orlando Furioso*. It develops an argument which draws on modern psychological and cognitive accounts of delusion, while maintaining a firm connection between the historical, the fictional and the cognitive. It forms a diptych with the following chapter, in which philosophers working on the frontier between philosophy and psychology (Bortolotti et al.) use case histories to discuss various kinds of delusional states and the relation between such states and other fixed beliefs not usually regarded as delusional. Chapter 3 (Chesters) further explores the question of counterintuitive beliefs (in particular, belief in ghosts) with the help of the notion of a 'limited counterintuitive violation' proposed by Pascal Boyer and of perspectives from relevance theory. It shares common ground with Chapter 4 (Maus de Rolley), where the focus is on early modern theories of the ways in which demons manipulate the mind. This chapter examines in particular the use of spatial metaphors in demonological discussions of delusions, using research on cognitive linguistics and philosophy of mind to shed new light on the early modern conceptualization of cognitive processes. Chapter 5 (Giglioni) places dreams and dreaming at the centre of attention. However, since dreams in the early modern period (and indeed in many cultures) are associated with supernatural visions and prophecy, it comprises a rich nexus of themes relevant to the volume as a whole. It also cites a wealth of materials from the history of ideas, encompassing the Platonist traditions of late Antiquity and the Renaissance, together with later figures such as Cardano and Sanchez who offer alternative views on dreams and their status. Its preoccupation with philosophical writing makes it a good (though also contrasting) companion for Chapter 6 (Helgeson), which is focused both on a canonic philosopher and on dreaming. The reference in this chapter to Descartes's 'demon' argument also associates it with the foregoing group. Chapter 7 (Banks) takes up the themes of prophecy and dreaming which are developed in Giglioni, but in the context of a literary work which interweaves several different cognitive and epistemic modes. This complex instance is analysed with the help of the cognitive anthropology and psychology of Cosmides and Tooby on the one hand and some aspects of relevance theory on the other. Themes of fictional belief and of dreaming reappear in chapter 8 (Sellevold). The approach adopted in this chapter combines relevance theory with the notion of stipulated or shared pretence (Kendall Walton, Harris, Schaeffer). That notion is developed in turn in chapter 9 (Smith), which draws additionally on Huizinga's classic *Homo ludens*. At the same time, the choice of a painting rather than a literary text as the focus of the chapter, together with literary texts used as secondary examples, provides (literally, as it were) a different angle of perception for the themes of illusion and cognitive confusion explored by the volume as a whole.

Note to the Preface

1. Those wishing to read more about cognitive approaches to literature should see his *Thinking With Literature: Towards a Cognitive Criticism* (Oxford: Oxford University Press, 2016). Other Balzan-funded publications on related topics include Marco Caracciolo and Karin Kukkonen, eds, 'Second-Generation Cognitive Approaches to Literature', *Style* 48.3 (2014), Special Issue; and Terence Cave, Karin Kukkonen and Olivia Smith, eds, 'Reading Literature Cognitively', *Paragraph*, 37.1 (2014), Special Issue.

INTRODUCTION

Terence Cave

> fatendum est humanam vitam circa res particulares
> saepe erroribus esse obnoxiam
> [it must be admitted that human life, in respect of particular
> things, is often fraught with errors]
>
> RENÉ DESCARTES[1]

The nine contributions to this volume address texts from a remarkably broad range of genres and sub-genres: philosophical treatises from several traditions (Platonist, Aristotelian, Democritan, Cartesian), theology, dialogues, ghost-stories offered as veridical, writings on the devil and on witches, apocalyptic visions, romance fictions, utopian fictions, dream narratives, classical epic and mythology, modern clinical case-studies, lyric and narrative verse, not to mention a painting celebrated for the perceptual trick it plays. They also deploy an almost equally broad range of methodological instruments: history of ideas, historical contextualization, philosophical analysis, literary analysis, linguistic analysis, psychological experiment and reasoning, together with a whole series of approaches derived from current cognitive research across the disciplines. Yet there is a single focus. At every point, this book explores the ways in which a given culture seeks to calibrate, control, and exploit the alarmingly inventive powers of human cognition. Promiscuity — the ability to improvise, to play games (often deadly serious ones) with the materials our perceptual systems offer to us, to imagine alternatives and counterfactuals, to hold beliefs that many might regard as irrational — is after all the distinctive feature of the human cognitive niche. The early modern period, subject as it is to rapid shifts of cultural ecology at every level (political, social, ideological, economic, geophysical), exhibits in remarkably complex and various ways the tensions and dissonances, the intuitions, insights and confusions that these capacities afford.

The object of this Introduction will be to provide an initial frame for the volume, focusing on certain of its methodological avenues of approach within a broadly cognitive perspective. I shall not provide summaries of the different chapters, follow their arguments in detail, or restrict myself to the materials and arguments they offer, although of course my reading of those materials and arguments will provide the direction and momentum of my remarks. Nor shall I offer a systematic review of the various methodological strategies used by the contributors; they make their assumptions and arguments sufficiently explicit within the context of their chosen set of materials. But I do need to say what is meant by a 'cognitive perspective' as the frame within which, in their different ways, all the contributions fall. I use the word 'cognition' here, not in the restricted sense that some dictionaries still specify (cognition *as opposed to* perception, emotion, imagination, or sensorimotor response), but rather as referring to the complete set of biologically based strategies and procedures by means of which humans think in and with the world. It designates above all the *focus* of everything the organism does actively to promote its survival and welfare in a given environment: cognition is alertness, the act of attending to the world and its demands. A cognitive approach to literature is thus one that regards literature as an instrument to think with, which includes thinking about literature as well as considering the objects and modes of thought that literary works individually afford.[2]

I have made the assumption throughout that literature plays a central role in the nexus of early modern reflections and imaginative representations gathered together in this book. I make it for reasons that will shortly become plain, but it is important to say from the outset that, in order to provide a sufficiently rich account of these issues, one cannot restrict oneself to works that fall unequivocally into the category 'literature' as it is understood nowadays. One of the distinctive features of the early modern archive is the degree to which its discourses are mixed, plural, generically fluid. Some of the contributors focus on what are broadly regarded as philosophical texts (the writings of Marsilio Ficino, or Girolamo Cardano, or René Descartes, to name only the most obvious examples). Agrippa d'Aubigné's *Les Tragiques* is an epic poem of a kind, but it is also an affect-driven history and a visionary scripture. Erasmus's *Praise of Folly* and Thomas More's *Utopia* both defy the presumed boundary between imaginative literature and theological, philosophical or political thought, and their successors explore this in-between terrain with remarkable exuberance. Montaigne's *Essais*, likewise, are notoriously resistant to generic classification: in order to 'place' them, in fact, it became necessary to invent a new genre, the 'essay'.[3]

It is a symptom of the highly fluid and exploratory nature of early modern writing, its love of the paradoxical and the counterfactual, that it returns over and over again to instances of cognitive confusion. The fascination with illusion, whether perceptual or ontological, goes deep, as does the intensive reflection on dreams, on prophetic modes of vision, and on mental aberration. It is to these modes of cognitive confusion and their presumed family likenesses that I now turn.

Illusions, delusions, dreams

Human cognition is in general fit for purpose; otherwise it wouldn't have survived the attrition of millions of years of evolution. Yet it is always approximate, prone to errors and confusions, and at times dangerously close to irreversible malfunction. The approximations and errors are already apparent at the level of immediate perception. The oar that seems to bend in the stream, the mirage that offers false hope in the desert, the distortions of vision, hearing and taste that can arise when the body is sick — all these examples are well known, and have been used, notably by sceptical philosophers from antiquity to modern times, to demonstrate the unreliability of our engagement with the physical world, and thence with the epistemological evidence on which our conceptual knowledge is based. Nowadays, cognitive psychologists like to point out the discrepancies between common beliefs about perception and the way the perceptual system actually works.[4] In addition to the many kinds of optical illusion which are easy to demonstrate, experiments that reveal phenomena such as 'change blindness' (the failure to notice a significant change in what is perceived because that feature is not salient at the moment of change) are now routinely adduced to counter the view that the eye is like a camera, and that we can form and maintain clear and coherent mental 'pictures' of the world. Some go so far as to suggest that all perceptual (and a fortiori imaginative) experience is a 'grand illusion', that what we think we see is 'only' a shifting model composed by the brain from the flow of partial, and always inadequate, perceptual fragments. The outer reaches of this type of argument rejoin the perennial philosophical argument about the metaphysical and epistemological status of the material world. Plato's famous myth of the cave was designed to persuade us that we will remain trapped in a world of illusions unless we learn to make the difficult ascent to the realm of higher forms, and such views were widely available in the early modern period (see Giglioni, this volume, on dreams as a way in which the soul can achieve freedom from the constraints of the body).

When we speak of 'illusion', we generally mean a cognitive error which is assumed to be correctable once the source of the error has been disclosed. If a conjurer invited you to go up on the stage and check her equipment (which she would normally be careful not to do), you would find that the assistant she appeared to have sawn in half is actually two people in separate boxes. In some cases, the perceptual error is hard to remove: in many common examples of optical illusion, the eye continues to 'see' the false image even after the subject has been convinced of its falsity. You are unlikely, however, to think that this misprision is a symptom of some psychotic state, still less that something supernatural is involved in such cases. On the other hand, your illusion may well have been deliberately provoked, whether with benign or malevolent intent. The Latin *illudere* carries the notion of play, but also of playing with someone, playing *on* them; *illusio* can mean a kind of mockery, making a fool of someone. In that sense, music-hall conjurers and Shakespeare's Iago have a good deal in common. And from Iago's devilry, it is only a short step to the common early modern belief that such tricks are liable to be the work of a malevolent force, a demon or devil.

'Delusion' shares with 'illusion' the etymological sense of 'play', but the Latin prefix 'de-' suggests *aberration*, a state of profound deception that is difficult if not impossible to reverse. This indeed is the everyday modern sense: the verb can be used to connote contempt, as in phrases such as 'the poor deluded fool', and the noun can be used to cover various states of mind that seem committed to persistent irrationality. Whereas 'illusion' is not a clinical term, 'delusion' is, although its definition is still controversial. Mac Carthy (this volume) cites the classic definition offered by Karl Jaspers (a false belief held with certainty and resistant to counter-argument), while remarking that modern clinical definitions have dropped the notion of 'falsity'. Central to the notion of delusion is the implication of cognitive inflexibility, a pattern of thought and behaviour that remains fixed regardless of changing contexts or circumstances. It typically appears, therefore, as a kind of imprisonment: like the magic domains of the Lorelei, the Snow Queen, or Hotel California,[5] it is a place where you are held as under a spell and from which you cannot escape. Since Bortolotti (this volume) provides a lucid and persuasive account of clinical delusion, I shall not elaborate further here, except to note the importance of her central hypothesis, namely that delusional states cannot be rigorously separated from other kinds of fixed belief, such as strongly held religious beliefs, which may to unbelievers appear to be 'irrational'. Cognitive confusions, like most other aspects of human cognition, are best understood as constituting a continuum or spectrum, where certain apparently distinct states may be shown to have uncertain or porous borders. That way of looking at the questions raised by the volume is amply supported by the early modern examples that its contributors put forward. Even though the texts themselves are for the most part not ones that are preoccupied with mental states as an object of specifically medical concern, the analyses of the supposed irruption of diabolic agency in human behaviour (witchcraft and other such practices) could be regarded as in some sense analogous to modern psychological and psychoanalytic enquiry, not least in their attempts to establish a firm diagnostic frame of reference. What is referred to by early modern theologians as 'discernment' (Giglioni, this volume; similar terms are cited by Maus de Rolley) — recognizing a demonic presence beneath an angelic disguise — is precisely such a diagnostic frame.

Where dreams and dreaming fit into the picture is much harder to pin down. Virtually everyone has dreams, and (as early modern oneirologists noted), animals can have them too. Their status as an activity of the mind that appears to be disconnected from everyday perceptual and cognitive engagements with the world implies an absence of control, and thus a kind of freedom: in dreams you can fly, commit crimes with impunity, encounter the dead, have a quite concrete experience of places and things that don't exist. Seeking to undo the popular view that dreams are always significant, that they demand and require interpretation, modern psychologists have suggested that they are simply the accidental by-product of the brain's self-monitoring or self-repair activities during sleep; at the Birmingham workshop,[6] Philip Gerrans went so far as to suggest that they are merely a kind of 'screen-saver', wallpaper that the brain affords while in default or resting mode. Yet the conviction that something more serious is going on in most of the dreams one remembers is hard to evacuate, and the industry of dream interpretation, even now that the heyday of Freudian and Jungian psychology is over, continues unabated. Early modern writers, like their classical and medieval precursors, take for granted that dreams are significant, and more specifically that they have a prophetic function (see Giglioni and Banks, this volume): the assumption seems to be that, since what happens in dreams doesn't correspond to any past or present experience of the world, it must adumbrate a future state of affairs.

To this function we need to add another: the dream affords a frame for allegorical narrative, whether in the form of a whole work (such as the medieval French *Roman de la Rose* or the fifteenth-century *Hypnerotomachia Poliphilii* attributed to

Francesco Colonna) or as a framed episode — Orlando's dream as discussed by Mac Carthy (this volume) is a classic case, but so is the utopian dream-world evoked by the Wise Man in Doni's *I Mondi* (Sellevold, this volume). Via this path, we move towards the attribution of dreams to characters within a fictional narrative. Such dream narratives — no less common in modern fictions than in earlier ones — are clearly invented by wide-awake authors, and very seldom succeed in conveying the radically strange feeling of actual dreams. They more often seem designed to suggest relevant psychological perspectives on the characters concerned, their fears, desires, and preoccupations. They may also act as a kind of prolepsis, intimating future events in the story, or at least drawing the reader's attention to likely plot development; in such cases, their function is the secular and fictional equivalent of prophetic dreaming.

Even if these invented dreams can tell us little about actual dreaming, the fact that the dream is used as a point of reference across a wide historical and cultural spectrum is surely of interest: it tells us something about the way cognition functions. Dreaming is, as Lakoff and Johnson might say, one of the metaphors we live by;[7] or perhaps it would be better to say that, like the ghost or the demon, it is one of the pan-human experiences we think with. Those strangely unintentional, ungoverned activities of the mind during sleep, remembered at best as fading fragments, provide an off-limits marker for what the mind can do when it is 'decoupled' from immediate in-the-world experience. It is neither illusion nor delusion, nor is it in itself a fiction; yet it clearly belongs to the spectrum of cognitive confusions, given that so many of the examples proposed in this volume combine dreaming with other modes of cognitive aberration or transcendence *as if that combination went without saying.*

Cognitive methodologies 1: the play of the imagination

One way of approaching this confluent set of mental modes, with their attendant flavours and colours and intimations of significance, is to see it as the cultural outgrowth of the capacity that, arguably, is fundamental to and distinctive of human thought as such. This is the ability, while the mind is not utterly preoccupied by the needs and pressures of the moment, to entertain alternative representations of the world, and not only to entertain them, but to improvise with them, *play* with them. As Smith (this volume) reminds us, the currently neglected *Homo ludens* (1938) of Johan Huizinga, who was also a biographer of Erasmus, presents an argument for the central role of imaginative play in human cognition that anticipates in many respects the views of cognitive scientists and philosophers of our generation such as Kendall Walton, Jean-Marie Schaeffer, Paul Harris and Ilona Roth.[8] The word 'play' can be misleading if it is taken to connote a marginal, frivolous or child-like activity. On the contrary, what we are speaking of here includes the ability to retrieve and compare memories, to predict future possibilities, and to imagine counterfactuals (what things might have been in different circumstances, what went wrong and what might be done to correct the error in a future recurrence of the same situation). Without such an ability and the complex additional neural networks that it implies, hominins could not successfully have moved out across the world, encountering and adapting to a bewildering variety of different natural environments and climates in a remarkably short time (a few tens of thousands of years). Of course the other capacity which is required in order for these cognitive powers to be activated, deployed and communicated is a rich syntactical language, with its tenses, conditional and subjunctive moods, its modalizing expressions and its procedurals.[9] This is not the place to explore the questions that then arise, such as the evolutionary priority of one or the other (it seems likely that they evolved simultaneously by some feedback process), but the fact that several of the contributions in this volume explore the linguistic underpinnings of Renaissance imaginings is testimony in itself to the synergy between language and the imagination.

The extraordinary possibilities afforded by this opening window in the neurology of the hominin brain come, however, at a price. First of all, there is the problem that the slower, reflective mode of thought that is required for counterfactual or imaginative thinking will inhibit the built-in streamlined systems of fast reaction that are common to all living creatures.[10] Secondly, cognitive fluidity can lead to cognitive dissonance, an unresolved conflict between different perceived representations, beliefs, or goals. And thirdly, where the brain fails adequately to map or tag the multiple scenarios it can imagine, the way is open for cognitive confusions of the worst kind, the kind that are destructive both for the individual and for the social group or family to which that individual belongs. This is the area where we begin to speak of 'madness', 'delusion' in a clinical sense, or other forms of mental breakdown such as schizophrenia. The ability to make the required distinctions, to know intuitively what is 'real' and what is 'imagined', what is an aberrant fantasy or delusion and what is a productive counterfactual representation, is fundamental to human cognition and must have evolved alongside the imagination,[11] but precisely because it is biologically evolved, it is approximate, imperfect. If the tags slip or the decoupling mechanism fails to operate correctly (see Banks, Mac Carthy, this volume), cognitive confusion is liable to ensue.[12]

Cognitive methodologies 2: affordances and beliefs

The early modern period is extraordinarily rich in imaginative representations of cognitive phenomena. From Ficino, Erasmus and More to Montaigne and Descartes, from Ariosto and Rabelais to Shakespeare and Cervantes, the problems and paradoxes of cognition are made salient in remarkably inventive ways. At the same time, the development of far-reaching perceptual affordances that have an immediate cognitive impact (optical instruments, experiments in perspective, anatomy and autopsy) prompts new kinds of engagement with the world and radically revised interpretations of nature. It is therefore not surprising that current cognitive methodologies have begun to demonstrate their value in the understanding of early modern culture. Indeed, these ventures were anticipated by a number of remarkable studies that include Walter Kaiser's *Praisers of Folly*, Rosalie Colie's *Paradoxia epidemica*, Ann Moss's *Printed Commonplace Books*, and — crucially for this volume — Stuart Clark's ground-breaking works on early modern demonology and visual perception.[13] Clark's powerfully argued thesis that supernatural creatures like demons are not irrational — still less 'primitive' — imaginings but instruments for thinking with (cited by Giglioni and Maus de Rolley) is both historically located and fundamentally anthropological. It goes hand in hand with his study of optical instruments in relation to forms of early modern thought (cited by Smith). Both enquiries presuppose the seriousness and relevance of a given culture's cognitive affordances, that is to say the instrumentation, whether material, imaginative or conceptual, by means of which that culture constructs an understanding of human agency and comportment within their ecological constraints.[14] Religious and philosophical beliefs that appear exotic, bizarre, or downright absurd from the perspective of a different culture may, within their own culture, be efficient, 'fit for purpose'. Of course many do not survive the pressures of cultural evolution, which requires that efficiency be preserved; they fall away, or represent the view of a small group or even a single individual. Yet we should assume that those that offer themselves to our view because they have been conserved through an enduring textual tradition are robust, and profoundly anchored in the emotional, intellectual and material needs of the cultures in which they arose: such are the theories of dreaming cited by Giglioni, the early modern demonologies cited by Maus de Rolley, the 'true' ghost story cited by Chesters, the prophetic and visionary thought-world cited by Banks. At times, the intrinsic sense of relevance and consonance of a belief-system will shine out in the aesthetic expressions that it affords: Dante's *Divine Comedy* is a supreme example, but so is the Renaissance art that feeds on Florentine neoplatonism of the late fifteenth century.[15]

We come now to a major issue which links modern and early modern perspectives: the status of belief or beliefs. Bortolotti's amply supported argument that delusion is not a distinct category, ontologically or epistemologically separate from other forms of perceived 'irrationality', is valid, as we have seen, for the whole spectrum of cognitive errors and confusions considered in this volume. When Doni reverses the polarities of the opposition between wisdom and folly or madness (see Sellevold, this volume), he is exploiting the celebrated paradox of Erasmus's *Praise of Folly*, defying common opinion on what it is to be 'wise' (or rational), and adding some flourishes of his own on the question of belief in the domain of the imaginary. We shall return shortly to that question, but for the moment we need to consider a further methodological argument that impinges primarily on the vexed issue of religious belief.

In order to approach the ways in which it is possible to imagine the ghost as a potentially credible phenomenon, Timothy Chesters (this volume) draws on Pascal Boyer's concept of a 'limited counterintuitive violation'. Partial infractions of the natural or rational order may be discounted, if only temporarily, where other aspects of the phenomenon in question remain anchored within the everyday world as we know it. Boyer reminds us that apparent aberrations of belief may be regarded as local cross-currents in the vast groundswell of what is shared, of beliefs that are *not* violated. These might be regarded as 'automatic' beliefs, acquired in early childhood: beliefs arising from the constraints of gravity, the body's recurrent need for food and sleep, sexual desire, the way the sun or its absence, rain or its absence, create comforts or discomforts for humans and their world. Religions of all kinds take on the colour of these abiding ecologies, become affordances for understanding them. The violations are always specific and limited, however spectacular (a god who acts like a human but is capable of bringing a dead person back to life; a murdered god who himself rises from the dead). All of them espouse and inflect common features of human experience — sexual behaviours, familial, social and tribal lines of force, ways of handling the environment, ways of living with disease, pain and death. Humans think with gods, demons, fairies, world-souls, spiritual beings, shamans; in most respects, thinking with modern medical and dietary beliefs, with modern forms of political control, with money, gold and petroleum, with agriculture and eugenically crafted animals, is entirely consonant with the kinds of interpretative grasp that religious beliefs afford.[16]

In consequence, any methodology designed to handle such materials should be careful about labelling beliefs 'irrational' according to (say) a post-Enlightenment conception of secular rationality. Beliefs people commonly hold about time, about money, about the climate, about their personal agency, about their friends and loved ones, are often ill-founded and may seem irrational to others, but they are in a rough sense fit for their purposes (it would cost them more to abandon the beliefs than to continue to hold them). More generally, a functional cognitive methodology needs to presuppose that we think with the world as it is and as it more or less consistently seems to be. The notion of 'extended' or 'distributed' cognition can be helpful here, since it understands cognition not as a rather abstract activity inside the mind, operating on an external environment that is separate from it, but as a bodily function (the brain is after all just another bodily organ, although an unusually complex one) that has evolved together with its changing environments.[17] In other words, we think with the world according to the way cognition is distributed in a given ecology, and our cognitive scope is remarkably flexible for the reasons outlined earlier. To return to Stuart Clark, Pascal Boyer, and the example of ghosts: it's easy to believe a ghost-story, even if nowadays we want a supporting this-worldly explanation (Sarah Waters's *Affinity*). It's easy, even if you're not a Puritan or a Catholic, indeed any kind of Christian, to read Marilynne Robinson's *Gilead* trilogy or Bernanos's *Journal d'un curé de campagne*, because the theologies that are explicitly referred to in those fictions are consonant, consilient with the human stories; they can be read figuratively, as the Judaeo-Christian Bible itself is now often read. The counterintuitive violations are perceived as intimations of an alternative way of thinking that, given a slight shift of cultural conditioning, the reader could easily have absorbed and become attuned to herself.

This volume contains a spectacular example of the way in which beliefs can be instrumental as a mode of explanation, and at the same time of the shifts that beliefs and their uses are liable to undergo as culture changes. The example can be constructed by juxtaposing Maus de Rolley's (also Giglioni's) analysis of demonological thinking with Helgeson's account of Descartes's famous thought experiment known as the 'evil genius' or 'evil demon' hypothesis, adding as a further coordinate the belief in alien abduction included among Bortolotti's case-histories.[18] As seen in retrospect from the viewpoint of a more secular age, the demon who undermines all phenomenal experience, spreading a radical doubt even about the existence of our own bodies, is a fiction, a pure conceptual instrument: we don't need to believe in the existence of demons to get the point of the argument. But Descartes was writing at a time when the age of demonology was not yet over; one has to assume that belief in the existence of demons who could deceive humans with their tricks and illusions was still widespread and perfectly familiar in European culture. What we see here, then, is a belief-affordance (the demon as a real being, capable of explaining otherwise mysterious phenomena or forms of behaviour) which is on the cusp of a shift towards a more secular conception while still preserving some of its praeternatural associations. One might say, adapting Boyer's model, that the counterintuitive violation has with Descartes shrunk until it is *potentially* (but not quite yet) no violation at all.

A similar overarching point can be made in relation to dreams as understood on the one hand by fifteenth- and sixteenth-century thinkers and on the other by Descartes. In the *Olympica*, a text posthumously revised in someone else's paraphrase, Descartes appears to assign to dreams a symbolic and indeed prophetic role in the inauguration of a whole philosophy, a move consonant with the strategies of an earlier period as described by Giglioni and others. Yet that philosophy has itself, retrospectively, been assigned an inaugural role in the development of a *rationalizing* Western philosophy. Therewith the dream becomes a new kind of affordance, shaped by the instrument of thought it allows to emerge. It is as if the capacity to construct a space in which the rational can have the untrammelled freedom to unfold required the irreducible mode of decoupling that only dreams can make possible. *Homo ludens* is about to embark on a new way of playing the great cognitive game.

How to handle cognitive confusions the literary way

When Montaigne asserts that all examples, whether or not they are fictional, count as valid materials for the understanding of potential human behaviour (see Chesters, p. 67), his inclusive gesture is clearly made for the sake of literature (or what he here calls 'fable'). It also sweeps in counterfactuals of all kinds, including what we would call thought experiments of the kind conducted by Descartes and many later philosophers, and it thus privileges imaginative discourse: the essay in question is called 'On the Power of the Imagination'. Although Montaigne is talking in that essay about the cognitive errors and confusions over which the imagination presides rather than the creative or 'Romantic' imagination, his work as a whole testifies to his ability to range across a number of problematic epistemic areas and topics while keeping his perspective flexible. The flexibility works at several levels, but one of the most critical is that of the articulation of the sentence, the use of delicately manipulated micro-tagging in the form of procedural and modalizing expressions.[19]

In that respect, and many others, Montaigne's open imaginative spectrum is distinct from the spectrum of beliefs that Bortolotti proposes. Beliefs are commonly regarded as being harder to negotiate: believing that someone loves you, as Ariosto's

Orlando does, despite all evidence to the contrary, or believing in the existence of a god together with accompanying supernatural beings and powers, may be porous at the edges, or subject to a dramatic collapse, but they have a hard epistemic core capable of resisting a good deal of opposition from the material and social worlds (and will typically take little account of procedurals or modalizing expressions). Such is generally not the case with the category 'fiction', which is a marker of shared pretence, and narrative instances on the fiction–history spectrum also have their own internal set of tags (history, epic, romance, fantasy, myth, realist fiction and so on). Yet the literary canon offers some striking instances of characters — Don Quijote and Emma Bovary are the best known — whose immersion in fictional worlds would count by most criteria as a mode of delusion, and Mac Carthy convincingly demonstrates that Ariosto's Orlando partakes fictionally in several modes of delusion. Amorous obsession provides the outer frame for these, but they are also held in place by Orlando's status as a character who holds a false belief (or becomes confused) about the storyworld he belongs to. As Mac Carthy succinctly puts it, 'Orlando is a hero who got lost in a forest' (p. 21). He also fails, unlike Fiordispina, to distinguish between the fiction of a dream and the real world.

The question of how it is that some people (perhaps more than are prepared to admit it) can appear to 'believe in' the existence of fictional characters such as Grace Archer, or Sybil Crawley in the *Downton Abbey* series, is often raised. The fictional death of such popularly favoured characters (although not of ill-favoured ones) does indeed seem to be a challenge to shared pretence.[20] Yet the critical view that only naïve and confused consumers of fiction are deceived or deluded in this way is not only arrogant but hypocritical. One can be sad that a favoured character is out of the story and hope that the scriptwriters will find a way of bringing her back without being critically naïve; the appearance of naïvety here is just an effect of the way it's expressed. Such forms of cognitive dissonance are not only largely benign: they are also essential to the way the multiform imagination works. The local confusions it gives rise to are a price well worth paying for its benefits. Kathryn Banks shows on the one hand that d'Aubigné in his ambitious seven-book poem *Les Tragiques* is promiscuous with his generic and epistemic categories (myth, personification, Biblical authority, historical and prophetic vision), but on the other that he uses authorial tagging to keep at bay the cognitive confusions that might so easily arise as the reader gropes her way through this constantly shifting epistemic and cognitive landscape. Thus the remarkable dream vision of the fifth book is presented as a 'pause' before the Scriptural eschatologies that will follow, especially in Book Seven:

> Mais premier que d'entrer au prevoir, et descrire
> Tes derniers jugements, les arrests de ton ire:
> Il faut faire une pause, et finir ces discours
> Par une vision, qui couronne ces jours:
> L'esprit aiant encor congé par son extase
> De ne suivre escrivant du vulgaire la phrase.

[But before I enter into foreseeing, and describing / Your last judgements, the sentences of your wrath: / I must pause, and finish these discourses / With a vision, which crowns these days: / My soul again given leave by its ecstasy / Not to follow, when writing, the everyday mode of expression.]

The 'pause' afforded (and performed) by this intervention is a metaphor taken from the proprioceptive domain, the sense of release and rest as the body disengages, decouples, from one mode of cognitive activity before engaging in another. At the same time, it allows space for an explicit tag that calibrates the status of the ensuing dream narrative in relation to the eschatological mode that will follow. With this tag firmly established, the reader is invited into a new and defamiliarizing segment of the storyworld.

D'Aubigné uses a further metaphor here which is again by no means purely conventional: he speaks of 'entering' the domain of prediction or prophecy. What is at issue this time is how to enter a new and strange storyworld without losing one's way. The most famous instance of such a tagging sequence is provided by the opening of the *Divine Comedy*, which has some affinities to a computer game, but with a player who is featured in the game and learns how to play it with the help of a guide. The narrator finds himself deep in a forest, having lost his way, and encounters a series of threatening wild animals, which he has to avoid. This, it turns out, is the forest of sin, and the narrator will find his way out of it. Being lost, however, remains the condition of playing the game (as the example of Ariosto's Orlando, lost in a forest, also shows), and the sequence, of course, begins in Hell. As Descartes puts it, human life is *obnoxia erroribus*, prone to errors, wanderings, confusions.

Dante's storyworld famously embodies a whole imaginative theology, parallel to but not reducible to the formal theologies of its day. The capacity correctly to enter a Utopian storyworld and to imagine its laws from the inside can similarly provide a basis for new insights which would not be available if societies and their political frames were regarded simply as matters of real-world pragmatics, or alternatively if the reader believed that the story was an account of a real place. So we need to know from the outset that it is an extended counterfactual: like *The Praise of Folly*, the *Utopia* is framed as a paradox, which is also a kind of counterfactual, since it challenges common opinion on questions of political, ethical and cultural value.[21] Thomas More set up his stipulation of pretence with a skill and an exuberance that continue to fascinate twenty-first century readers, and More's epigones have done their best to equal if not outdo his achievement. François Rabelais's comic fictions feature a perpetual dialogue between wisdom and folly that includes the bravura sequence of chapters in the *Third Book* where Panurge delivers his paradoxical praise of debt; but they also feature explicit references to Utopia as the homeland of the giants, together with the utopian Abbey of Thélème.[22] The Italian humanist Anton Francesco Doni includes among the fictional 'worlds' of his *I Mondi* a version of Utopia, staging it as the object of a dialogue between a wise man (*Il Savio*) and a fool or madman (*Il Pazzo*).[23] As Sellevold shows, these latter change places (or rather characteristics) in bewildering fashion, as if the author wanted to outdo the tour de force of Erasmus himself, while also invoking the storyworld of More's *Utopia*. Something very interesting is going on here, an intensive appraisal of the modalities of belief. Oddly, it is the madman who most often calls in question the wise man's invitation to participate in the imagination of the utopian world he says they have both visited in a dream. And the Lucianic 'celestial dialogue' that constitutes the second part of Doni's chapter features as a parallel character Jupiter's sidekick Momus, whose epistemic vigilance[24] is set at an even higher level than the madman's. He denies that dreams can sometimes be true, and rejects Jupiter's claim to have descended to earth. His remark at this point, quoted by Sellevold (p. 157), is an involute *reductio ad absurdum* of the cognitive dissonance that arises where one believes something one knows is impossible; it provokes Jupiter to riposte with a version of the ontological argument that opens the door wide to the imagination: 'man cannot imagine things that haven't been or that ought not to be.' These various statements of position can be placed on a spectrum that runs from the wise man's advocacy of shared pretence and of the imagination to a hard-core scepticism.[25]

Doni thus explores the potentialities of fictional belief within a complex context where other kinds of belief are also at stake. The same could be said of the narrator of the ghost story cited by Chesters. Although his intervention is quite brief, he does take care to tag the story as a mythical story (*fabula*) like that of Orpheus, only to correct himself immediately ('if "mythical story" is the right expression...')[26] with the admission that many believe it to be a true account (*historia;* Chesters, p. 65); at the end of the story, he again cites sources he claims are reliable. In this case, too, the supernatural is at issue: the ghost, as it turns out, is something like a diabolic appearance, a *quasi-fantasma* (p. 65), although one that leaves a bodily trace in the form of an unspecified number of uncanny children.

In such ways, the contributors to this volume demonstrate that early modern writers and readers knew that the game of shared pretence, the mode of entry into storyworlds, is infinitely complex and variable, and that fictional belief is at the heart of the question of belief itself. They knew that one could both believe and not believe at the same time, without necessarily regarding that as a contradiction: cognitive dissonance, benign or otherwise, is intrinsic to the way the human mind works. And they knew that the fictional imagination belongs to the spectrum of imaginative or counterfactual modes that characterizes human cognition. When Rabelais prefaces *Gargantua* (1534) with a poem 'To the Reader', the last line of which declares that laughter is the distinctive feature of the human ('Le rire est le propre de l'homme'), laughter stands in, as do Folly and her avatars, for the literary imagination, which in turn provides a crucial model for that higher level of cognitive confusion we all inhabit in our different cultural ways.

Notes to the Introduction

1. See Helgeson, this volume, p. 116. I have retranslated the quotation for the purposes of the Introduction.
2. I have sketched out an approach of this kind in my book *Thinking with Literature: Towards a Cognitive Criticism* (Oxford: Oxford University Press, 2016). Most of the cognitive approaches adopted in this volume are referred to and discussed in more detail there.
3. Montaigne's title does not designate the genre but the content of the work: an open-ended series of 'trials', 'soundings', explorations of the writer's own way of thinking.
4. An accessible review of recent work on perceptual and cognitive illusion is offered by Chris Frith, *Making up the Mind: How the Brain Creates our Mental World* (Oxford: Blackwell, 2007), Part I. See

also the references provided by Emily Troscianko in her richly documented article, 'Reading Kafka Enactively', in *Reading Literature Cognitively*, ed. by Terence Cave, Karin Kukkonen, and Olivia Smith, special issue of *Paragraph* (37.1, March 2014), especially pp. 17–19.
5. I owe this last reference to Shaun Gallagher, who used the analogy in a paper delivered at a Balzan project workshop organized by Timothy Chesters at Royal Holloway, University of London, in January 2013.
6. I refer here to the Balzan project workshop held at the University of Birmingham in April 2014, organized by Ita Mac Carthy, at which earlier versions of most of the papers included in this volume were presented and discussed; see above, Preface.
7. See George Lakoff and Mark Johnson, *Metaphors We Live By* (Chicago: Chicago University Press, 1980); cited by Maus de Rolley, this volume, p. 79.
8. See Kendall L. Walton, *Mimesis as Make-Believe: On the Foundations of the Representational Arts* (Cambridge, MA, and London: Harvard University Press, 1990); Jean-Marie Schaeffer, *Pourquoi la fiction?* (Paris: Seuil, 1999; English version *Why Fiction?*, trans. by Dorrit Cohn, University of Nebraska Press, 2010); Paul Harris, *The Work of the Imagination* (Oxford: Blackwell, 2000); Ilona Roth (ed.), *Imaginative Minds* (Oxford and New York: Oxford University Press for the British Academy, 2007). Harris is cited by both Sellevold and Smith, who also cites Walton: this volume, p. 161, n. 26, and pp. 174–75, 179, n. 42.
9. Modalizing expressions are those that allow the speaker to qualify her assent to the content of her utterance ('It seems that...', 'It seems to me that...', 'perhaps', 'arguably'). Procedural expressions are the features of language that guide the interlocutor in the interpretation of the conceptual or propositional content of the utterance. The procedural–conceptual distinction is not always easy to preserve and is the subject of controversy, but it has the merit of drawing attention to cognitively important elements that are often ignored in favour of 'content'. See Sellevold, Chesters and Helgeson, this volume.
10. See Daniel Kahneman, *Thinking, Fast and Slow* (New York: Farrar, Straus and Giroux; London: Penguin Books, 2011).
11. I am using the word 'imagination' here in the broad-brush sense of a mental representation that is distinct from immediate perception; it includes 'imagining that' something is the case as well as sensory imaginings of the kind often referred to in discussions of the literary imagination. For early modern accounts of the imagination, see Giglioni and Maus de Rolley (this volume).
12. On the concept of tagging, see Lena Cosmides and John Tooby, 'Consider the source: the evolution of adaptations for decoupling and metarepresentation', in *Metarepresentations: A Multidisciplinary Perspective*, ed. by Dan Sperber (New York: Oxford University Press, 2000), pp. 53–111; on the related concept of epistemic vigilance, see Dan Sperber, *et al.*, 'Epistemic vigilance', *Mind and Language*, 25 (2010), 359–93; on fictional decoupling, see Schaeffer, *Pourquoi la fiction?*. See also my study *Thinking with Literature*, esp. ch. 5, on the question of the imagination and its constraints.
13. Walter Kaiser, *Praisers of Folly: Erasmus, Rabelais, Shakespeare* (Cambridge, MA: Harvard University Press, 1963); Rosalie Colie, *Paradoxia epidemica: The Renaissance Tradition of Paradox* (Princeton, NJ: Princeton University Press, 1966); Ann Moss, *Printed Commonplace-Books and the Structuring of Renaissance Thought* (Oxford: Clarendon Press, 1996); Stuart Clark, *Thinking with Demons: The Idea of Witchcraft in Early Modern Europe* (Oxford: Oxford University Press, 1999), and *Vanities of the Eye: Vision in Early Modern European Culture* (Oxford: Oxford University Press, 2007).
14. On affordances, see James J. Gibson *The Ecological Approach to Visual Perception* (Hillsdale, NJ: Lawrence Erlbaum Associates, 1986; first published 1979); for an account of affordances in the context of literary studies, see my study *Thinking with Literature*, ch. 4.
15. I refer here to the iconographical studies of Edgar Wind and others; see in particular Wind's *Pagan Mysteries in the Renaissance* (London: Faber, 1958 and later editions). Although his interpretative methodology has subsequently been contested by some art historians, I believe that such studies convincingly demonstrate the way in which a symbolic and conceptual repertory could, when powerfully articulated in visual images or in literary forms of expression, perform an essential cognitive function, becoming an affordance for an illuminating vision of the world and of the human presence within that world.
16. It is perhaps necessary to emphasize that this equation of religious and secular beliefs is not

intended to discount the religious domain, to deny its value and function, in the manner associated with Richard Dawkins (an approach that Pascal Boyer also shares); on the contrary, it suggests that all types of belief, the ones that last and the ones that don't, may be regarded as more or less viable and productive ways of explaining the world and living with its intractability.
17. On the notion of distributed cognition, see in particular Andy Clark, *Supersizing the Mind: Embodiment, Action, and Cognitive Extension* (Oxford: Oxford University Press, 2008).
18. One might object that belief in alien abduction is delusional; but, if one accepts Bortolotti's argument for a spectrum of belief in 'irrational' or counterintuitive phenomena, that objection is invalidated. Such a belief would in any case have a function for the individual who holds it, allowing him or her to make sense of his or her perceived world (cf. the unrequited lover who continues to believe that the beloved reciprocates his affections).
19. On procedural and modalizing expressions, see n. 9 above.
20. Children's games, and computer games, manage it differently: there can be a shared pretence that a player is allowed one or more additional 'lives'. This also happens, though less systematically, in soap operas and other serial fictions: characters thought to be dead may reappear, more or less plausibly, in later episodes. We know that that will not happen, however, to Grace Archer or Sybil Crawley; no amount of special tagging will allow them to return from the fictional dead. Brody of *Homeland* also seems irreversibly dead after the final episode of Series 3, where he is publicly hanged, but he appears to return in Series 4, confusing the viewer momentarily, as a delusion brought on when Carrie is tricked into taking the wrong medication.
21. I use the term 'paradox' in the classical (Ciceronian) and early modern sense, out of which arose the conception of a reversal of values, a *coincidentia oppositorum*, and ultimately the modern sense ('a contradiction in terms', or even the rhetorical paradox also known as 'oxymoron').
22. On Rabelais's *Third Book* and the *Praise of Folly*, see Kaiser, *Praisers of Folly*.
23. As Sellevold points out (p. 162, n. 37), the relation between these two is not unlike that between Pantagruel and Panurge, especially in the 1546 *Third Book*, where it takes the form of a constantly renewed dialogue.
24. On this concept, see above, note 12; also Sellevold, note 14.
25. I use the word in the non-technical sense, i.e. an unwillingness to accept beliefs not based on tangible, this-worldly knowledge. The relation of this sense to the philosophical scepticism that plays a major role in early modern thought lies outside the frame of this discussion.
26. I have slightly modified Chesters's translation here.

CHAPTER 1

Reverse Othello Syndrome by Another Name: Ariosto's Deluded Hero

Ita Mac Carthy

Ludovico Ariosto's *Orlando furioso*, first published in 1516, is a 46-chapter epic romance that centres on a delusion and its consequences.[1] The delusion, which eventually drives the knight Orlando completely insane, reaches its climax exactly half way through the poem in canto 23, so that the first half of the poem deals with the cause and mechanics of the hero's loss of sanity while the second half concerns its retrieval. Delusion is also at the heart of the poem's thematic concerns. From the outset, the poet declares his intention to sing of 'cosa non detta in prosa mai ne in rima' ['things untold in prose or in rhyme'], that is to say, the story of how Orlando is driven mad by love 'd'uom che sí saggio era stimato prima' ['and he a man who had always been esteemed so wise'] (I. 2).[2] Orlando's delusion and eventual madness have, of course, been explored from multiple viewpoints over the five hundred years since its publication, but never before has a cognitively inflected reading of the poem been attempted.[3] This chapter revisits Orlando's delusion in light of recent studies in cognitive philosophy, psychiatry and psychology and observes, in part I, the striking similarities it shares with symptoms of the cognitive disorder known as reverse Othello syndrome. It suggests, in part II, why aligning Orlando's madness with reverse Othello syndrome might be useful to Ariosto scholarship before going on to show, in part III, how it stands to advance the most up-to-date thinking on pathological delusions as well. This final part of the chapter argues that reverse Othello syndrome is actually misnamed and should be called Orlando syndrome instead. It explains the change in emphasis this new name would bring to our understanding of the condition and argues that the *Furioso* serves as a test case for a certain kind of delusion. In so doing, it affirms the power of literature to encapsulate phenomena that are otherwise hard to explain.

Part I — Orlando and 'Reverse Othello Syndrome'

The Italian words for 'delusion' ('delirio' / 'credenza delirante') post-date Ariosto and do not appear in the *Orlando furioso*, which features instead the more generic terminology of its age ('pazzia' / 'furia' / 'errore', etc).[4] It is not hard to argue, however, that 'deluded' is the contemporary word that best describes Orlando's frame of mind for the first half of the *Orlando furioso*. Until canto 23, he believes that the exotic princess from the East, Angelica, loves him as he loves her. Despite her constant elusiveness, a prophetic dream that tells him to abandon all hope of her, and ample proof to the contrary, he persists in this belief till it becomes an obsession: he abandons his duty as Charlemagne's foremost champion in the defence of the Christian world against Saracen attack and devotes himself entirely to pursuing Angelica across Europe. At the mid-way point in the poem, Orlando's delusion reaches its climax as he comes face to face with unassailable evidence that his beloved is in love with Medoro, a lowly foot soldier of the pagan army. Despite this evidence, though, he is convinced for some time longer that she loves him.

Orlando's behaviour at this point bears all the hallmarks of what we would call a pathological delusion. He has come to a pleasant meadow where he had hoped to rest for a while, but his peace is shattered when he notices inscriptions on the trees in Angelica's handwriting: the names 'Angelica' and 'Medoro' written in a hundred places, united by a hundred love-knots. His first response is denial: he tries 'non creder quel ch'al suo dispetto crede: / ch'altra Angelica sia, creder si sforza, / ch'abbia scritto il suo nome in quella scorza' ['not to believe that which he could not help believing: and to force himself to believe that it was some other Angelica who had written her name on the bark' (my trans.)] (23. 103)'. He looks for alternative explanations: 'Finger questo Medoro ella si puote: / forse ch'a me questo cognome mette' ['Can she perhaps be inventing this Medoro? Perhaps by this name she means me?'] (23.104). When he stumbles upon the cave where the lovers sought shade from the mid-day sun, he finds carved on the rock further proof that he has lost Angelica to Medoro. Despite being perfectly able to decipher Medoro's Arabic verse praising the spot where 'la bella Angelica che nacque / di Galafron, da molti invano amata, / spesso ne le mie braccia nuda giacque' ['fair Angelica, daughter of Galafron, and loved in vain by many, often lay naked in my arms' (23. 108)]; he clings to his false belief, reasoning 'che voglia alcun cosí infamare il nome / de la sua donna e crede e brama e spera, / o graver lui d'insoportabil some / tanto di gelosia, che se ne pèra' ['that someone was trying in this way to besmirch his lady's name — and this he believes and desires and hopes — or to charge him with a burden of such jealousy that he would die of it' (my trans.)] (23. 115). Overwhelming evidence to the contrary notwithstanding, he manages to leave the spot with his false belief intact: 'In cosí poca, in cosí debol speme / sveglia gli spiriti e gli rifranca un poco' ['With such meagre, such puny hopes he roused his spirits and found a little courage'] (23. 115).

Orlando's belief is certain (he comes to hold it with absolute conviction); incorrigible (it does not change despite compelling counterarguments or proof to the contrary); and false (it is patently untrue that Angelica loves him), thereby corresponding closely to the first definition of delusions by Karl Jaspers in 1913.[5] The definition has evolved since Jaspers, but the two outstanding features of certainty and incorrigibility remain constant. Beliefs no longer have to be false to be delusional, but they do need to be held with unmovable conviction. As the most recent edition of the *Diagnostic and Statistical Manual of Mental Disorders* (the standard classification used by mental health professionals, also known as the *DSM–5*) states, 'delusions are fixed beliefs that are not amenable to change in light of conflicting evidence'.⁶ They are faulty hypotheses generated and maintained when a person is unable to test or revise them on the basis of contradictory information; they are errors in reading the sensory evidence that should inform, update or change one's beliefs about the world.

This perfectly describes Orlando. Despite encountering information that should change his beliefs, he safeguards his faulty hypothesis about Angelica. With notable success, he manages 'not to believe that which he could not help believing' of Angelica and 'force[s] himself to believe' that she does indeed love him, just as he 'believes and desires and hopes'.⁷ The narrator's repetition of the verb 'to believe' here gives the sense that Orlando's delusion is voluntary, a deliberate act of conviction. He struggles against an undesirable belief and imposes a more acceptable one wrought out of desire and hope. Self-generated and wilful though it may be, the view that Angelica loves him is, nonetheless, a belief — the keystone of any delusion — and pathological too in that Orlando holds tight to it, even when he should acknowledge that it is wrong.⁸ This is not an error in reading, since the narrator makes it clear that the knight is perfectly able to decipher the evidence before his eyes and to decode the signs inscribed on the trees and stones, but in receiving the significance of what he reads. He can make sense of the words, but his strong desire prevents him from accepting them for the truth they signify. The cognitive dissonance between his belief that Angelica loves him and the new information proving that she does not prompts a malfunction in the processes that modulate his beliefs and results in what cognitive philosophers call faulty 'reality testing'.⁹

Cognitive philosophy and psychology has a specific name for the type of faulty reality testing Orlando suffers from: reverse Othello syndrome, which Peter V. Butler defines as 'a delusional belief in the fidelity of a romantic partner'.¹⁰ First documented by Butler in an article published in 2000, reverse Othello syndrome was used to describe a 49-year-old man, B.X., who sustained a severe brain injury in a car crash in August 1995.¹¹ Almost a year after the accident, B.X. began to develop 'an intense delusional belief' that the woman who had been his romantic partner before the accident was now his wife (86). Despite the fact that the woman (known as N.) had actually ended their relationship as a consequence of his injuries, B.X. was able to describe their (imagined) wedding in detail and to describe the emotional and physical fulfilment he had enjoyed since that day. Physicians put it to him that his recollections were false, that there was no evidence to prove the wedding had occurred, that there were no photographs, wedding presents or witnesses to corroborate his belief. Yet still the delusion persisted. On the physicians' prompt, N. wrote a long letter to B.X., telling him unequivocally that she did not love him, that she felt 'nothing but anger and disgust' and that she never wanted to see him again (88). Following some initial upset, however, B.X. insisted that the letter 'had been a mistake' and that his relationship was 'back to normal' (88): N. 'remained sexually faithful and continued as his lover and life partner' (86).

The striking similarities between the cases of B.X. and Orlando lead irresistibly to the conclusion that Butler and Ariosto are describing the same type of phenomenon, albeit from different perspectives. Both subjects (one clinical, one fictional) continue to believe in their beloved's fidelity 'on inadequate grounds' and are unaffected by 'rational argument or contrary evidence' (Butler, 86). Both fail to revise their versions of reality despite written proof that their perception is wrong. Just as Orlando ignored the names inscribed on trees and stones, B.X. rejected the truth value of N.'s letter. Despite initial tears, the two men roused their spirits and found the courage to move on, maintaining (to use Butler's words) 'total faith' in their beloved's fidelity while 'retrospective misinterpretations of coincidental and insignificant events' served only to affirm that faith (86). Butler's recourse here to the language of faith and fidelity is most pertinent to Orlando since the progression of his madness hinges on his choice to elevate Angelica's (perceived) fidelity to him and his to her above his *fede* or loyalty to Charlemagne and the Holy Roman Empire.[12] Preferring private (though delusional) vows of fidelity to public contracts of faith in God and King, Orlando demonstrates clear signs of reverse Othello syndrome, albeit five centuries before it was so named and nearly one hundred years before William Shakespeare wrote the play whose eponymous hero lent it his name.

Part II — the Power of Names

It might seem strange — anachronistic — to think of Orlando's madness in terms of a twenty-first-century syndrome and in relation to another fictional character about whom Shakespeare was yet to write. Yet there is an obvious fascination in identifying themes and topics that pervade literature (fictional and otherwise), and a certain comfort in the realization that the things that puzzle us today preoccupied our predecessors, too. It is striking that the phenomenon Ariosto describes in relation to his fictional character bears such close resemblance to the 1996 case described by cognitive psychiatrists and philosophers from Butler to Bortolotti and humbling to remember that we all live beneath the same sky.[13]

More importantly for the purposes of this chapter, thinking of Orlando's delusion alongside reverse Othello syndrome reminds us of the power of literature to encapsulate real-life phenomena that are hard to express. For nearly fifty years before the term was coined, its counterpart, Othello syndrome, had provided an eloquent means of describing individuals who were irrationally and pathologically convinced that their partners were unfaithful.[14] Othello syndrome denoted delusional jealousy, in other words, which the *DSM*–5 defines in the following terms:

> In *jealous type* [delusional disorders], the central theme of the delusion is that of an unfaithful partner. This belief is arrived at without due cause and is based on incorrect inferences supported by small bits of 'evidence' (e.g., disarrayed clothing). The individual with the delusion usually confronts the spouse or lover and attempts to intervene in the imagined infidelity (p. 91).

Other scientific literature describes Othello syndrome as a rare disorder with 'high-risk implications' that is also referred to as 'delusional, pathological, morbid or erotic jealousy'.[15] Leong et al. define it as 'a psychiatric condition in which the degree of jealousy and / or belief in [the] infidelity of one's spouse reaches delusional intensity'.[16]

Aligning this distressing psychiatric disorder with Shakespeare's tragic hero was a powerful act of naming because it communicated in one speech act more than the sum of its various definitions in the scientific literature. In fact, Shakespeare shows up manuals like the *DSM–5* as the relatively blunt instruments they are when it comes to encapsulating psychotic jealousy. Diagnostic manuals, in fact, have been criticized by health professionals for their inability to account for the many different ways in which conditions manifest themselves and for the multiple background factors that contribute to their development (amongst other things).[17] In 2011, the British Psychological Society criticized the *DSM–5* for its 'top-down' approach to mental health which means that patients are required to 'fit' a diagnosis, rather than the other way round.[18] Manuals fail to take specific experiences, histories, feelings and problems as their starting point: but this is precisely what good literature specializes in. Shakespeare's talent for evoking real-life variety and complexity is celebrated in the preference by many clinicians for the term 'Othello syndrome' over the flatter 'delusional jealousy'. Othello syndrome conjures up a vivid picture of what the *DSM–5* calls 'the theme of an unfaithful partner' since — as everyone knows — the title-character in Shakespeare's play suspects his innocent wife, Desdemona, of infidelity. It expresses the scantiness of the evidence required to sustain the delusion, as Othello exaggerates the importance of his wife's misplaced handkerchief, and it also communicates the potential danger of erotic jealousy since Shakespeare's play famously ends with both homicide (Othello suffocates Desdemona in her bed) and suicide (he runs himself through with his own dagger). Moreover, as it charts the course of Othello's downfall, the name Othello syndrome encapsulates the humiliation and degradation of pathological jealousy, and the ravaging effects it can have on individual lives. Starting out as an esteemed military general in the Venetian army and elevated to high social standing by his marriage into a patrician family, Othello is progressively stripped of all dignity during the play as he is consumed by the ugly passion, jealousy. At a crucial point in his degradation, his scheming confidante, Iago, offers a most evocative insight into the predatory nature of that emotion and the insatiability of its appetite:

> O beware, my lord, of jealousy!
> It is the green-eyed monster, which doth mock
> The meat it feeds on. That cuckold lives in bliss
> Who, certain of his fate, loves not his wronger,
> But O, what damned minutes tells he o'er
> Who dotes yet doubts, suspects yet strongly loves! (III, iii).

Jealousy breeds jealousy and needs no sound cause to sprout, as Desdemona's maid, Emilia, says when Desdemona proclaims her innocence. Jealous souls, she says, 'are not jealous for the cause, but jealous for they're jealous. It is a monster begot upon itself, born on itself' (III, iv). The Shakespearean name, therefore, is the perfect epitome of the irrational, self-generative and highly destructive nature of morbid jealousy.

Othello syndrome expresses pathological jealousy's complex manifestation as well, its combination of physiological, psychological and social factors that make it notoriously hard to comprehend and to treat. For *Othello* is not just about the 'green-ey'd monster' and the pitiless way it humiliates the people it assaults. It is also a play about social maladjustment. As a powerful general in the Venetian army, Othello is more at ease on the battlefield than in the domestic household he enters into on marrying Desdemona. A stranger to the patrician culture of Venice, he is ethnically foreign too, a Moor whose social alienation is marked by the colour of his skin. As A. D. Nuttall puts it, Othello 'left the arena proper to tragedy, the battlefield, and entered a subtragic world for which he was not fitted. *Othello* is the story of a hero who went into a house'.[19] Finding himself in an alien environment and unable to interpret the words and actions of its inhabitants, he relies on the advice of Iago. Yet though the lieutenant's Venetian background makes him better equipped than Othello to decipher the alien codes of love and marriage, he chooses instead to manipulate them out of hatred for his general. Keenly aware that the bourgeois company of Othello's married life is radically different from the military company of his profession, Iago preys upon his vulnerability and sows the seeds of suspicion that become his undoing. At the source of Othello's tragedy, then, is an untranslatable disjuncture between two worlds. A major theme of the play is social integration and the ways in which individuals adjust or fail to adjust to realities at odds with their experience. Othello syndrome expresses a similar disjuncture in individuals who lose their social bearings, misread the codes of their community, and are no longer able to discern truth from falsehood or to temper their passions with reason.[20]

What of reverse Othello syndrome: does it, too, evoke the power of literature to express the inexpressible in human experience? Peter Butler affirms that it also takes its name from the Shakespearean play in which 'the initially trusting Othello is consumed by suspicion and eventually jealously murders his guiltless wife, Desdemona, at the prompting of an evil courtier' (p. 86). Beyond this one sentence, Butler expands no further on the connections between the play and the disorder that he is the first to name in this way. Presumably, the 'reverse' in the title refers to the direction of the beloved's affections: Othello fears that Desdemona, who truly loves him, has turned away from him, while B.X. believes that N., who has withdrawn her affections, loves him still. It refers, as well, to the effects of the syndrome, which in one case are catastrophic, and in the other, inversely, altogether more pleasant for the duration of the delusion of fidelity. Rather than being devoured by jealousy, B.X. basks in the glow of his imagined partner's love and describes the sexual and emotional satisfaction he has felt since their imagined marriage. Orlando is not quite so self-satisfied (in fact the narrator describes him as 'fraude a sé medesmo' ['self-deluded'] and 'malcontento' ['unhappy'], 23. 104), but he remains, nevertheless, hopeful that Angelica will raise him to the level of the gods as soon as he is reunited with her. Though not exactly basking in a glow of happiness, he lives in hope (albeit fragile), which is the reverse of living with despair. Like Othello syndrome, then, reverse Othello syndrome expresses beliefs about intimate relationships that are irrational, incorrigible and indicative of an epistemological rift between the individual and the real world. Unlike its counterpart, though, reverse Othello syndrome conjures up love where there is none and — paradoxically — brings its sufferers hope (if not the realization) of happiness, gratification and relief from pain.

Thinking about Orlando's delusion in relation to reverse Othello syndrome is useful to Ariosto scholarship because it draws attention to the fact that his 'furia' begins early on in the poem. The critical tendency has been to consider his madness as the cataclysm that takes place following his encounter with the shepherd who proves beyond all doubt that Angelica has married someone else. Jane Everson, for example, calls it the kind of *furor* that involves 'a sudden madness sent by a god in punishment for some fault'.[21] Yet Orlando began losing his wits long before canto 23: it is not sudden but progressive. Considering Orlando in terms of reverse Othello syndrome serves to remind us that the theme of human reason is constant in the poem whose central concern is the ways and means by which a wise man (or woman) can become 'furioso'. Moreover, taking the long view of his 'furia' stresses the complexity of this process and reinforces the fundamental point that madness is on a spectrum with 'normal' experience.[22] Neither God's punishment alone, nor a sudden mind-body collapse, Orlando's madness develops gradually along emotional, physiological, divine and social axes. What Butler said of B.X., in fact, might equally be applied to him since he too displays 'the interaction and interpenetration of an array of biopsychosocial elements in the crystallization of his delusion' (p. 90).

Like B.X.'s, Orlando's is a two-factor delusion in origin, the first factor being emotional (his love for Angelica), and the second being social (his excessive adherence to the chivalric code, which promises the worthy knight his lady).[23] There is a physiological side to Orlando's case too, not brain injury (as in the case of B.X.) but an imbalance of humours that Orlando himself describes as his 'vitale umore' ['vital spirit'], which 'fugge per quella via ch'agli occhi mena' ['which escapes by the ducts that lead to the eyes' (my trans.)] and as ardour that keeps his heart burning, though never consumed by the flames (XXIII, 126–27).[24] However, this comes into the picture only after the delusion has taken hold. God's punishment is a fundamental element as well, but it is the result rather than the cause of his obsessive love for Angelica. God's judgment is exacted only after Orlando has been 'acceccato' ['blinded'] by 'l'incesto amore / d'una pagana' ['his lustful passion for a pagan woman' (34, 62)] and because 'torse / dal camin dritto le commesse insegne' ['he misappropriated the standards committed to him'] (34, 64). Divine intervention, in other words, comes as a consequence of the primary error of loving the wrong woman too much and of the secondary impairment of deserting his epic duty in favour of a knight errant's role. As this statement suggests, Orlando's transgression in the poem is not only social but generic as well. Whereas Othello 'left the arena proper to tragedy, the battlefield, and entered a subtragic world for which he was not fitted', as Nuttall puts it, Orlando abandons the battlefields of Christian epic for the wooded landscapes of chivalric romance. If Othello is a hero who went into a house, Orlando is a hero who got lost in a forest.

Orlando's 'amor' for Angelica is announced in the eleventh line of the poem, and his over-zealous conformity to the conventions of chivalric romance are first hinted at in the ninth octave of Canto I when Charlemagne offers Angelica as a prize to the worthiest of his champions. From the very beginning, then, these two factors spur on his actions and define his character. Initially they are perfectly acceptable.

His two-part delusion does not disrupt normal functioning and, on the contrary, motivates great acts, audacious deeds and a healthy desire to out-perform his peers in Charlemagne's army. Inspiring the everyday work of a hero, it is what cognitive philosophers would call an 'everyday delusion', that is to say, an irrational belief that does not adversely affect the believer's life. One could go so far as to call it positively beneficial since it not only inspires Orlando to win 'infiniti et immortal trofei' ['countless and immortal trophies'] (1. 5), but it also motivates him to rid Europe of foreign invaders as he takes up Charlemagne's challenge to be the one who 'in quel conflitto, in quella gran giornata, / degli infideli piú copia uccidessi, / e di sua man prestassi opra piú grata' ['slaughtered the greater number of Infidels and wrought him the worthiest assistance in the vital conflict of that day' (1, 9)] in order to win Angelica's hand.[25] Ariosto seems perfectly aware of the benefits of a healthy dose of self-delusion, but over the course of the poem the 'everyday' delusion turns increasingly 'psychotic' (to use the contemporary lexicon) as it starts to impinge on his ability to fulfil his social and professional roles.[26] It is in canto 8 that Orlando exits Charlemagne's camp and leaves his role as Carolingian hero behind. Yet even as the more Arthurian-style knight-errant he becomes thereafter he shows signs of impaired judgment and dangerously delusional behaviour. When he meets Olimpia in canto 9, for example, he neglects to consider the petulance of the Dutch countess who appeals for help in saving her from the violent King Cimosco and reuniting her with her 'beloved' Bireno. Olimpia had been captured by the neighbouring tyrant, Cimosco, who wanted her to marry his son. For love of Bireno, though, she had slit the offending son's throat, sacrificed her own father, brothers and kinsmen (all killed by Cimosco), and left her country under the neighbouring king's control. Orlando fails to comprehend the blinkered individualism in her story and to consider the real source of 'la guerra / che tutto il sangue mio cacciò sotterra' ['the war which sent all my kindred to the grave' (9.27)], Olimpia's childish and misguided crush. Caught up in a fantasy of chivalric romance, he focuses on the love story instead, reading Olimpia as a straightforward damsel in distress and intervening unthinkingly at her bidding.

In so doing, Orlando consigns Olimpia to a fate that is, in fact, worse than the one he 'saves' her from. For Olimpia's 'beloved' turns out not to love her at all. She, like Orlando, has been deluded. In this respect, and in the extremity of her initial love for Bireno (which the narrator says — with characteristic and untrustworthy hyperbole — makes her 'a paragon of fidelity'), she acts as an analogue for Orlando and gives Ariosto a further chance to explore the emotional and social consequences of love madness. What happens next presages Orlando's fate: Bireno abandons her Ariadne-like on a deserted beach where her anguish pre-echoes the depths of Orlando's pain once he realizes that Angelica has 'abandoned' him. Olimpia is 'punished' for her delusion by being picked up by pirates and offered in sacrifice to a sea monster that feeds on beautiful young women, just as Orlando will be punished by being driven insane. Both are stripped naked of clothing and of all outward signs of their aristocratic status. Sacrificial Olimpia and mad Orlando become cautionary figures in a tale designed to warn against misguided (deluded) love and over-investment in the conventions of chivalric romance. In failing to reflect on the possible consequences of their actions, they have shown themselves incapable of evaluating the world around them. They behave not according to the evidence of their surroundings, but according to a type — the damsel in distress for Olimpia and the knight-errant for Orlando — and are controlled more by the probabilities of the chivalric romance genre than by the anomalies they encounter in the fictional world they inhabit.

Like most knights of chivalric romance, Orlando relies on the probability that if he performs brave feats and saves damsels in distress, he will get his reward. Fervently anticipating Angelica's love, he brooks no evidence that might sway that conviction.[27] As such, his delusion is a form of personal narrative-making (as is Olimpia's), the practice that cognitive psychologists suggest we all engage in as we use stories and scenarios to make our experience of the world intelligible. As neuroscientist Vilayanur S. Ramachandran comments:

> Each of us has a tremendous need to impose consistency, coherence and continuity in his / her behavior. In other words, we need a script — a thread of continuity in time.[28]

Early moderns, too, were no strangers to the idea of selfhood being a script, as Erasmus makes clear in *The Praise of Folly*:

> Now what else is the life of mortal men but a kind of fable in which the actors appear on stage under the disguise of different masks? Each plays his assigned part till the stage manager comes forth and takes them off stage (p. 28).[29]

Orlando spins an account of himself that chimes with his sense of the world and if 'all the world's a stage, and all the men and women merely players', as Shakespeare writes in *As You Like It* (II.vii), one might expect that a knight errant in a tale of 'le donne, i cavallier, l'arme, gli amori' ['ladies, knights, arms, loves'] (I, 1) would be perfectly within his rights to play the part of the archetypal chivalric hero. The problems are, though, that the world Orlando lives in does not really match his script and the *Furioso* is not the chivalric romance its opening line purports it to be. Written in the context of a sixteenth-century Italian court where chivalric ideals were all but obsolete, it is a hybrid genre that is neither epic nor romance but that blends features of both.[30] Ariosto draws his inspiration for Orlando from romance and epic, from Classical, Carolingian, and Arthurian precedents, but he places him in a fictional universe that is unique. It is a world in crisis, neither heroic nor governed by the rules of chivalry; the literary counterpart, in other words, of the real world of the poet.

Reassessing Orlando in the light of reverse Othello syndrome might at first seem absurd to those who consider the poem an escapist fiction and Orlando's madness a dramatic device designed for effect. Yet though the poem contains flights of fancy, supernatural marvels and certain unbelievable occurrences, it is nonetheless grounded in reality and represents the world of the poet in imaginative but concrete ways. Ariosto wrote the *Furioso* during a period of great political turbulence in Italy. In 1494, Charles VIII of France had invaded the country in an effort to take control of the Kingdom of Naples, which he had 'inherited' from his father. This was an incursion that triggered thirty years of war in the Italian peninsula. As Guicciardini, who held the prestigious communal office of Gonfaloniere di Giustizia in Florence, wrote, Charles VIII put an end to an Italian 'Golden Age' of peace and political stability and Ariosto lived through three decades of foreign aggression and domestic tension which culminated in the 1526 League of Cognac and the 1527 Sack of Rome.[31] Throughout the *Furioso*, there is an undercurrent of uncertainty that reflects this political turmoil. The narrator complains about professional soldiers, who have replaced the knights of old.[32] In the Olimpia episode mentioned above, he criticizes the new warfare technologies that kill indiscriminately, unlike the more discerning swords and spears of history. He expresses anxiety about Italy's vulnerability against foreign attack and attaches great hope to the figure of Charles V who he hopes will unite Italians against future invaders and also against internal disintegration. The poet uses his poem to dramatize this set of circumstances, which affect him profoundly, so that it becomes anything but an escapist work of fiction. It is a means of coming to terms with a world in transition. Viewed in this light, Orlando's incompatibility with the post-chivalric world of the poem is no idle narrative trick designed for impact.[33] It is a metaphor for anyone who struggles with a world in transition and for those who suffer when the harsh realities of the world clash with their expectations of how it ought to be. It is a metaphor, in other words, for the poet himself as well as an eloquent analogue for other real-life characters like B.X.

Thinking about his madness as an early modern equivalent of reverse Othello syndrome, therefore, focalizes the etiology as opposed to just the climax of the crisis around which the *Furioso* revolves. It provides a new appreciation of the admixture of social, emotional, physiological and divine factors that lead to that crisis and triggers a fresh assessment of the hero's inability to evaluate effectively information about the world and to adjust his belief system accordingly. Moreover, reading Orlando's delusion alongside cognitive literature of this kind highlights the verisimilitude of a poem rich in fantasy but anchored in reality and replete with insights of real-life relevance.

Part III — The Orlando Syndrome

Emphasizing the similarities between B.X. and Orlando in this way raises an irresistible question: Since they have so much in common, should not the condition be called 'Orlando Syndrome'? In fact, B.X. has far more in common with Ariosto's deluded hero than with Othello who, strictly speaking, is not really deluded at all. In an essay entitled 'Did Othello have "the Othello syndrome"?', consultant psychiatrist Paul Crichton suggests that Othello did not have Othello syndrome since his jealousy is neither irrational nor deluded.[34] He was deceived, rather than deluded, about Desdemona's infidelity. Indeed, alongside jealousy and social maladjustment, *Othello* explores deceit and enmity as well through the figure of Iago, who does an excellent job of showing bad faith in friendship. When he first suggests Desdemona's infidelity, Othello demands material proof which Iago supplies by planting her handkerchief amongst her supposed lover Cassio's things. The misplaced handkerchief — a gift from her husband — is, in itself, inadequate evidence of Desdemona's infidelity. If that were all he had to go on, Othello could well be considered deluded. But the handkerchief is the material counterpart to Iago's cunning construction of a lie. It is evidence to 'thicken other proofs that do demonstrate thinly' (III.iii). 'Thus', reveals Iago 'credulous fools are caught and many worthy and chaste dames even thus, all guiltless, meet reproach' (IV, i). As Crichton suggests, 'it seems perfectly plausible that Othello should believe this evidence, especially when combined with Iago's report of his having overheard Cassio speaking in his sleep of his love for Desdemona' (p. 162). Othello, therefore, 'did not have "the Othello syndrome"', he concludes; 'it is a misnomer and should be abandoned' (p. 168).

Since the Oedipus complex (and before), literature has played a crucial role in naming and encapsulating aspects of the human condition.[35] In psychology and psychiatry, as well as in social theory and medicine, literary figures embody complex phenomena and make rich and complicated realities instantly communicable. Yet the namers do not always get it right. Anti-Freudians have pointed out that Oedipus did not have an Oedipal complex,[36] and — as Crichton points out — Othello may not have suffered from Othello syndrome. Yet despite Crichton's conclusion, there is much that can be said in favour of retaining the Othello syndrome name. For one thing, the word 'delusion' originally contained connotations of deception — the Latin *delusio* meaning 'a deceiving' or the 'act of misleading someone' — so that to say that Othello was deluded amounts to saying that he was both misled by someone and tricked by his own mind.[37] Even if contemporary usage has allowed those original connotations to disappear, aligning Shakespeare's character with delusional jealousy is still useful because it does more than any other name to encapsulate the humiliation of the condition, the interweaving of social, psychological and emotional factors that underpin it, and the potential for danger of patients who suffer it (as I have argued above). The same, however, cannot be said of reverse Othello syndrome, whose name offers no insights at all into the potentially positive feelings elicited by a conviction in the imagined fidelity of an intimate partner. As a title, reverse Othello syndrome lacks the evocative force of 'Othello syndrome', a fact that may go some way towards explaining why it describes just one case in the scientific literature whereas Othello syndrome applies to countless examples. Orlando syndrome, on the other hand, would offer far better purchase on the composition and presentation of delusions of fidelity.

Apart from making poetic sense, what difference would this new name produce? Calling what happened to B.X. the Orlando Syndrome would have immediate communicative benefits. It would express in one instant not just his deluded belief in N's fidelity, but also the status of his delusion as a coping strategy. Butler concludes that B.X.'s erotic fantasy was 'self-motivated', serving as a defence against 'depressive overwhelm' for a man struggling to cope with the life-changing consequences of his car accident: 'B.X.'s erotic fantasy system seemed to go some way toward reconferring a sense of meaning to his life experience and reintegrating his shattered sense of self' (p. 89). Orlando's erotic delusion, too, is self-motivated, protecting him from the loss of self-esteem and extreme emotional consequences that facing the truth about Angelica and about the post-chivalric world would bring.[38] In the sense that it frees the mind from anxiety and worry and relieves distress about an unmanageable reality, the name 'Orlando syndrome' is far more expressive of B.X.'s condition than 'reverse Othello syndrome'.

Ariosto's deluded hero provides a better analogue for B.X. when considering the most appropriate therapeutic approach as well. Given its psychological benefits, B.X.'s clinicians decided not to challenge his delusion: 'It was concluded that B.X.'s fantasy system functioned to protect him from massive narcissistic injury and attendant depressive overwhelm. All members of the treating team were instructed not to aggressively challenge B.X.'s delusional beliefs but were also cautioned not to become complicit in his elaboration of them' (p. 88). Orlando's delusion, on the other hand, was challenged and eventually collapsed — with dire consequences. On meeting the melancholic Orlando in an inn, a well-intentioned herdsman tries to cheer him up by telling him the love story of Angelica and Medoro who had sheltered in his house. To end the story, the herdsman produces the bracelet that Angelica gave him to thank him for his hospitality (23. 118–120). At the sight of the bracelet, originally a gift from him, Orlando can sustain the delusion no longer and he experiences a total breakdown. As the narrator puts it, 'questa conclusion fu la secure / che 'l capo a un colpo gli levò dal collo' ['this evidence shown in conclusion proved to be the axe which took his head off his shoulders at one stroke'], (23, 121). The blow that takes Orlando's head off his shoulders and propels him into a furious rage, the bracelet, in other words, shatters the delusion that kept his reason misguided but intact. Once dispelled, the fantasy ceases to serve its function of self-preservation. Unlike B.X., he is no longer protected by the fiction that serves to reconfer 'a sense of meaning to his life experience' and he lacks the means to reintegrate 'his shattered sense of self' (Butler, 89). Calling B.X.'s delusion the 'Orlando syndrome', therefore, encapsulates much more than the fact of his erotomanic fantasy. It expresses its function as a psychological fuse that blows when B.X.'s emotional and psychological wellbeing are threatened by the intolerable burden of the accident's aftermath.

The analogy with fuses is McKay and Dennett's, who also describe self-motivated delusions as 'shear pins', those parts of machines that are designed to break in the case of a mechanical overload and to safeguard other more valuable parts from damage. Like shear pins, 'components of belief evaluation machinery' are designed to break 'in situations of extreme psychological stress (analogous to the mechanical overload that breaks a shear pin or the power surge that blows a fuse)'.[39] In extreme circumstances, delusions act as sacrificial mechanisms occurring to protect the rest of the subject's mental health. This is the case for both B.X. and Orlando. Renaming the type of delusion they share the 'Orlando syndrome' underlines the adaptive function of their romantic fantasies and it emphasizes, too, the crucial fact that the shear pins of self-motivated delusions should be allowed to do their job. In the case of B.X., the delusion remains unchallenged and so preserves him from 'massive narcissistic injury' and 'depressive overwhelm'. In Orlando's case, however, it does not: The truth causes a breakdown in reason far more extreme and damaging than any psychologically and epistemically 'innocent' fantasy.[40] In a visible manifestation of the invisible disintegration of his selfhood and social identity, he sheds his clothes and armour on the forest floor and embarks on a bestial rampage through the forests.

As the author of a literary text, Ariosto does what medical ethics prevents clinicians from doing: he challenges Orlando's delusion and pushes it to its limits within the safe — and not entirely unscientific — environment of a literary experiment. The result is a poetic manifestation of what Butler et al. hypothesized would happen to B.X. had he been similarly challenged. Literary anecdotes — as opposed to clinical test cases — are usually disparaged in contemporary science, but the case of Orlando (amongst others cited in this volume and throughout works of literary criticism) shows that this is not entirely justified. Literary experiments like Ariosto's can have their value too if informed by careful observation of human behaviour, and carried out with integrity according to the principles of verisimilitude. Sixteenth-century medical writers saw this value and often quoted literary cases to exemplify particular diseases and conditions.[41] In treatises dealing with love-melancholy or love madness especially, medical authorities combined literary, philosophical and medical source texts with empirical evidence to give as complete a picture of the condition as they thought possible. Ariosto's *Furioso* featured alongside Virgil's *Georgics* and Ovid's *Remedia Amoris*, demonstrating the profound impact it had on medical experts studying the effects of love and desire on mental health as well as on lovers of literature. One such expert, Domenico Leoni, comments on the 'skilful' ('*graphice*') way in which Ariosto described 'wandering melancholy' (*melancholia errabunda*) suffered by Orlando, suggesting that it was his rhetorical skill that was most useful to physicians.[42] Equally important, though, was the poetic licence held by him and other writers of literature to conduct the kinds of experiments on their subjects that medical practitioners could only dream of.

In this sense, early modern medical writers precede by many years contemporary calls within the mind sciences for interdisciplinary collaboration. Lisa Bortolotti, for example, commends the 'fertile' cooperation between philosophers, psychiatrists and psychologists in the investigation of 'the nature of mental states' and 'the conditions of their attributions'.[43] For Bortolotti, however, only 'real-life cases' and not 'anecdotal evidence, outlandish [*sic*] thought experiments, or references to works of fiction' can act as the proper objects of study for such collaborations: works of literature and of literary criticism should have no place therein (p. 5). Yet the distinction between real-life cases, anecdotes and works of fiction is not always as clear-cut and straightforward as it might seem (as oft-quoted maxims about life being stranger than fiction, and art imitating life — and vice versa — suggest). For one thing, the evidence provided in 'real-life cases' is often narratives reported to clinicians by sufferers; narratives that are related to anecdotes and works of fiction in that they represent but are not reducible to lived experiences (see, for example, the narratives of thought-insertion quoted in Bortolotti et al.'s article in this volume). Moreover, interpretation in the scientific literature of such narratives is also a literary exercise that departs further from the 'hard' facts in order to produce the general statements about the mind that is their aim. At the same time, certain works of fiction, though not necessarily based on 'real-life' examples, are governed by real-life probabilities and by the laws of verisimilitude. Formed in the minds of authors, they spring from real-world contexts and are bound by real-world constraints and conventions. Early modern medical writers recognized the literariness of medical writing as well as the valuable insights offered by fictional writing, and contemporary mind sciences would do well not to dismiss works of fiction outright as useful instruments for thinking about the human mind. Bortolotti's criticism, it must be clarified, is not directed at writers of fiction: it is directed at those scientists who draw on clinical cases only to confirm and consolidate pre-established conceptual frameworks, often missing the particularities of those cases and the ways in which they deviate from the frameworks. She argues for methodological approaches that question 'well-established principles' relating to human nature and that are willing to revise and revisit them in the light of individual cases. This, I would suggest, is what literature and literary criticism does best, and it is what makes them such valuable partners in collaborative investigations into how the mind works.

Orlando's *furia* inspires early modern medical writers and, it is worth pointing out, becomes a model for Othello's jealous rage in Shakespeare too. Both Orlando and Othello are possessive but capable of holding their jealousy at bay up until the point when they are presented with their discarded love gifts in unexpected places. Like Angelica's bracelet, Desdemona's handkerchief provides the material evidence of infidelity, the proof 'to thicken other proofs that do demonstrate thinly' (*Othello*, III iii). It 'speaks against her with the other proofs' (III, iii), just as the bracelet had combined with the inscriptions on trees and rocks to demonstrate Angelica's 'betrayal'. Othello is rendered incoherent and rambling by the concrete evidence in the same way that Orlando lost his former eloquence, and there is no doubt that Shakespeare drew on Ariosto's once-wise hero for this recognition scene and for the way in which Othello 'breaks out to savage madness' (*Othello*, IV, i).[44] Orlando syndrome, therefore, is a capacious title that encapsulates both the shear pin of delusions of fidelity *and* the axe-blow of delusions of infidelity. As well as replacing reverse Othello syndrome, in other words, it could well replace Othello syndrome itself as well.

The heuristic value of *Orlando furioso*, therefore, is great when it comes to thinking about B.X. in particular and about erotomania more generally. It offers a fictional analogue for real-life cases, but it offers counter-examples too. One of the ways in which Ariosto explores madness is through characters who are not mad, who do not commit Orlando's error, and whose contrasting behaviour sheds further light on his failure to patrol the boundaries between reality, fantasy and delusion.[45] The character of Fiordispina, for example, offers a light-hearted example of someone who, though also madly in love, retains her sanity and gets her prize. The Spanish princess mirrors Orlando in useful and insightful ways. In particular, her story sheds greater light on the role played by dreams in fuelling Orlando's delusion. It is, after all, a dream about Angelica that triggers the knight's first serious 'reality-testing' malfunction in Canto 8. His reaction to this dream contrasts with and is understood better by the way in which Fiordispina reacts to a comparable dream in canto 25.

In Orlando's dream, he sees Angelica's lovely face, 'il bello avorio, e la nativa / purpura ch'avea Amor di sua man tinta, / e le due chiare stelle onde nutriva / ne le reti d'Amor l'anima avinta' ['ivory-white blent with a flush of crimson painted by

Love's own hand and her eyes, a pair of limpid stars whose light nourished his soul, caught in Love's toils'] (8. 80). Feasting his eyes upon the apparition, he is filled with the deepest sense of happiness and well-being. Happiness turns to despair, however, when a storm blows up and the vision is dispersed. Orlando wanders through the wilderness in search of shelter and of his damsel till a voice calls out, 'Non sperar più gioirne in terra mai' ['Look no more to have joy from her here below'] (8. 83). He wakes in a sweat and leaps, fulminating, out of bed. He clads himself in armour and sets off in search of Angelica, abandoning Charlemagne in his hour of greatest need.

Of interest here is the narrator's comment when Orlando awakes. Orlando, he says, is unmindful 'che sian l'imagin false / quando per tema o per disio si sogna' ['that the pictures must be false that fear or hope projects in the dreaming mind'] (8.84). Troubled by the thought that Angelica is out in the world, all alone and in need, he acts on his dream as if it were real. Confronted with this vision of a damsel in distress, he sees himself, once again, as her knight in shining armour and fails to check either the truth of his dream, or the validity of his chosen account of things. This cognitive error is hugely significant in Orlando's story since it marks the moment when he abandons his epic persona, that is to say, his role as the valorous servant of God and Emperor Charlemagne, and flings himself wholeheartedly into the Romance mode. It also marks the beginning of the process that will ultimately lead to his madness. In this respect, his post-dream decision to discard his 'insegna del quartiero / distinta di color bianchi e vermigli' ['his distinctive emblem of red and white quarterings' (trans. mine)] (8. 85) and to sneak off in the night disguised in a black emblem presages the moment when he will strip himself entirely naked and run through the forest like a wild beast.

In this respect, Orlando is an example of the importance of epistemic vigilance — even in relation to the fabrications of our own mind (our dreams and personal narratives) — and of the dangers of an unchecked imagination.[46] Fiordispina, by contrast, provides an example of how to keep delusions under control with concrete evidence from the world around us. The Fiordispina episode appears in canto 25 of the *Orlando furioso* and offers light relief after canto 24 in which the full extent of Orlando's madness is described. As well as offering a change of mood, it extends a semi-serious counterpoint to Orlando's story as well. The story goes like this: Fiordispina falls in love with the damsel warrior, Bradamante, mistaking her for a man and brings her to her palace. Though Bradamante makes it clear that she is a woman, despite her masculine appearance, Fiordispina continues to desire her, perhaps all the more. They spend an evening together in the castle, then share a bed for the night, during which time Bradamante sleeps but Fiordispina tosses and turns, despairing of her 'impossible' desire for a woman. During this restless night, she dreams.

Hers is not the Petrarchan dream suffused with Neoplatonic undertones that Orlando had. If there is a literary model for it, it is Boccaccio with his emphasis on sensory authenticity and the value of everyday experience. In her dreams, 'le par veder che 'l ciel l'abbia concesso / Bradamante cangiato in miglior sesso' ['it seemed to her that Heaven had allotted to her a Bradamante transformed into a preferable sex'] (25.42). Her dreaming mind threw up images to 'far sue voglie liete' ['to requite her desires'], just as a thirst-tormented invalid, 'ne l'interrotta e turbida quïete' ['in his turbid, fitful rest'] will call to mind every drop of water he ever saw (25.43). It is not, in other words, Bradamante's ivory-white face, crimson lips and star-like eyes she dwells upon but that other part of her anatomy which, if improved by the gods, would satisfy her longing. Then Fiordispina would wake, the narrator says, and reach out — only to find 'pur sempre il sogno vano' ['that what she had seen was but an empty dream'] (25.43). So while Orlando, unmindful that the images projected in his dreaming mind were false, jumps out of bed and acts on his dream without further reflection, Fiordispina reaches out to test the veracity of hers and finds that it is indeed untrue. Through her, Ariosto playfully explores the role of embodied cognition (or situatedness) in the acquisition of beliefs and the testing of reality.[47]

Fiordispina's dream is clearly provocative. Ostensibly an expression of her frustrated desire, her groping of Bradamante's lack (combined with her sighs and moans) doubles as mild titillation, designed to suggest not the impossibility but the possibility of woman-to-woman love. As well as exploring questions of gender and sexuality (and the relationship between appearance and truth), the episode also makes a point about dreams. Though they may be a projection of fears and hopes, it reiterates, dreams are nonetheless compelling and on waking can feel real and significant. Sensible people will test the significance of their dreams before acting on them, deluded people will not because they no longer have the capacity to verify the reality of their imaginings (waking and not).

Certain cognitive theories of dreams arrive at similar conclusions though via very different routes. V. S. Ramachandran, for example, evokes the model of hemispheric specialization to compare dreams and dreaming with the process by which our alert mind tries to 'impose consistency, coherence and continuity' on our day-to-day experiences.[48] Hemispheric specialization is the idea that one hemisphere of the brain has specialized functions and that it takes greater charge than the other of particular types of mental activity. When we are awake, Ramachandran says, the left hemisphere of the brain (specializing in verbal and analytical activities) weaves a narrative that makes sense of the jumble of sensory inputs received by the right hemisphere (specialized in non-verbal activities such as visual and spatial thinking).[49] In order to make sense of the superabundance of information the brain receives every waking moment, the 'conservative' left hemisphere selects some sensory inputs and represses others and generally succeeds, thereby, in 'imposing consistency on to the storyline' of our lives.[50] When we sleep, however, the 'revolutionary' right hemisphere is allowed to escape the control of the 'die-hard conservative left' and to entertain alternative storylines that might, during waking hours, destabilize our sense of selfhood and of the world. It rehearses alternative scripts, which may range from the verisimilar to the bizarre. The left hemisphere's task, on waking, is to decide whether those nighttime scripts have any place in the daytime self-narrative, whether they chime with what stored memories and sensory evidence tells us is true or not. The *Furioso* makes no mention of the architecture of the brain and its division into hemispheres, of course. Orlando and Fiordispina's dreams are clearly invented by a wide-awake author and their primary function is almost certainly 'to suggest relevant psychological perspectives on the characters concerned, their fears, desires, preoccupations', as Cave puts it in his Introduction to this volume (p. 5). They manage, nonetheless, to present dreams in ways that resonate with contemporary cognitive psychology and to make a serious point: Dreams — like the narratives we produce to make the waking world intelligible — spring from the imaginative faculties and need to be regarded with caution (call it epistemic vigilance) — but not with neglect. As it turns out, both Orlando and Fiordispina's dreams are true / prophetic (though not in the sense Guido Giglioni discusses in his chapter in this volume). Orlando does fail to 'gioire' ['have joy from'] Angelica (8.83) and Fiordispina's Bradamante is, for all intents and purposes, transformed into the 'miglior sesso' ['better sex'] (25.43) when her identical twin brother Riciardetto appears in the palace the following night and opportunistically takes his sister's place in Fiordispina's bed. Truth-value, however, is not the real issue at stake here. What is at stake is that very Ariostean concern: the need to constantly check our impressions, dreams and imaginings against our senses and stored memories of the world, and vice versa.

The process of monitoring applies to the dreaming mind as much as to the wakeful story-telling mind and one's ability to exercise judgment and executive control over dreams is a likely indicator of one's ability to regulate the other processes that govern personal story-making too. When speculating on the source of B.X.'s fantasy of marital bliss, in fact, Miyazono, Bortolotti and Broome suggest that it must have come to him in a dream or a hallucination (p. 38). Like his fictional counterpart, Orlando, he was unable to tell the difference between his dreaming and waking experiences, taking his night-time fantasies to be more reliable than the written corroboration he received in N.'s letter of the external world. It is this that makes his disorder pathological. Simply believing that N., who does not love him, does love him would not be pathological, since this is likely to be a common misunderstanding in the general population. Being unable to distinguish his dreams from reality, however, is pathological because it demonstrates a dysfunction in his reality-testing mechanisms with the harmful consequence that he is no longer able to maintain a reasonable relationship with the woman who used to be his partner.[51] Calling his disorder the 'Orlando syndrome', therefore, captures perfectly not just the fact, but also the way and the reasons for which he was driven mad for love.

★ ★ ★ ★ ★

Ariosto's poem abounds with characters and stories full of insights that readers have enjoyed for five hundred years. It is especially perceptive on human reason and the distinction between the real, the imaginary and the pathological, thanks in no small way to the poet's own investment in and self-professed acquaintance with these topics. It is striking, though not surprising, to see how it resonates with subsequent literature (e.g. Shakespeare) and enriches the most up-to-date theories about the mind. For Ariosto, the poem is a fictional space within which to make some sense of the delicate negotiations between the mind and the world. For readers, it echoes with imperfectly acknowledged intuitions of our own about human reason and the human experience. Introducing the 'Orlando syndrome' to the cognitive sciences, therefore, is worthwhile because it evokes afresh the power of literature to create those alternative worlds in which many of us, much of the time, find it useful to live.

Notes to Chapter 1

1. The *Furioso* appeared in two later editions, one in 1522 (with minor changes, mainly linguistic) and another in 1532 (significantly revised and with numerous additions). This chapter refers to and quotes from the final 1532 version in the following edition: Ludovico Ariosto, *Orlando furioso*, ed. by Lanfranco Caretti (Turin: Einaudi, 1992). The English translations are mine or, if not marked as 'my trans.', the following: Ludovico Ariosto, *Orlando furioso*, trans. by Guido Waldman (Oxford: Oxford World Classics, 1983).
2. Back in 1965, Robert M. Durling asserted that 'madness is... the richest and most important theme of the poem' (p. 175), but the poem's focus on madness (and delusions) is only one part of its broader investigation of the powers and limits of human reason. As Eduardo Saccone asserted, 'piuttosto che un poema sulla pazzia, infatti, il *Furioso* è un'epica che ha per protagonista la ragione umana [...] i suoi limiti e le sue difficoltà' ['Rather than a poem about madness, in effect, the Furioso is an epic whose protagonist is human reason, its limits and its challenges'] (p. 169). Robert M. Durling, *The Figure of the Poet in Renaissance Epic* (Cambridge, Mass: Harvard University Press, 1965); Eduardo Saccone, *Il 'soggetto' del* Furioso *e altri saggi tra Quattro e Cinquecento* (Naples: Liguori Editore, 1974) [the translation is mine].
3. Studies of Orlando's madness are too numerable to list exhaustively, since most major studies of the poem deal with madness in some way or another. A list of those studies which treat madness as their central topic, however, should include the texts by Durling and Saccone cited above and the following: Giulio Ferroni, 'L'Ariosto e la concezione umanistica della follia', in *Ludovico Ariosto: Convegno Internazionale* (Rome: Accademia Nazionale dei Lincei, 1975), pp. 73–92; Elizabeth Chesney, 'Folly in Rabelais and Ariosto', *The Journal of Medieval and Renaissance Studies*, 7 (1977), 67–93; Andre Rochon, 'La folie d'amour dans le Roland furieux', in *Visages de la folie 1500–1650*, ed. by Augustin Redondo and Andre Rochon (Paris: Sorbonne, 1981), pp. 93–100; Enrico Musacchio, *Amore, ragione e follia: una rilettura dell'Orlando furioso* (Roma: Bulzoni, 1983); Elissa B. Weaver, 'A Reading of the Interlaced Plot of the *Orlando furioso*', *Ariosto Today: Contemporary Perspectives*, ed. by Donald Beecher, Massimo Ciavolella and Roberto Fedi (Toronto: University of Toronto Press, 2003), pp. 126–54; Marion A. Wells, '"Solvite Me": Epic, Romance and the Poetics of Melancholy in the *Orlando furioso*', *The Secret Wound: Love-Melancholy and Early Modern Romance* (Stanford: Stanford University Press, 2007), pp. 96–137; Rafaella Anconetani, 'L'*Orlando furioso* e l'*Elogia della Follia*: alcune note', *Bollettino di italianistica*, 2 (2009), 117–46.
4. See Saccone for an analysis of 'furioso' in the poem's title (pp. 201–04).
5. Karl Jaspers, *General Psychopathology*, trans. by J. Hoenig and Marian W. Hamilton (Baltimore: Johns Hopkins University Press, 1997), p. 106.
6. *Diagnostic and Statistical Manual of Mental Disorders, DSM-5* (Arlington, Va.: American Psychiatric Association, 2013), p. 87.
7. In this sense, I disagree with Elissa B. Weaver for whom Orlando is 'an exemplary reader', 'able to arrive at the truth in literary texts (the names of Angelica and Medoro united by love-knots — the simplest form of literary message he was to encounter, the Petrarchan poem written in Arabic, the oral text narrated by the shepherd)', p. 138. What is most striking in this episode is not Orlando's acceptance of the truth in what he reads, but the emphasis placed on his unwillingness to do so. Ariosto explicitly describes a man at pains to defend his prior beliefs from attack and to reject the truth of the words before him.
8. The success of Orlando's campaign to defend his beliefs against assault chimes with the distinction the *DSM-5* makes between delusions and non-pathological strongly held ideas which 'depends in part on the degree of conviction with which the belief is held despite clear or reasonable contradictory evidence regarding its veracity' (p. 87).

9. Richard P. Bentall, *Madness Explained* (London, 2003: Allen Lane); Allan Hobson, 'The Neurobiology of Consciousness: Lucid Dreaming Wakes up', *International Journal of Dream Research* 2.2 (2009): 41–44; Cristopher Moulin, 'Disordered Recognition Memory: Recollective Confabulation', *Cortex*, 49.6 (2013): 1541–52; and Phillip Gerrans, 'Pathologies of Hyperfamiliarity in Dreams, Delusions and Déjà Vu', *Frontiers in Psychology*, 5 (2014): 1–10.
10. Thanks to Kengo Miyazono for pointing me in the direction of Reverse Othello syndrome.
11. Peter V. Butler, 'Reverse Othello syndrome Subsequent to Traumatic Brain Injury', *Psychiatry*, 63.1 (2000), p. 86.
12. On the crucial importance of the theme of 'fede' in the *Furioso*, see Eduardo Saccone, 'Cloridano e Medoro, con alcuni argomenti per una lettura del primo *Furioso*', in *Il 'soggetto'*, pp. 161–200.
13. All citations of the 'reverse Othello syndrome' relate back to Butler's article from 2000. These include Ryan McKay, Robyn Langdon, and Max Coltheart, '"Sleights of Mind": Delusions and Self-Deception', *Delusion and Self-Deception: Affective and Motivational Influences on Belief Formation*, ed. by Tim Bayne, Jordi Fernandez (Hove: Psychology Press, 2009), pp. 165–85; Alfred R. Mele, 'Delusional Confabulations and Self-Deception', *Confabulation: Views from Neuroscience, Psychiatry, Psychology and Philosophy*, ed. by William Hirstein (Oxford: Oxford University Press, 2009), pp. 139–59; Lisa Bortolotti, 'The Epistemic Innocence of Motivated Delusions', *Consciousness and Cognition*, 33 (2015), 490–99.
14. Todd and Dewhurst were the first to use the term in their article: 'The Othello Syndrome: A Study of the Psychopathology of Sexual Jealousy', *Journal of Nervous and Mental Disease*, 122 (1959), 367–74.
15. Marcia A. Miller, Andreas M. Kummerow, and Tennyson Mgutshini, 'Othello Syndrome: Preventing a Tragedy when Treating Patients with Delusional Disorders', *Journal of Psychosocial Nursing and Mental Health Services*, 48.8 (2010), p. 21.
16. Gregory B. Leong, et al., 'The Dangerousness of Persons with the Othello Syndrome', *Journal of Forensic Sciences*, 39 (1994), p. 1445.
17. The *DSM–5* is discredited, too, for its links with pharmaceutical companies (that is to say, for the way in which it can be said to match descriptions of conditions to the actions of marketable cures); its 'medicalisation' of certain natural and normal responses to experiences; and its inability to account for the social, biological and other causation of many mental health problems. See Lisa Cosgrove and Darrel A. Regie, 'Toward Credible Conflict of Interest Policies in Clinical Psychiatry', *Psychiatric Times* (2009), <http://www.psychiatrictimes.com/articles/toward-credible-conflict-interest-policies-clinical-psychiatry#sthash.etWvz2pA.dpuf> [accessed 12 October 2015]; and the British Psychological Society's response to the *DSM–V* (referenced below).
18. The British Psychological Society, 'Response to the American Psychiatric Association: DSM-5 Development' (2011), <http://apps.bps.org.uk/_publicationfiles/consultation-responses/DSM-5%202011%20-%20BPS%20response.pdf> [accessed 12 October 2015].
19. A. D. Nuttall, *A New Mimesis: Shakespeare and the Representation of Reality* (London and New York: Methuen, 1983), p. 134
20. A number of studies of Othello syndrome emphasize the 'organic' nature of the condition, that is to say, its origins in brain defects or the use and/or abuse of medicinal and recreational drugs and alcohol. In this sense, too, Othello is an eloquent metaphor since the play says he suffers from epilepsy, one of the conditions that predisposes humans to delusional disorders of this kind.
21. The fault in question is his 'deluded pursuit of Angelica'. Jane Everson, *The Italian Romance Epic in the Age of Humanism* (Oxford: Oxford University Press, 2001), p. 346.
22. This is the point made by Bortolotti et al. whose chapter in this volume sets out 'to illustrate the continuity between clinically and non-clinically significant beliefs' and delusions, p. 39.
23. 'Two-factor delusions' is the technical term used to describe delusions that feature a first factor, which explains where a delusion comes from (e.g. Orlando's enamourment with Angelica), and a second factor or impairment that explains why the delusion is not rejected (e.g. Orlando's excessive adherence to the chivalric code). See Anne Aimola Davies and Martin Davies, 'Explaining Pathologies of Belief', *Psychiatry as Cognitive Neuroscience: Philosophical Perspectives*, ed. by Matthew Broome and Lisa Bortolotti (Oxford: Oxford University Press, 2009), pp.

285–323; and Kengo Miyazono, Lisa Bortolotti and Matthew Broome, 'Prediction-error and Two-factor Theories of Delusion: Competitors or Allies?', *Aberrant Beliefs and Reasoning*, ed. by Niall Gilbraith (Hove: Psychology Press, 2015), pp. 34–55.
24. See Marion A. Wells on the ways in which the physiological features of Orlando's madness chime with early modern medical authorities on love-melancholy, 'Solvite me: Epic, Romance and the Poetics of Melancholy in the *Orlando furioso*', *Italian Studies*, 59 (2004), p. 24. This essay and her subsequent book, *The Secret Wound* (cited above in footnote 3), emphasize the previously under-valued influence of medical — as well as literary — accounts of erotomania on Ariosto's construction of Orlando's madness.
25. There have been a number of cognitive studies recently of the benefits and powers of delusions. See Bortolotti et al.'s chapter in this volume, for example, and also Lisa Bortolotti, 'The Epistemic Innocence of Motivated Delusions', *Consciousness and Cognition*, 33 (2015), 490–99. Other examples include David E. Raskin and Kathleen E. Sullivan, 'Erotomania', *American Journal of Psychology*, 131.9 (1974), 1033–1035; Richard P. Bentall, 'Cognitive Biases and Abnormal Beliefs: Towards a Model of Persecutor Delusions', in Anthony David and John P. Cutting (eds), *The Neuropsychology of Schizophrenia* (Hove: Lawrence Erlbaum Associates Ltd., 1994), pp. 337–60; Vilayanur S. Ramachandran, 'The Evolutionary Biology of Self-Deception, Laughter, Dreaming and Depression: Some Clues from Anosognosia', *Medical Hypotheses*, 47.5 (1996), 347–62; Ema Sullivan-Bisset, 'Implicit Bias, Confabulation and Epistemic Innocence', *Consciousness and Cognition*, 33 (2015), 548–60); and Butler, 2000.
26. For the distinction between 'psychotic' and 'everyday' delusions (i.e. between those false belief systems which have distressing effects on the subject's health, social and professional life and those which do not), see Andy Hamilton, 'Against the Belief Model of Delusion', in Cheung Chung, Bill Fulford and George Graham (eds), *Reconceiving Schizophrenia* (Oxford: Oxford University Press, 2007), pp. 217–34.
27. It is Orlando's propensity to adopt a chivalric (and unsuitable) personal narrative and to reason on the basis of fictional probabilities that became the inspiration a hundred years later for Cervantes's *Don Quixote*. Like Orlando, the knight from La Mancha falls hostage to narratives drawn from literature and not from the world around him and, like his predecessor, he comes a cropper each time reality clashes with the fictional codes he adheres to. Reasoning on the basis of fictional and not realist probabilities has come to be called, in fact, Quixotic reasoning and is a common literary *topos* from the seventeenth century onwards. For more on this, see Karin Kukkonen, 'Quixotic Reasoning: Counterfactuals, Causation and Literary Story Worlds', *Paragraph*, 37 (2014), 47–61.
28. Vilayanur S. Ramachandran, 'The Evolutionary Biology of Self-Deception, Laughter, Dreaming and Depression: Some Clues from Anosognosia', p. 351.
29. Desiderio Eramus, *The Praise of Folly and Other Writings*, trans. by Robert M. Adams (New York and London: W. W. Norton and Company, 1989).
30. For the best recent studies of the way in which Ariosto straddles romance and epic genres, see David Quint, 'The Figure of Atlante: Ariosto and Boiardo's Poem', *Modern Languages Notes*, 94 (1979), 77– 91; Patricia Parker, *Inescapable Romance: Studies in the Poetics of a Mode* (Princeton: Princeton University Press, 1979, rev. edn, 2015); Albert Ascoli, *Ariosto's Bitter Harmony: Crisis and Evasion in the Italian Renaissance* (Princeton: Princeton University Press, 1987); Daniel Javitch, 'The Grafting of Virgilian Epic in *Orlando furioso*', in *Renaissance Transactions: Ariosto and Tasso*, ed. by Valeria Finucci (Durham & London: Duke University Press, 1999), pp. 56 –77; and Sergio Zatti, *Il Furioso fra epos e romanzo* (Lucca: Maria Pacini Fazzi Editore, 1990).
31. For an account of these years, see Jane Everson, *Italy in Crisis: 1494* (Oxford: Legenda, 2000).
32. This is not to confuse the narrator of the poem with Ariosto himself because, as Stefano Jossa points out, 'non si deve far l'errore [...] d'interpretare la poesia ariostesca in chiave biografica, perché la sua lirica, come tutta la lirica cortigiano, è prima di tutto un gioco di società' ['we should never commit the error of reading Ariosto biographically because his poetry, like all court poetry, is first and foremost a sort of parlour game' (my translation)]; Stefano Jossa, *Ariosto* (Bologna: Il Mulino, 2009), p. 15. There is no way of knowing how much of Ariosto's life and circumstances are invested in Orlando, with whom the narrator identifies and, indeed, in the narrator himself. What is certain, though, is that the narrator acts as a spokesperson for the

society in which Ariosto lives and writes, just as Orlando acts as a figure for the narrator's self-confessed madness.
33. As Elizabeth Chesney put it, Orlando's folly is 'polemic in value, used largely to question the sanity of society's comfortable institutions, those inessential edifices which lull man into unconsciousness' (p. 85).
34. Paul Crichton, 'Did Othello have 'the Othello Syndrome'?', *Journal of Forensic Psychiatry*, 7 (1996), 161–69.
35. It is worth taking a look at the encyclopedia of literary names that lend themselves to medical phenomena to test the extent to which this is true. *Medicine, Literature and Eponyms*, ed. by Alvin E. Rodin and Jack D. Key (1989).
36. On Oedipus's lack of an Oedipus complex, see A.D. Nuttall's essay on 'Freud and Shakespeare: Hamlet' in John Batchelor, Tom Cain, and Claire Lamont (eds), *Shakespearean Continuities* (Basingstoke: Macmillan Press, 1997), pp. 123–37.
37. See Cave's Introduction to this volume, which highlights this aspect of delusion by emphasizing its roots in the Latin 'ludere' (to play, to mimic, to mock or to deceive).
38. It is an example of the sort of 'genial aberration' that Erasmus's Folly says is to be desired because it frees the mind 'from anxiety and worry while at the same time imbuing it with the many fragrances of pleasure' (p. 39). This type of 'mental error', says Folly 'is what Cicero, writing to Atticus, wishes for his friend as a special bounty of the gods, a delusion that will relieve his distress over the evils of the age' (p. 39).
39. Ryan McKay and Daniel Dennett, 'The Evolution of Misbelief', *Behavioural and Brain Sciences*, 32.6 (2009), p. 494.
40. 'Innocent' here is meant in the judicial sense of an act that may be blameworthy in its own right but that is freed of blame because of its role in preventing greater harm from happening in the circumstances. Bortolotti describes as 'epistemically innocent' those delusions that carry a significant epistemic benefit, despite their epistemic costs. For more on the epistemic 'innocence' and possible benefits of self-motivated delusions, see Lisa Bortolotti, 'The Epistemic Innocence of Motivated Delusions' and and Sullivan-Bisset, 'Implicit Bias, Confabulation and Epistemic Innocence'.
41. For more on this, see Monica Calabritto, 'Examples, References and Quotations in Sixteenth-Century Medical Texts', *La parola ritrovata: Fonti e analisi letteraria*, ed. by Costanzo di Girolamo and Ivano Paccagnella (Palermo: Sellerio Editore, 1982), pp. 58–93.
42. 'Quod si ex tali amore cutubut, seu melancholia errabunda: vel mania affectus omnino fuerit (ut Rolandus ex Angelicae amore olim laborasse a Ludovico Ariosto in suo poema graphice describitur) pro eius cura adhibe quae in superioribus capitibus in cura melancholiae, cutubut, & maniae posita sunt' ['And if an individual is affected by 'cutubut' — or 'errabund melancholy' — or mania (of the kind Orlando felt for Angelica as Ludovico Ariosto skilfully describes in his poem), let him be cured by the remedies that have been outlined in previous chapters on melancholia, cutubut, and mania' (trans. mine)]. Quoted in Calabritto, p. 72.
43. Lisa Bortolotti, *Delusions and Other Irrational Beliefs* (Oxford: Oxford University Press, 2010), p. 4.
44. Honigmann, in fact, cites the *Orlando furioso* as a source for Othello's epileptic fit in his glossary on IV, i, ll. 35–40: 'Othello's fit in some ways represents [...] the raging hero in Greene's *Orlando furioso* (printed 1594).' William Shakespeare, *Othello*, ed. by Ernest Honigmann (London, New Delhi, New York, Sydney: Bloomsbury, first edn 1997, repr. 2014), p. 256.
45. Though I disagree with some of her conclusions (see footnote above), Elissa B. Weaver's comparison of three cases of love madness (the cases of Orlando, Rodomonte and Bradamante) is highly effective in showing how Ariosto enriches his development of themes by conducting similar narratives along different trajectories and towards different conclusions. The technique of *entrelacement*, 'which does not allow a continuous, linear presentation of the plot', isolates single episodes enabling readers 'to appreciate what is unique about' each one. At the same time, it sets up connections between those single episodes, so that readers are also encouraged to cross-compare and, in so doing, allow new meanings to emerge (Weaver, 2003, p. 144).
46. The term 'epistemic vigilance', proposed by Sperber, Wilson et al., refers to 'a suite of cognitive mechanisms' which play the fundamental role in human communication of protecting against 'the risk of being accidentally or intentionally misinformed'. Dan Sperber, Fabrice Clément,

Christophe Heintz, Olivier Mascaro, Hugo Mercier, Gloria Origgi and Deirdre Wilson, 'Epistemic Vigilance', *Mind and Language*, 25.4 (2010), p. 359.
47. For a concise overview of embodied cognition, see Michael Dawson, 'Embedded and Situated Cognition', *The Routledge Handbook of Embodied Cognition* (2014), pp. 50–67. The idea that cognition depends on aspects of the body beyond the mind would not have been alien to early modern thinkers for whom the role of the senses and sense perception in the acquisition of knowledge was increasingly important. Guido Giglioni points out that there was a period between the late Middle Ages and the seventeenth century 'when it seemed that the senses could somehow realign themselves with the reality of things.' He goes on to argue that 'during the Renaissance, a number of important authors in such diverse fields as philosophy, medicine, literature and the visual arts had become increasingly persuaded that the faculty of sense could convey knowledge of nature, ethical discernment and aesthetic acumen'. Guido Giglioni, 'Sense', *Renaissance Keywords*, ed. by Ita Mac Carthy (Oxford: Legenda, 2013), p. 15.
48. Ramachandran, 'The Evolutionary Biology of Self-Deception, Laughter, Dreaming and Depression', p. 351.
49. Ramachandran concedes that hemispheric specialization is 'almost certainly a gross over-simplification' and reminds us that the human brain also has a front and back, an up and down and countless other subdivisions' that affect its functioning (347). It is, however, a useful means of thinking about the ways in which the human brain receives, sorts and organizes the information about the world that it receives.
50. Ramachandran notes that the left hemisphere, in this respect, might be said to correspond roughly to that which Freud calls the ego.
51. For a discussion of what makes a delusional belief pathological, see Jerome C. Wakefield, 'The Concept of Mental Disorder: On the Boundary Between Biological Fact and Social Facts', *American Psychologist* (1992), 373–88. Wakefield argues that delusional beliefs are pathological when they involve harmful malfunctions of the mind.

CHAPTER 2

What Makes a Belief Delusional?[1]

Lisa Bortolotti, Rachel Gunn, Ema Sullivan-Bissett

Introduction

In philosophy, psychiatry, and cognitive science, definitions of clinical delusions are not based on the mechanisms responsible for the formation of delusions, since there is no consensus yet on what causes delusions. Some of the defining features of delusions are *epistemic* and focus on whether delusions are true, justified, or rational, as in the definition of delusions as fixed beliefs that are badly supported by evidence. Other defining features of delusions are *psychological* and focus on whether delusions are harmful, as in the definition of delusions as beliefs that disrupt good functioning. Even if the epistemic features go some way towards capturing what otherwise different instances of clinical delusions have in common, they do not succeed in distinguishing delusions as a clinical phenomenon from everyday irrational beliefs. Focusing on the psychological features is a more promising way to mark the difference between clinical and non-clinical irrational beliefs, but there is wide variability in the extent to which delusions are psychologically harmful, and some everyday irrational beliefs can affect functioning in similarly negative ways. In this chapter we consider three types of belief that share similar epistemic features and exhibit variation with respect to how psychologically harmful they are: (1) delusions of thought insertion, (2) alien abduction beliefs, and (3) self-enhancing beliefs. In the light of the similarities and differences among these cases, we highlight the difficulty in providing an answer to what makes an irrational belief *delusional*.

1. Definitions and Examples of Clinical Delusions

In psychiatry some disorders of cognition are distinguished from instances of 'normal' cognitive functioning and from other disorders in virtue of their *surface features* rather than in virtue of the underlying mechanisms responsible for their occurrence. Aetiological considerations about psychiatric disorders are the object of study and debate, but they often cannot play a significant classificatory and diagnostic role, because there is not sufficient knowledge or consensus about the causal history of those disorders. Moreover, it is not always possible to identify a pathological behaviour as the symptom of a certain disorder, as disorders that are likely to differ both in their causal histories and in their overall manifestations may give rise to very similar patterns of behaviour.

Delusions are a good example of how symptoms of psychiatric disorders are defined in terms of their surface features.[2] Such features are largely *epistemic*. Key terms include 'belief', 'proof', 'evidence', 'judgement', 'warrant', 'falsehood', and 'incorrectness'.

> Delusion. A false belief based on incorrect inference about external reality that is firmly held despite what almost everyone else believes and despite what constitutes incontrovertible and obvious proof or evidence to the contrary. The belief is not ordinarily accepted by other members of the person's culture or subculture (i.e. it is not an article of religious faith). When a false belief involves a value judgment, it is regarded as a delusion only when the judgment is so extreme as to defy credibility. Delusional conviction can sometimes be inferred from an overvalued idea (in which case the individual has an unreasonable belief or idea but does not hold it as firmly as is the case with a delusion).[3]
>
> A person is deluded when they have come to hold a particular belief with a degree of firmness that is both utterly unwarranted by the evidence at hand, and that jeopardises their day-to-day functioning.[4]

Consider the following examples of delusions. A man comes to believe that his parents were replaced by impostors when he was a baby (*Capgras delusion*). Family members and healthcare professionals attempt to persuade him that his parents have not been substituted, but they fail. The man becomes hostile and aggressive towards his parents, trying to choke his mother on one occasion.[5]

A woman comes to believe that she is surrounded by alien forces controlling her actions and slowly taking over people's bodies (*delusion of persecution*). She has a number of different delusional beliefs that are interrelated and affect her interpretation of most events occurring in her life. To protect herself and her loved ones, she breaks contact with her family and moves to a different city.[6]

A young woman is convinced that a fellow student is in love with her although the two have never spoken to each other (*erotomania*). She takes TV messages, the colour of dresses, licence plates on cars, and other sources as evidence that the young man is planning to marry her.[7]

Definitions of delusions that are largely epistemic are successful in highlighting what is common among the three cases we have briefly described above. People who report delusions seem genuinely to believe what they are saying. Reports are endorsed with conviction even if they are not plausible given the person's other beliefs. Delusions are tenaciously maintained in the face of challenges. The epistemic features of delusions exemplified by the three cases we have described are found in other clinical delusions, but also in a variety of everyday irrational beliefs.

Some of the definitions of delusions helpfully include some reference to the psychological features of delusions, that is, their effect on wellbeing or good functioning (see the definition above by McKay and colleagues). Delusions such as Capgras, delusions of persecution, and erotomania are often acted upon; they can become very disruptive and distressing, with pervasive and lasting negative effects on people's lives.

Our goal here is to show how the similarities across the clinical/non-clinical spectrum make it difficult to demarcate delusions sharply. Beliefs epistemically similar to clinical delusions include prejudiced beliefs, such as racist beliefs about black waiters offering a worse service and being less worthy of tipping;[8] superstitious beliefs, such as beliefs about nights with a full moon causing accidents;[9] and self-enhancing beliefs, such as excessively positive beliefs about one's own qualities.[10] Such beliefs are akin to delusional beliefs with respect to their epistemic features: their contents seem to be genuinely believed and held with conviction; moreover, beliefs are not only implausible, but also held in the face of apparent counter-evidence or counter-argument. Differently from delusional beliefs found in the clinical population, prejudiced, superstitious, or self-enhancing beliefs are not associated with a psychiatric diagnosis and are not generally accompanied by psychological distress.

In the rest of the chapter, we want to illustrate the continuity between clinically and non-clinically significant beliefs by reference to a delusion associated with a diagnosis of schizophrenia, *the belief that a thought has been inserted in one's head* (section two); a belief that is common in certain sub-cultures, but is not mainstream, the *belief that one has been abducted by aliens* (section three); and a set of beliefs that are very widespread in the non-clinical population, *self-enhancing beliefs* (section four). Our goal is to show that similar deviations from norms of truth, justification, and rationality can be found across the clinical/non-clinical spectrum, and that there is also variability in the psychological effects of such beliefs. In the light of this, identifying what makes a belief delusional poses a major challenge, a challenge we return to in section five.

2. The Delusion of Thought Insertion

In this section, we consider the case of thought insertion. Thought insertion is a symptom regularly associated with a diagnosis of schizophrenia. A thought is inserted when it has the quality of not being one's own and is ascribed to an external agency.[11]

In thought insertion, people (1) experience a thought as alien or foreign (*experience of an alien thought*), and (2) offer an explanation for this experience, that is, that some third party is inserting thoughts into their head (*the delusional explanation of the experience in terms of literal, non-metaphorical insertion*). We are going to offer some examples of thought insertion that have been taken from various threads about thought insertion on mental health forums on different websites.[12]

> Often, in a quiet place, and all the time at night when I am alone, I experience thoughts that do not 'feel' like my own. It's like they come out of a part of my brain that is not the part that controls my 'normal' thoughts and into my awareness from there. It is hard to describe. These 'false thoughts' are usually about random subject matter and usually make little sense, but are extremely distracting. Back when I first experienced them, I thought I was psychic and that I was picking up other people's thoughts (telepathy?). However, now I know that they are a part of psychosis because I experience them around the times I hallucinate.[13]

> Yes, I get thought insertion all the time. Mine is pretty bizarre though and I have enough insight to realize this. I get thoughts directly from the government

and sometimes even alien beings from another world. There were times that it was very severe. Sometimes it is scary because they tell me things and what to do. I haven't been getting thought insertion that recently since I have been doing better though. I get these thoughts because of a chip in my head[;] even though this technology is being used against me, I am still fascinated by technology all around me good and bad. People see technology around them but they don't realize that the gov has technology that is 200 years more advanced than our own and the aliens are even further along than that. I have psychic powers as well, but not picking up thoughts from others around me (except this has happened a few times) but my psychic powers are mainly telling the future and influencing events around the world. I am not proud of this power.[14]

i truly do have unwanted thoughts that are forced into my head from somewhere... I mean I will have a thought saying my grandmother is a bitch. I would never ever think of my grandmother as a bitch. She is one of the greatest women I know and I adore her. So how is that a delusion? It is an intrusive thought! I sure didnt imagine it!.... i really do not think my grandmother is a bitch. i think these thoughts are evil and came from an evil being. Some thoughts however that pop into my head all of a sudden are my own thoughts and i can recognize that even though they are unwanted, but some are just plain ridiculous and mean and i know must be from an outside force. That's just what i believe. probably has nothing to do with my illness.[15]

The first two examples above (from Alienonite and Firebird) highlight that there is a real phenomenon with perplexing features. The person believes that some thoughts have been 'inserted' and have an alien quality to them. The thoughts are described as 'different from my usual thoughts' or 'false'. Alienonite previously believed that she must be psychic. Firebird claims he has the insight to realise that his experiences are bizarre, yet he still believes that thoughts entering his stream of consciousness are coming from aliens and from the government via a chip in his head. Both Alienonite and Firebird lack a sense of ownership and agency regarding these thoughts. Alienonite says that the thoughts 'do not feel like her own', and Firebird is certain the thoughts come from others. They also have other anomalous experiences and beliefs: Alienonite has hallucinations, and Firebird believes he has special powers. The third example (from Star-28) is of a thought that the person *does not like* and *does not want to have*. Star-28 insists that she would not think about her grandmother in the way the alien thought suggests, and says that the thought 'must be from an outside force'.

Ordinarily one does not question ownership of one's experiences — if one picks up a pen to write something, one does not have to ask *who* picked up the pen; if one feels happy about eating an ice-cream in the sun, one does not have to ask *who* is feeling happy. Arguably, it is self-evident that the physical and mental actions involved in doing things, feeling emotions, and having thoughts are one's own. Those actions could not be but *one's own*. That is why it is so hard to grasp what people mean when they say that they 'experience' and access by introspection thoughts that are not their own.[16]

There are some obvious features that make the belief that a thought has been inserted into one's head a delusion. The belief is usually firmly held, resistant to challenges, and accompanied by other unusual experiences that could be associated with a diagnosis of schizophrenia. But what is commonly called 'thought insertion' is a complex and heterogeneous phenomenon and there are multiple ways in which it might manifest itself. The experience of a thought being alien does not itself count as a delusional belief. For instance, the experience of a thought which is not owned can be one which is relatively neutral. Consider a person experiencing thoughts that seem alien but have a content she might well think anyway. The content of the thought is not threatening or problematic, and it does not contain distressing or unwanted ideas. Whilst the experience of having a thought that feels alien may be distressing, the content of the thought itself might not have a detrimental effect on the person. A person experiencing thought insertion with extremely distressing or unpleasant content might find it difficult to ignore her experience, and live with it. The nature or strength of the threat to the self (or threat to the ego) and the way a person responds to it determines whether the alien thought becomes problematic or detrimental.

This kind of experience is not yet a delusion (even if the person is certain that the thoughts are not hers). If the phenomenon persists and no explanation is found, then the person may search for relief from the strange experience, and come to a personally salient explanation, for example, that another is contacting her *telepathically*. A belief about how the thought is inserted qualifies as a delusion in some of the definitions we considered earlier if it seems to be a genuine belief, is held with high conviction, has an implausible content, and is resistant to counterevidence. Prior to the development of the belief about having been telepathically contacted, the phenomenon might have been described as a mere perceptual anomaly.

The phenomenon of thought insertion has differing degrees of intrusion or influence, from little or no influence to a compulsion to think (and perhaps do) what the voice or thought commands. The level of intrusion, distress, and influence might be regarded as a secondary phenomenon. In psychiatry (as in the rest of medicine) a value judgment which relates to the harm or potential harm that the experience of thought insertion has for the person is made by the clinician to determine diagnosis and therapeutic intervention.[17]

3. Alien Abduction Belief

In this section we will consider claims made by some people that they have been abducted by aliens, and reflect on the similarities and differences between their beliefs and clinical delusions. As is the convention in the literature, we will refer to people who believe that they have been abducted by aliens as 'abductees'. Consider three representative reports from Richard McNally and Susan Clancy's studies of abductees' experiences:

> A female abductee was lying on her back when she woke up from a sound sleep. Her body was completely paralyzed and she experienced the sensation of levitating above her bed. Her heart was pounding, her breathing was shallow, she felt tense all over. She was terrified. She was able to open her eyes, and when she did so, she saw three beings standing at the foot of her bed in the glowing light.

> [A] female abductee was lying on her back when she woke up in the middle of the night. She was completely paralyzed, and felt electrical vibrations throughout her body. She was sweating, struggling to breathe, and felt her heart pounding in terror. When she opened her eyes, she saw an insect-like alien being on top of her bed.
>
> A male abductee awoke in the middle of the night seized with panic. He was entirely paralyzed, and felt electricity shooting throughout his body. He felt his energy draining away from him. He could see several alien beings standing around his bed.[18]

An initial reaction to these reports is to question whether people actually believe their bizarre claims. Aside from the sheer implausibility of abductees' claims, there are no reasons for thinking that they disbelieve them or are lying with respect to them. Additionally, McNally and Clancy found that the physiological responses of abductees when listening to recordings of themselves reporting their abduction experience were larger than the responses that subjects with Post Traumatic Stress Disorder (PTSD) exhibited when listening to scripts of their experiences.[19] They take this finding to 'underscore the power of emotional belief', and though abductees may not qualify for a diagnosis of PTSD, their psychophysiologic profiles will 'resemble that of PTSD patients'.[20] These experimental results might be indicative of abductees *believing* the reports in the scripts they listen to, and their doing so would explain their reactions to them which are in line with reactions people with PTSD have to hearing scripts of their traumatic experiences.

How do abductees come to hold these bizarre beliefs? A typical case is described by McNally as involving the following: a person has the kind of experience given in the reports above; she wonders what happened, starts reading about the kind of experience she had, sees a therapist who endorses the abduction explanation for such an experience, and enters into memory recovery sessions via hypnosis. That person may then start generating more details under hypnosis about the experience and what happened thereafter, such as being 'whisked through walls up into the sky into the spaceships', being 'sexually probed by aliens', and 'involved in hybrid breeding experimentation' before being 'brought back down to the bedroom, before the break of dawn'.[21]

Some theorists working on abduction beliefs explain why abductees have the experiences that they do by appeal to awareness during sleep paralysis (ASP) and hypnopompic hallucinations. During Rapid Eye Movement (REM) sleep, the sleeper is immobilized, insofar as motoric output is blocked. Sometimes a sleeper can wake up before the paralysis has disappeared, and they can become aware that they are unable to move.[22] ASP can be accompanied by an increase in heart rate, difficulty breathing, and feelings of dread.[23]

Sleep paralysis can be accompanied by hypnopompic hallucinations, so the sleeper is unable to move and is also hallucinating sights and sounds in this state. Visual hallucinations might include 'lights, animals, strange figures, and demons', and auditory hallucinations might include 'heavy footsteps, humming or buzzing noises, and sounds of heavy objects being moved'.[24]

Imagine opening your eyes shortly before dawn, attempting to roll over in your bed, and suddenly realizing that you are entirely paralyzed. While lying helplessly on your back and unable to cry out for help, you become aware of sinister figures lurking in your bedroom. As they move closer to your bed, your heart begins to pound violently and you feel as if you are suffocating. You hear buzzing sounds, and feel electrical sensations shooting throughout your body. Within moments, the visions vanish and you can move again. Terrified, you wonder what has just happened.[25]

Having an experience of this kind leads some people to search for an explanation. Some people may know the real cause of the experience and so search no longer. However, though awareness during sleep paralysis and hallucination is relatively high among the general population, knowledge of these states is not common. For this reason, it is unlikely for the experience to be explained by appeal to such states.[26]

We now turn to the epistemic surface features which typically characterize abduction beliefs, in order to show similarities between abduction beliefs and delusions with respect to their deviation from ideal epistemic standards. We saw earlier that delusional beliefs are firmly held despite contrary evidence. In her book *Abducted*, Clancy notes that

> Once the seed of belief was planted, once alien abduction was even suspected, the abductees began to search for confirmatory evidence. And once the search had begun, the evidence almost always showed up. [...] Once we've adopted the initial premises ('I think I've been abducted by aliens'), we find it very difficult to disabuse ourselves of them; they become resilient, immune to external argument.[27]

We might also think that the evidence abductees have does not strongly support the content of a belief, since oftentimes there are alternative explanations available to them. Even when abductees are aware of the naturalistic explanations for their experiences, they do not adopt these explanations. This also suggests that alien abduction beliefs are similar to delusional beliefs with respect to their epistemic features.

It might be thought that alien abduction beliefs are different from delusional beliefs since beliefs with alien abduction content are shared within a culture, and rather culture-specific (most abductees are to be found in the US). As we saw earlier, the *DSM-5* definition of delusion suggests that a belief cannot be a delusion, or at least cannot be a bizarre delusion, if it is shared within a culture: 'Delusions are deemed bizarre if they are clearly implausible and not understandable to same-culture peers and do not derive from ordinary life experiences. [...].' Alien abduction beliefs are 'clearly implausible', but they are held by many people; indeed there are mini-cultures of abductees. Typically, alien abduction beliefs are not *collective* beliefs (comparable to *folie à deux* cases). Rather, they are *individualized*, but held by many individuals.

Here we do not take a stand on whether alien abduction beliefs *are* delusional beliefs. We just observe that the stipulation in the *DSM* which rules out that alien abduction beliefs are delusions because they are widely held does not speak against the epistemic similarities we have drawn between cases of alien abduction belief and cases of delusion.

4. Self-enhancing Beliefs

In this section, we want to focus on self-enhancing beliefs. So-called 'positive illusions' are defined as 'enduring patterns of beliefs' about self, world, and future, and are prevalent in the non-clinical population. There are at least three types of positive illusions.[28]

Some beliefs are about the capacity that the person has to control external events (*illusion of control*). Subject to such illusory perceptions, the person tends to believe that her thoughts affect the external world more than they actually do and that it is in her power to bring about positive events. Further, positive illusions affect self-perception, self-evaluation, and autobiographical memory. The person interprets her past performance as better than it actually was, and sees herself as more attractive, skilful, talented, and virtuous than average (*self-enhancement*). Interestingly, the biases affecting self-perception seem to apply to the person's romantic partner as well. What psychologists call 'the love-is-blind bias' is the tendency to see romantic partners as more attractive, intelligent, and talented than they actually are. This is generally thought to contribute to satisfying and lasting relationships. Finally, the person believes that her future will bring progress, and that it will not feature negative events that are statistically very common, such as a serious illness or a break-up (*unrealistic optimism*).

Although positive illusions are a robust phenomenon in people of different sex, age, economic status, and culture, they can manifest differently across individuals, and some illusions seem to be culture-dependent. In Japanese culture, for instance, evidence for illusions of control has been found, but there is little evidence for positive self-regard or enhanced self-esteem, and more evidence for self-criticism in comparison with Western samples.[29] Some psychologists argue that positive illusions are biologically adaptive and improve people's chances to survive, reproduce, and have lasting relationships that ensure protection for their offspring.[30] One of the most discussed findings is that positive illusions promote *mental health*, helping people find meaning in their lives, be caring, motivated, creative, productive, and develop resilience, that is, the capacity to 'bounce back' after adversities.[31]

Unrealistic optimism about health prospects can have immediate psychological benefits, as people are less worried about their future if they think that they are unlikely to suffer from a disease. But there are also significantly bad consequences when people underestimate risks and fail to adopt preventive measures that would improve their prospects. For instance, the belief that one is at low risk of negative outcomes may lead to the decision to continue smoking due to the belief that one is unlikely to suffer from lung cancer, or the decision not to use contraception due to the belief that one is unlikely to contract sexually transmitted diseases.[32]

Originally, Taylor distinguished positive illusions from delusions on the basis of positive illusions being more flexible and more sensitive to evidence, but it has been shown that not only are positive illusions implausible given the available evidence, they also are resistant to negative feedback. Here is a telling example. In one interesting study, medical students' assessment of their own ability at the end of medical school correlates with their initial assessment of their ability in their first year, irrespective of supervisors' ratings or exam results.[33] One interpretation of how students manage to maintain positive self-evaluations is that they redefine the criteria for medical ability to match the criteria they can comfortably satisfy, and thus preserve a sense that they are medically able.[34]

Recently, further evidence has suggested that there are several strategies for maintaining positive illusions in the light of challenges or negative feedback (Hepper and Sedikides 2012): (1) regarding positive evaluations as more reliable than negative ones; (2) interpreting ambiguous or neutral feedback as positive; (3) when failure is expected, behaving in a way that could be used to justify future negative feedback (for instance, drinking too much before an important exam); (4) when failure is experienced and negative feedback received, focusing on different aspects of one's performance that are positive. Such strategies make positive illusions resistant to a variety of potential challenges.

This suggests that the difference between delusional beliefs and self-enhancing beliefs is not epistemically significant.

5. What Makes a Belief Delusional?

As we said, clinical delusions are characterized by surface features of two kinds, epistemic (fixity, implausibility) and psychological (negative impact on functioning). As it has already been observed,[35] epistemic features alone are not sufficient to demarcate delusions from other irrational beliefs. We have looked at three cases of irrational belief which share these epistemic features. In this section, we want to consider whether the psychological criterion is more promising for distinguishing delusions.

People working on the diagnostic manuals used in psychiatry rely on levels of distress to establish what a disorder is:

> In the absence of clear biological markers or clinically useful measurements of severity for many mental disorders, it has not been possible to completely separate normal and pathological symptom expressions contained in diagnostic criteria.... a generic diagnostic criterion requiring distress or disability has been used to establish disorder thresholds, usually worded 'the disturbance causes clinically significant distress or impairment in social, occupational, or other important areas of functioning'.[36]

Here we would like to suggest that it is not straightforward to base the distinction between delusional and non-delusional beliefs on psychological effects. This is because not all the phenomena classified as delusional impair good functioning, and alien abduction beliefs and self-enhancing beliefs that are not delusional can compromise good functioning.

In the psychological and psychiatric literature it has been suggested that some delusions enhance the sense that one's life is meaningful,[37] and that there are 'successful psychotics'.[38] In some cases, people are able to find additional meaning in life thanks to the formation of a delusion, and their functioning is not seriously impaired as a result. One such case is Simon, a lawyer with a happy family life and a good career:

> [...] Out of the blue, he was threatened by a malpractice legal action from a group of his colleagues. Although he claimed to be innocent, mounting a defence

would be expensive and hazardous. He responded to this crisis by praying in front of an open bible placed on a small altar that he set up in his front room. After an emotional evening's 'outpouring' he found that wax from two large candles on the altar had run down onto the bible marking out various words and phrases (he called these wax marks 'seals' or 'suns'). [...] From this time on, Simon received a complex series of 'revelations' largely conveyed through the images left in melted candle wax. They meant nothing to anyone else including Simon's Baptist friends and family. But for Simon they were clearly representations of biblical symbols particularly from the book of Revelations signifying that 'I am the living son of David... and I'm also a relative of Ishmael and... of Joseph'. [...] His special status had the effect of 'increasing my own inward sense, wisdom, understanding, and endurance' which would 'allow me to do whatever is required in terms of bringing whatever message it is that God wants me to bring'.[39]

The description above stresses the role of delusions in giving the agent a sense of purpose and meaning, and downplays the negative effects on wellbeing that delusions are often characterized as having. This is probably due to the self-enhancing content of the delusions reported (e.g. Simon thinks of himself as gifted and invested with special responsibilities) and the support provided by the person's immediate social circle.

In the context of thought insertion, there are some relevant sub-clinical cases. An example is that of people who run or attend spiritualist churches where it is a special skill to have access to the thoughts of the dead in one's stream of consciousness. To experience alien thoughts is not only culturally *normal* (within the sub-culture of the spiritualist church) but culturally *desirable*. The belief that one can access the thoughts of the dead is implausible and badly supported by evidence, but it does not have an adverse impact on the person's functioning and well-being. The fact that no adverse impact is observed may be due to intrapersonal or interpersonal factors.[40]

Intrapersonally, the person may not have any other experience or belief that would count as bizarre outside her sub-culture, and her belonging to the church may serve as an explanation of her having inserted thoughts. The psychological history of the person developing the delusion is important when we are interested in the difference between clinical and non-clinical irrational beliefs. Interpersonally, the *local acceptability* of the belief and the fact that it does not lead to social isolation but potentially to better integration may be a powerful antidote against psychological harm. A person who believes that she is receiving the thoughts of the dead but (a) does not belong to a spiritualist church, (b) has no desire to experience these thoughts, and (c) has no background that might explain why this seems to be happening is likely to be more distressed by these experiences than the spiritualist church-goer.

Let us look back to alien abduction belief. Alien abduction belief can be characterized by distress and preoccupation. Although formal psychiatric interviews with abductees uncover little pathology (for example see McNally and Clancy, 'Sleep Paralysis, Sexual Abuse, and Space Alien Abduction'), some abductees display acute distress: three of ten abductees in McNally and Clancy's study nearly met the criteria for a diagnosis of PTSD following their abduction experience. Mean scores on questionnaires relating to depression and anxiety, though, put abductees within normal limits, such that they were indistinguishable from control groups.[41]

As we saw, McNally and Clancy's abductees displayed a similar physiological profile when listening to scripts of their experiences to that of subjects suffering from PTSD. Abductees were also found to report 'heightened ratings of arousal, fear, surprise, and imagery vividness during exposure to scripts featuring their most traumatic abduction memories'.[42] Reporting on this work, Clancy notes that '[n]ot only were the physiological reactions of abductees similar to those of documented trauma victims, such as combat vets and rape victims; in some cases, they were even more extreme'. And the 'alien abduction memories that emerge under hypnosis generate intense emotions — pain, terror, helplessness, awe'.[43]

Interestingly though, just like successful psychotics, some abductees do rather well out of having their beliefs. As McNally reports:

> when I ask these subjects if you could do it all over again would you rather not have been abducted and they said well, when it first happened I was terrified, I had ontological shock, some of them would say, the whole fabric of my sense of the world was torn asunder. But then I realized that there are beings out there who care for us, for the fate of the earth, so on balance, yeah I think it's a good thing.[44]

Finally, as suggested in section four, positive illusions have been considered as psychologically beneficial, and even adaptive, as they enable people to develop coping strategies and maintain motivation in the face of challenges. Could this be the telling difference between positive illusions and delusions? Focusing on functioning is definitely helpful to map out the differences between clinical and non-clinical irrational beliefs, as we saw, but it is important to notice that self-enhancing beliefs have been exposed as potentially (physically and psychologically) harmful in some circumstances.[45]

More to the point, positive illusions that are especially resistant to negative feedback can give rise to excessively high expectations, and then disappointment, when the expected targets are not achieved. This may lead to agents being unprepared for set-backs.[46] In the light of this, the recent psychological literature has suggested that psychological wellbeing and success (measured in terms of an agent's capacity to pursue and achieve one's goals) are not the default effects of positive illusions, but come from other characteristics (which may be, but do not need to be, positively correlated with self-enhancing beliefs), such as 'sense of coherence' and 'hardiness'.

> Sense of coherence has three components: '*Comprehensibility*, the extent to which an individual can make sense of adversity; *Manageability*, the extent to which an individual perceives that resources are at her or his disposal to meet the challenges of inordinate demands; and *Meaningfulness*, the extent to which an individual feels that the challenges faced are worth engagement with.'[47]

> Hardiness has been defined as 'a pattern of attitudes and strategies that together facilitate turning stressful circumstances from potential disasters into growth opportunities'.[48] It supports personal growth and a sense of control: events are seen as stressful when the agent does not get a sense that she can control them,

while people who are curious and engaged see challenges as opportunities to grow and improve. Hardiness has been described as including (1) a commitment to oneself and work, (2) a sense of personal control over one's experiences and outcomes, and (3) the perception that change represents a challenge and should be treated as an opportunity for growth rather than a threat.[49]

This is especially interesting as some people with elaborated delusions in the context of schizophrenia are found to have an increased *sense of meaningfulness* and *sense of coherence* with respect to non-clinical controls, when they find themselves in the acute stage of psychosis.[50] Enhanced sense of meaningfulness and sense of coherence are due to the person feeling empowered by the delusion as a potential explanation of a puzzling experience, and are correlated with high levels of wellbeing. The sense of meaningfulness and the sense of coherence drop, for instance, in remission, because the delusion is no longer thought to provide a satisfactory explanation of the person's experience. Levels of wellbeing also drop, and depression is likely to ensue, because the person realizes that the meaning she had ascribed to her experience was delusory.

Conclusions

Based on epistemic and psychological considerations, the prospect of arriving at a principled way to distinguish delusional from non-delusional beliefs is not promising. Delusions are a paradigmatic instance of irrationality and are generally harmful, impairing good functioning and causing anxiety and distress. But delusions are not *always* harmful and distressing. Also, other irrational beliefs (such as alien abduction beliefs and self-enhancing beliefs) share some epistemic features with delusions, and can have psychologically adverse effects in at least some contexts.

This suggests caution in the project of demarcating delusions, and supports the view that there is more continuity than is commonly thought between experiences and beliefs that are classified as clinically significant, and those that characterize the non-clinical population.

Notes to Chapter 2

1. In the preparation of this chapter, Lisa Bortolotti and Ema Sullivan-Bissett acknowledge the support of a European Research Council Consolidator Grant (grant agreement 616358) for a project entitled 'Pragmatic and Epistemic Role of Factually Erroneous Cognitions and Thoughts' (PERFECT). Lisa Bortolotti also acknowledges the support of the Hope and Optimism funding initiative for a project entitled 'Costs and Benefits of Optimism'.
2. Lisa Bortolotti, 'Psychiatric Classification and Diagnosis: Delusions and Confabulations', *Paradigmi*, 1 (2011), 99–112.
3. American Psychiatric Association DSM-5 Task Force, *Diagnostic and Statistical Manual of Mental Disorders, Fifth Edition* (Washington, D.C: American Psychiatric Publishing, 2013), p. 819.
4. Ryan McKay, Robyn Langdon, Max Coltheart, 'Sleights of mind: Delusions, defences and self-deception', *Cognitive Neuropsychiatry*, 10.4 (2005), 305–26, p. 315.
5. J. Arturo Silva, Gregory Leong, Robert Weinstock and Catherine L. Boyer, 'Capgras Syndrome and Dangerousness', *Bulletin of American Academy of Psychiatry and the Law*, 17.1 (1989), 5–14.
6. Roberta L. Payne, 'First Person Account: My Schizophrenia', *Schizophrenia Bulletin*, 18.4 (1992), 725–28.
7. Harold W. Jordan and Gray Howe, 'De Clerambault Syndrome (erotomania): A Review and Case Presentation', *Journal of the National Medical Association*, 72.10 (1980), p. 983.

8. Zachary W. Brewster and Sarah Nell Rusche, 'Quantitative Evidence of the Continuing Significance of Race: Tableside Racism in Full-Service Restaurants', *Journal of Black Studies*, 43.4 (2012), 359–84.
9. David E. Vance, 'Belief in Lunar Effects on Human Behavior', *Psychological Reports*, 76.1 (1995), 32–34.
10. Shelley E. Taylor, *Positive Illusions: Creative Self-Deception and the Healthy Mind* (New York: Basic Books, 1989).
11. Daniel R. Weinberger and Paul Harrison (eds), *Schizophrenia*, 3rd edn (Chichester: Wiley-Blackwell, 2011), p. 18.
12. This may seem a dubious choice of methodology, but the reports of thought insertion in the psychiatric literature are few and far between, and they often lack detail and context. Extracts from first-person accounts give us some insight into the experience people are having and reinforce that there is heterogeneity in the types of thoughts that are claimed to have been inserted, and in the feelings associated with the experience. Online searches were undertaken by one of us (RG) looking for 'thought insertion' on six mental health forums in the summer of 2011 and in the autumn of 2014. These forums were the Crazyboards forum, the Schizophrenia forum, the Ehealth forum, the Psychcentral forum, the Depersonalization Community Self Help Forum and the Mental Health forum.
13. Alienonite, 'Crazyboards Forum', *Crazyboards* (2010), <http://www.crazyboards.org/forums/index.php/topic/37139-thought-insertion/> [accessed 14 April 2016].
14. Firebird, 'Crazyboards Forum', *Crazyboards* (2010), http://www.crazyboards.org/forums/index.php/topic/37139-thought-insertion/> [accessed 14 April 2016].
15. Star-28, 'Forum', *Mental Health Forum* (2010), http://www.mentalhealthforum.net/forum/showthread.php?15811-intrusive-thoughts-thought-insertion> [accessed 14 April 2016].
16. Rachel Gunn, 'On thought insertion', *Review of Philosophy and Psychology* (2015), 1–17 <http:link.springer.com/article/1007/s13164-015-0271-2>.
17. K. W. M. Fulford, *Moral Theory and Medical Practice* (Cambridge, New York: Cambridge University Press, 1989).
18. Richard J. McNally and Susan A. Clancy, 'Sleep Paralysis, Sexual Abuse, and Space Alien Abduction', *Transcultural Psychiatry*, 42. 1 (2005), p. 116.
19. McNally and Clancy, 'Sleep Paralysis, Sexual Abuse, and Space Alien Abduction', p. 117.
20. Ibid.
21. Richard J. McNally, 'Aliens', *The Forum*, BBC World Service, 29 September 2014 <http://www.bbc.co.uk/programmes/p0270hy2>. See Thibaut Maus de Rolley's chapter in this volume for descriptions of analogous experiences, e.g., '[w]itches believed they were flying to and attending the sabbath, when they were actually watching independently, immobile in their beds' (p. 78). One interesting question is whether so-called 'witches' in the early modern period are comparable — or even equivalent — to abductees now.
22. McNally and Clancy, 'Sleep Paralysis, Sexual Abuse, and Space Alien Abduction', p. 114.
23. Katharine J. Holden and Christopher C. French, 'Alien Abduction Experiences: Some Clues from Neuropsychology and Neuropsychiatry', *Cognitive Neuropsychiatry*, 7.3 (2002), p. 166.
24. Holden and French, 'Alien Abduction Experiences: Some Clues from Neuropsychology and Neuropsychiatry', p. 167.
25. McNally and Clancy, 'Sleep Paralysis, Sexual Abuse, and Space Alien Abduction', p. 114.
26. Holden and French, 'Alien Abduction Experiences: Some Clues from Neuropsychology and Neuropsychiatry', p. 166.
27. Susan A. Clancy, *Abducted: How People Come to Believe They Were Kidnapped by Aliens*, new edn (Cambridge, Mass.: Harvard University Press, 2007), p. 51.
28. See Maus de Rolley and Olivia Smith, this volume, for a discussion of different kinds of illusion from those we are interested in here.
29. See, for example, Steven J. Heine and others, 'Is There a Universal Need for Positive Self-Regard?', *Psychological Review*, 106 (1999), 766–94; and Miki Toyama, 'Benefits and Costs of Positive Illusions. Changing Children's Stress Responses and Aggressive Behavior', *Japanese Journal of Educational Psychology*, 54 (2006), 361–70.
30. Tali Sharot, *The Optimism Bias: A Tour of the Irrationally Positive Brain* (New York: Pantheon,

2011); Ryan T. McKay and Daniel C. Dennett, 'The Evolution of Misbelief', *Behavioral and Brain Sciences*, 32 (2009), 493–510.
31. Taylor, *Positive Illusions*.
32. See for instance: Kate Sweeny, Patrick J. Carroll and James A. Shepperd, 'Is Optimism Always Best? Future Outlooks and Preparedness', *Current Directions in Psychological Science*, 15 (2006), 302–06; and James A. Shepperd, William M. P. Klein, Erika A. Waters and Neil D. Weinstein, 'Taking Stock of Unrealistic Optimism', *Perspectives on Psychological Science*, 8.4 (2013), 395–411.
33. Louise Arnold, Lee Willoughby, and Virginia Calkins, 'Self-Evaluation in Undergraduate Medical Education: A Longitudinal Perspective', *Journal of Medical Education*, 60.1 (1985), 21–28.
34. Clayton R. Critcher, Erik G. Helzer and David Dunning, 'Self-Enhancement via Redefinition: Defining Social Concepts to Ensure Positive Views of Self', in *Handbook of Self Enhancement and Self-Protection*, ed. by Mark Alicke and Constantine Sedikides (New York: Guilford Press, 2011), pp. 69–91.
35. See for instance Bortolotti, 'Psychiatric Classification and Diagnosis: Delusions and Confabulations'.
36. American Psychiatric Association, *DSM-5*, p. 21.
37. Glenn Roberts, 'Delusional Belief Systems and Meaning in Life: A Preferred Reality?', *The British Journal of Psychiatry*, 159 Suppl. 14 (1991), 19–28.
38. Gary Hosty, 'Beneficial Delusions?', *Psychiatric Bulletin*, 16.6 (1992), 373. A number of essays in this volume deal with cases where delusions are seen to have long or short-term benefits. See Ita Mac Carthy, for example, for an early modern case of erotomania (more specifically, 'reverse Othello syndrome'), where the delusion protects its sufferer from otherwise unbearable realizations about his personal circumstances (pp. 15–18). Reverse Othello syndrome has also been discussed in some detail in Lisa Bortolotti, 'The Epistemic Innocence of Motivated Delusions', *Consciousness and Cognition*, 33 (2015), 490–99.
39. Mike Jackson and K. W. Fulford, 'Spiritual Experience and Psychopathology', *Philosophy, Psychiatry, & Psychology*, 4 (1997), pp. 44–45.
40. Compare this case with the phenomenon of dream divination described by Giglioni in the present volume. In certain early modern contexts, Giglioni reports, the ability to tell the future and influence events (which contemporary philosophers might liken to the kind of thought insertion reported by Firebird above) is not negative but God-given, an instance of divine intervention in the minds and lives of ordinary individuals. There is much to be said about the social anthropology of thought insertion and cognitive impairment in general and the ways in which they present and are interpreted differently (or similarly) across different social contexts and time. This, however, falls beyond the scope of this chapter.
41. McNally and Clancy, 'Sleep Paralysis, Sexual Abuse, and Space Alien Abduction', p. 116.
42. Richard J. McNally et al., 'Psychophysiological Responding During Script-Driven Imagery in People Reporting Abduction by Space Aliens', *Psychological Science*, 15. 7 (2004), 493–97, p. 495.
43. Clancy, *Abducted: How People Come to Believe They Were Kidnapped by Aliens*, p. 77.
44. McNally, 'Aliens'.
45. For a brief review of the recent literature, see Lisa Bortolotti, and Magdalena Antrobus, 'Costs and Benefits of Realism and Optimism', *Current Opinion in Psychiatry*, 28.2 (2014), 194–98.
46. See James A. Shepperd and Javad H. Kashani, 'The Relationship of Hardiness, Gender, and Stress to Health Outcomes in Adolescents', *Journal of Personality*, 59.4 (1990), 747–68; and Daniel L. Schacter, and Donna Rose Addis, 'On the Constructive Episodic Simulation of Past and Future Events', *Behavioral and Brain Sciences*, 30.3 (2007), 331–32.
47. Astier M. Almedom, 'Resilience, hardiness, sense of coherence, and post-traumatic growth: All paths leading to "light at the end of the tunnel"?', *Journal of Loss and Trauma*, 10.3 (2005), p. 259.
48. Salvatore R. Maddi, *Hardiness Turning Stressful Circumstances into Resilient Growth* (Dordrecht: Springer, 2013), p. 8.
49. See Suzanne C. Kobasa, 'Stressful Life Events, Personality, and Health: An Inquiry into Hardiness', *Journal of Personality and Social Psychology*, 37.1 (1979), 1–11; and Suzanne C. Kobasa, Salvatore R. Maddi, and Stephen Kahn, 'Hardiness and Health: A Prospective Study', *Journal of Personality and Social Psychology*, 42.1 (1982), 168–77.

50. See Glenn Roberts, 'Delusional Belief Systems and Meaning in Life: A Preferred Reality?', *The British Journal of Psychiatry*, 159, Suppl. 14 (1991), 19–28; and Moshe Bergstein, Abraham Weizman, and Zehava Solomon, 'Sense of Coherence among Delusional Patients: Prediction of Remission and Risk of Relapse', *Comprehensive Psychiatry*, 49.3 (2008), 288–96.

CHAPTER 3

Cognition, Relevance and Early Modern Ghosts

Timothy Chesters

Introduction

Historians and critics routinely interpret early modern ghost stories — fictional ones as well as purportedly 'true accounts' — primarily in relation to the beliefs that produced them. Beliefs about ghosts invite special scrutiny in an age where these — so it is thought — betrayed one's theological position.[1] To take only the best-known example, a long tradition of Shakespeare criticism has understood Hamlet's equivocations before his father's ghost to reflect those of the Anglican psychology more broadly: between a Catholic teaching that held fast to the doctrine of Purgatory (from which ghosts might be permitted a temporary return) and a Reformed soteriology that vigorously denounced it. Unusually attuned to these broader questions as to so much else, Shakespeare felt this tension, which found its way into his play.[2]

This critical methodology seems so routine as scarcely to qualify as a 'methodology' at all. Ghosts, unlike (say) tables and chairs, are or were once objects of belief; apparitions have the character of epistemic events; naturally we refer literary occurrences to the intellectual and ideological commitments of authors and their readers. The religious crisis occasioned by the Reformation makes the study of the period's ghost stories especially attractive. A properly attuned historicist criticism can show how disturbances in the early modern religious sphere might ripple into the literary one.

Yet seeing a ghost in any historical period, or hearing or reading a story about someone else who does so, is not simply an epistemic event; it is also a *cognitive* one. That is, before I even get as far as reflecting on my convictions about ghosts, the concept GHOST will have impinged in my cognitive environment in a form that appears relatively invariant across human culture: roughly, a person-like being not dissimilar to me, but with unusual physical properties.[3] This much I cannot help. Irrespective of historically or geographically localised commitments to ghosts at the level of belief (e.g. whether they exist, return to the living, demand reburial or intercession, etc.), the information contained in the concept GHOST is composed of similar intuitions, and triggers similar basic inferences, in all human minds — of all beliefs and none. Regardless of what people might believe about ghosts, the concept GHOST is everywhere — a sometime visitor in the mental experience of practically everybody in the world.

Like certain other magical or religious concepts, GHOST has travelled well across our species; and recent work in cognitive anthropology has begun to suggest some reasons why. One possibility is that it has proven unusually *relevant* to human minds — that is, we might attribute its spread and historical tenacity not to any special properties inhering independently in GHOST itself, but rather on account of the 'fit' between the concept and a human cognitive machinery adapted to accept it. On this view magical concepts would perhaps appear not so very different from tables and chairs after all: just as domestic furniture affords the human body certain kinds of action, so GHOST has become an affordance for the mind. Below I shall return to the notion of 'relevance', in the technical sense of that term. For now we might acknowledge a methodological possibility arising from this shift in focus from beliefs onto concepts: that when reading early modern ghost stories, it may be worth dwelling on their cognitive effects.

Despite the relative stability of GHOST as a cross-cultural concept, describing these effects in a given context is far from straightforward. This is because, as I shall argue here, ghosts are purveyors *par excellence* of cognitive confusion. This chapter examines a specific feature of this confusion: our contradictory intuitions about the physical properties of ghosts. It begins with a canonical instance in Ovid's *Metamorphoses*, before introducing recent work on GHOST as a magical concept. The dominant perspective throughout will be that of Relevance Theory, a radical form of cognitive pragmatics that, as well as being influential in the anthropology of religion, seeks to explain how human minds handle ostensive communication (necessarily including literary communication). The final part of the essay offers a detailed case study of an early modern variant on Ovid's narrative — and one of the most unusual ghost stories of the European Renaissance.

The Limping Shadow

Ovid's retelling of the Orpheus and Eurydice story (*Metamorphoses* X) includes a touching detail not present in other versions. Dancing through the grass after her wedding, Eurydice is suddenly killed by a poisonous snakebite to the ankle. Orpheus descends into the underworld, through the 'unsubstantial throngs' (*per leves populos*), and prays for the return of his dead bride. The 'bloodless spirits' (*exsangues animae*) weep at his song and then Eurydice appears, falteringly:

> She was among the new shades and came with steps halting from her wound.[4]

Eurydice *limps*. Her shade labours under the weight of a body it no longer possesses. While pagan ghosts often bear the mark of injuries incurred while still alive (scars, bloodied faces, etc.), there is something especially poignant about these 'halting' steps which, as the reader imagines them, necessarily invoke physical heft and strain, the careful distribution of weight across space. For of course there is no weight — only a trace of the prior corporeal life that Eurydice may now possibly regain.

Much hinges on what we are to understand by 'and' in this sentence ('she was among the new shades *and* came with steps halting...'). Some readers, depending on their existing assumptions about the fate of the dead in the afterlife (as well as their assumptions about Ovid's assumptions), might infer a cause-effect relation: Eurydice's is a 'new' shade *and so* limps because her passage from life to death, from body to pure shadow, is not quite complete. Perhaps this transition, being only recent, really is reversible: perhaps there really is a way back to the living. But ultimately — and here the poignancy is redoubled — Eurydice's limp condemns her. The path out of the underworld is steep (*adclivis*) and difficult (*arduus*). Orpheus does not know if his struggling wife will endure it. So he looks back to make sure...

Ovid's story illustrates what appears to be a widespread contradiction in how we think about the afterlife, and one that intensified in early modern Europe. For thousands of years, and across cultures, people have professed a conviction in the immateriality of the soul while remaining seemingly unable to imagine its post-mortem existence — its punishments or pleasures — as anything other than corporeal. Such incongruities are so frequent in Hades that we barely notice them: moments before the appearance of limping Eurydice Ovid refers to Tantalus's thirst, Sisyphus's rock, and the vultures pecking eternally at Tityus's liver.[5] In epic, visitors to the underworld are armed with swords to fight off shadows or, seeing the ghost of a loved one, try vainly to embrace it.[6] These contradictions were not irresolvable. The shades of the classical underworld were to be understood as 'simulchra' (Ovid's word) — i.e. shadows that exhibit pain or pleasure *as if* they maintained their material existence. This idea left a clear legacy in the Christian imaginary of the afterlife: in Dante's *Inferno*, for example.

In early modern Europe, the Reformists' challenge to the traditional doctrine of Purgatory blew wide open debates about ghosts and the afterlife, and the picture became especially confused.[7] Humanist scholarship exposed an increasingly literate society to an array of ancient visions of the dead: not simply the *eidola* or *umbrae* of Greek and Roman myth but also, in authors such as Apuleius, Heliodorus, or Phlegon of Tralles, tales of departed men and women returning in their bodies. The transmission of Neoplatonic philosophy promoted by Marsilio Ficino raised the possibility that some spirits might be susceptible to pain.[8] Journeys to new worlds and old, and the growth of comparative ethnography, revealed a widespread strain of ancestor-worship which placed its dead on the side of matter and, often, violence: the deceased Inca (emperor) Guyanacape, still feared by the Amerindians of Peru 'as if he were still alive'; the terrifying *draugr* of the Northern peoples, rising out of their graves; or in the Far East, as the Jesuit missionaries reported, the Japanese festivals of the dead, where relatives left victuals on tombstones.[9] Closer to home, the animistic lore of rural populations — in which the dead came to inhabit a tree, a hill, a toadstool — continued to flourish beyond the reach of any Church.[10]

This recurrent urge to impose material form on the spirit world, even while professing its immaterial nature, deserves explanation. One approach would be to ascribe it to competing beliefs about the dead. Thus one might speculate in the sixteenth-century context that this confusion has its roots in the imperfectly reconciled claims of lay and 'official' spirituality, for example. This is the view of the historian Walter Stephens, who argues that late-sixteenth century theologians emphasise the palpability of spirits as a means of rendering them more real to an ever more sceptical populace.[11] The alternative explored here seeks an explanation not simply among people's beliefs, but additionally among their *concepts* and *intuitions*. These intuitions influence the ways we think about the dead regardless of our stated beliefs on the subject, and sometimes in spite of them. The following section will offer a simplified account of this process as it applies to magical concepts such as GHOST.

Relevant Mysteries

The most thoroughgoing cognitive account of magical concepts is offered by Pascal Boyer, a French anthropologist influenced by Relevance Theory.[12] His *Religion Explained* (2001) opens with an invitation: to take a list of supernatural concepts and try to intuit which of them might plausibly form the basis for a religious system:

(1). Some people are dead but they keep walking around. They cannot talk any more, they are not aware of what they are doing.

(2). Some ebony trees can recall conversations people hold in their shade.

(3). This wristwatch is special and will chime when it detects that your enemies are plotting against you.

(4). If you drop this special ritual object it will fall downwards until it hits the ground.

(5). The gods are watching us and they notice everything we do. But they forget everything instantaneously.

(6). There is only one God. He has no way of finding out what goes on in the world.

For Boyer, (1)–(3) are examples of 'successful' supernatural concepts. (1) and (2) are integral concepts within real-world religious systems; (3) describes an invented concept, but one which, according to Boyer's prediction, most people would consider a good candidate. By contrast (4)–(6) do not quite hit the mark. The problem is not, of course, that these concepts seem implausible in relation to scientific or rational standards (on that basis the whole list would be disqualified); rather, something in the shape or structure of the concepts seems awry. How might our intuitions about the probable success or failure of religious concepts be accounted for?

For Boyer a successful concept, or mental representation, is simply one that has been widely transmitted via multiple acts of human communication. This success is not attributable to pure chance, he argues, but more plausibly ascribed to some form of 'transmission advantage'. In attempting to explain what this advantage might consist of, Boyer adopts what the anthropologist Dan Sperber has termed an 'epidemiological' approach to cultural representations.[13] The analogy with the spread of infectious diseases is a suggestive one. For scientists investigating the cause of disease transmission, knowledge of the pathogen itself is insufficient on its own; equally essential is understanding those features of human physiology that allows it to spread throughout the population. By the same token, anthropologists seeking to explain the transmission of supernatural representations must not simply attend to the representation itself, but also the mental architecture which allows it to take hold. Hence the need for a two-step description: of the successful concepts themselves, and of a cognitive system geared to act as their host.

In Boyer's account, successful magical concepts display two elements in a specific relation. The first — a feature of all concepts — is membership of what he calls a basic ontological category (PERSON, TOOL, NATURAL OBJECT, PLANT, etc.). Each of these can be thought of as a kind of template, membership of which triggers its own routine intuitions. For example, PLANT calls to mind an entity that is inanimate (in the sense of lacking a mind or soul), has typical shape, grows and dies, needs water, sunlight and soil, and so on; any concept belonging to this category (ELM, DANDELION, etc.) will be instantly assumed to possess these characteristics. The second ingredient is a counter-intuitive violation that contradicts a *strictly limited* amount of information provided by the ontological category. Recall Boyer's example, encountered among the Uduk-speaking peoples of Sudan, of the ebony tree which remembers conversations people hold in its shade. This tree belongs to the ontological category PLANT; and by exhibiting animacy — more specifically, the ability to produce mental representations — it flouts an important intuition we have about that category. Notice, though, that only this element is affected by the violation. All our other intuitions about PLANT are left untouched: we go on inferring that, in spite of its counterintuitive property, the magic tree still has typical shape, that it still grows, still needs water, sunlight and soil, and so forth. It is not the case that with successful magical concepts simply 'anything goes'. Just one element has changed; everything else remains the same. This Boyer calls the principle of *limited counterintuitive violation*.

According to Boyer, magical concepts that obey this principle are those most likely to be stored, accessed and transmitted by a human cognitive system adapted for optimal efficiency. Why should this be so? Key to cognitive efficiency are the mechanisms of what he calls 'default reasoning'. Default reasoning is vital in processing novel concepts of all kinds, not just magical ones. For example, upon encountering the concept KANGAROO for the first time, the cognitive system automatically carries across a wide range of default assumptions attached to the ontological category ANIMAL and applies them to the newcomer. Thus we infer that KANGAROO must be a physical entity, that it is animate, grows, feeds, dies, has internal organs identical to other members of the same species, has live young that will grow up to resemble its parents, and so on. The efficiency gain from proceeding in this way is considerable: default reasoning dispenses us from re-learning the same information every time we encounter a new member of the category. The process is akin to completing a template with most of the spaces already filled in. Although a new concept might specify only a very small number of unique features, the template enriches these to complete a highly informative picture. For this reason, as Boyer puts it, *'people have detailed representations even though they are not told much'*.[14]

This drive towards cognitive efficiency continues to apply in the case of magical concepts, for which Boyer offers the analogous case of irregular shapes:

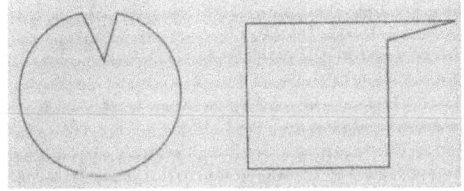

FIG. 1. Limited counterintuitive violation.
Reproduced by kind permission of Pascal Boyer.

These two figures represent a visual analogue for limited counterintuitive violation. Although it may be just about possible to conceive of them as an entirely novel form, they are most easily perceived and stored in the memory as something like CIRCLE-minus-segment and SQUARE-plus-spike; this would also be the most efficient way of communicating their general features to another person unfamiliar with them. As with the magic tree concept, the reason such 'counterintuitive' figures are handled — perceived, remembered, transmitted to others — so efficiently by the cognitive system is that, because the adjustment is highly constrained, we can confidently activate all the default assumptions that the adjustment leaves untouched (e.g. that the right-hand figure is composed for the most part of solid lines meeting at right angles). Note in addition that the negative corollary also holds true: i.e. if more irregularities were added to the shapes above, fewer inferences could be carried over as defaults. These new figures would likely prove harder to perceive as shapes at all; we would also struggle to commit them to memory or communicate their structure verbally to someone else who has not seen them. Having forfeited the transmission advantage conferred by the limited violation, these would quickly prove to be 'unsuccessful' shapes.

Why should human cognition set such store by efficiency? It does not seem a matter of conscious volition. An important aspect of Boyer's account is that the human mind does not *choose* to handle concepts in this way; on the contrary, the vast majority of people would find it difficult *not* to do so. Something about our cognitive architecture compels us. (From this we can see that the potentially misleading phrase 'default *reasoning*' should not be taken to imply conscious deliberation, but a subpersonal cognitive routine.) Boyer's insistence on the mandatory aspect of default reasoning signals his debt to evolutionary accounts of cognition and, more narrowly, to the Relevance Theory of Deirdre Wilson and Dan Sperber. Elsewhere in *Religion Explained* he enlarges on his debt to Sperber and Wilson, according to whom human cognition is always geared towards those inputs from its environment that yield optimal *relevance*. The primary goal of Relevance Theory is to propose an account of human communication, not cognition. But the notion of relevance, and the evolutionary hypothesis on which it rests, may still be helpful in explaining why some conceptual inputs gain greater traction than others in the mental life of humans.

'Relevance' should here be understood in its strictly technical sense.[15] Any number of potential inputs to cognition compete for an organism's attention at a given time. No organism enjoys limitless attentional resources — least of all humans, whose cognitive environment includes at any moment not only what is currently available to them in perception, but also the vast data-store available in memory. Sperber and Wilson argue that humans must have evolved some mechanism to allocate these resources efficiently. From this supposition they derive their 'cognitive principle of relevance':

> **Cognitive Principle of Relevance**
> Human cognition tends to be geared towards the maximisation of relevance.

Relevance is here to be understood as a function of two factors: cognitive effects (or reward) and processing effort. For Sperber and Wilson, those inputs we deem most relevant in any given environment will be the ones that, when combined with other contextual information and our existing assumptions, are liable to provide *maximum cognitive effects for minimum cognitive effort*. Inputs, including concepts, that fit this criterion become relevant, and as such produce a change in the subject's cognitive environment; other, less relevant potential inputs recede into the background.

Transposing this idea into Boyer's account, we might suggest that certain magical concepts do not succeed because they are any more *true* than their less successful rivals — that is, better reflections of our external reality; they do so because they are more *relevant*. They offer a better fit with a human mind adapted to harvest maximum information from its environment at minimum cognitive expense. Tested over thousands of years of storytelling, GHOST has proved an especially clear example of fitness in this sense, and of the principle of limited counterintuitive violation on which it depends. Boyer's own analysis of GHOST is worth quoting in full:

> The concept is that of a PERSON that has counterintuitive physical properties. Unlike other persons ghosts can go through solid objects like walls. But notice that, apart from this, these ghosts follow very strictly the ordinary intuitive concept PERSON. Imagine a ghost suddenly materialises in your home as you are having dinner. Startled by this sudden appearance, you drop your spoon in your bowl of soup. In a situation like this your mind creates a whole lot of assumptions that you do not necessarily represent consciously. For instance, you assume that the ghost *saw* you were having dinner so that he now *knows* that you were eating. Also, the ghost probably *heard* the sound of your spoon landing in your soup and can now *remember* that you dropped it. You assume that the ghost *knows* you are here since he can *see* you. It would be unsettling but not too surprising if the ghost asked you whether you were enjoying your dinner. It would be very weird if he asked you why you never had dinner at home or why you never have soup. In other words you assume that this ghost has a mind. All the italicised verbs above describe the sort of thing a mind does: it perceives actual events in the world and forms beliefs on the basis of these perceptions.[16]

If we were to reformulate Boyer's example in Relevance-Theoretic terms, we could say that understanding the concept GHOST comes at only a limited cognitive price: we simply take the ontological template PERSON and subtract from it 'has a normal human body'. As with the magical tree, every other inferential mechanism normally prompted by the source category continues to yield a rich array of cognitive effects: we go on inferring the same range of perceptual and mental states, such as *seeing, hearing, thinking, remembering*, etc., as would usually be generated by the concept PERSON. Compared to the counterintuitive element (the ghost that 'suddenly materialises'), these default inferences may appear banal, as Boyer notes. Nonetheless, that very banality suggests how much default reasoning silently undergirds our supernatural concepts. No special cognitive mechanism is required to process GHOST, no unique programme that applies only to it. Ghosts may be mysterious, but they are a relevant mystery — conceptual grist to the default operations of our ordinary mental life.

Cognitive Confusions

What kind of insights might Boyer's understanding of supernatural concepts bring to bear on the problem of ghostly bodies? Before addressing this question directly it is worth returning briefly to the difference between intuitions and beliefs. One important distinction concerns degrees of awareness and commitment. Beliefs imply conscious adherence, however uncertain or provisional, to a set of propositions at least potentially available for self-report: I believe that 'dead souls are disembodied', that 'the soul dies with the body', and so on. These may be buttressed by institutional support (doctrine), or may operate outside it (folk beliefs). By contrast my intuitions about the concept GHOST — as a PERSON minus a body + the application of default inferences — function for the most part under the threshold of consciousness. (Indeed, if this kind of procedure were to operate with our full awareness it might become difficult to go on thinking at all.) Intuitions are not acquired either by a process of rational deliberation or by an outbreak of emotional conviction; they are a product of the explanatory mechanisms I wield by virtue of having the kind of mind that human beings have. I can to some extent choose my beliefs, but I cannot choose my intuitions. And I possess the concept GHOST, and a set of intuitions about it, irrespective of whether I possess the belief.

A corollary of this difference between beliefs and intuitions concerns degrees of variability. Beliefs vary. They vary across cultures and history; they can also do so within a single individual. I can be ideologically coerced, or simply persuaded, to increase or decrease my commitment to my current beliefs, or transform them altogether. Furthermore, I can temporarily revise or suspend my beliefs (say, about the fate of the dead) in order to entertain somebody else's. When I willingly enter the storyworld of Ovid's *Metamorphoses*, for example, I may temporarily try on a set of beliefs not my own: recent work in cognitive narratology has investigated the mechanisms of 'tagging' and 'decoupling' required to sustain (but also keep in check) readers' immersion in fictional worlds.[17] By contrast the intuitions and inferences that drive default reasoning are not so malleable. Whatever my conscious beliefs, it would be difficult, if not impossible, to shut down the inferential system that, say, attributes mental states to PERSON-like concepts: the witness to the ghost in Boyer's example would struggle to do so even if he tried. In this respect, our cognitive system places important constraints on supernatural thinking. While beliefs in ghosts and the afterlife vary widely, their conceptual underpinnings remain very consistent from one culture to another.

We might wish to conclude from all this that our beliefs about ghosts are messy and variable, while our basic intuitions about them are stable and unchanging. This might hold true at the anthropological level of description; but in specific instances such a claim would be quite wrong. The dead pose a particular challenge to the normal operation of human inferencing systems. This challenge is felt most viscerally in the presence of human corpses. Although, conceptually speaking, CORPSE ought properly to belong to the category OBJECT, most people treat CORPSE as a limited modification of the concept PERSON, with animacy (and with it goal-directed action and intentional states) subtracted. Executing this subtraction in the presence of a real instance is less straightforward than this description makes it seem, however. Inference mechanisms that operated prior to the person's death often continue to function in spite of it, especially in the case of someone to whom we felt emotionally attached. The so-called 'person-file' system, with which we recognise familiar faces, is not easily switched off: the system continues to deliver the usual sense of recognition, and with it a host of affective responses, despite our conscious awareness that the person is no longer 'there'. Similarly, our so-called 'Theory of Mind' mechanism may continue to run inferential routines geared towards attributing mental representations to the corpse: e.g. perceptual or affective states (such as anger). This is especially likely to occur if its eyes remain open: gaze-tracking is among our most ancient modes of intuiting others' goal-directed actions. The compulsion to go on imputing intentional states to something we 'know' to be an object does much to explain the uncanny sensation produced by not just corpses, but also portraits, dolls, puppets, and masks.

The cognitive confusion induced by corpses also arises in response to other states we imagine for the dead. ZOMBIE has proven a highly successful magical concept, and obeys Boyer's rule of limited counterintuitive violation: ZOMBIE is conceptualised as a PERSON minus intentional states. And yet, like CORPSE, this concept is liable to induce cognitive contradictions. However deeply embedded the intuition that zombies lack volition, personal identity, and so on, we may find it unnervingly difficult to resist making these attributions when confronted with (or just imagining) an actual example. Film-makers such as George A. Romero play on exactly this disjunction for dramatic effect. Most zombie movies contain some version of the chilling moment at which the audience spots, among the anonymous hordes, a familiar character from earlier in the film who has now joined the legions of the dead. Such moments achieve their shock because familiar characters are likely to prompt the inference of emotions and purposes — more especially if we had felt sympathetic to these while the character was still alive — even though this inner life is the very element excluded by the concept ZOMBIE. The impact of such instances is a product of cognitive confusion, of multiple inference systems running out of synch.

A similar disjunction may affect the way we think of ghosts. Recall Boyer's characterisation of the GHOST concept as PERSON with counterintuitive physical properties. Though this structure may be relatively stable in our conceptual archive, in some specific instances the counterintuitive violation seems inhibited. As with ZOMBIE, the countervailing pull of the ontological category is especially felt by those with strong attachments to the deceased. The ancient epic trope of 'the vain embrace', in which a visitor to Hades (Aeneas, Achilles) tries and fails to grasp a beloved ghost (Creusa, Patroclus etc.), illustrates the point:

> Thrice I strove to throw my arms around her neck; thrice the form, vainly clasped, fled from my hands, even as light winds, and most like a winged dream.[18]

However firm Aeneas's conviction that he is in the presence of a shade, he feels no less compelled to reach out and touch it. PERSON-inferences discarded in the magical subconcept have begun to reassert themselves, such that Creusa — at least in his confused understanding — is momentarily endowed with something like a body. The hero's confusion is only 'corrected' when the ghost suddenly takes flight, cruelly reaffirming the counterintuitive element.[19]

The story of Orpheus and Eurydice shares the affective atmosphere of these epic episodes — limping Eurydice appears amid tears and laments — and can be read as a distended version of the same motif: eventually Orpheus too will reach out, and Eurydice vanish. But not before PERSON inferences have been allowed to linger far longer than is usually the case. Eurydice does not disappear straight away; instead the possibility of her reversion to the ontological category is held open as an integral feature of the plot and its suspense. Her limping gait, a vestige of the body she might yet recover, emerges as a mark of this reversion — one that occurs not as the sudden substitution of one concept (PERSON) for another (GHOST), but a step-wise inferential adjustment between them. If Boyer's analysis is right, GHOST and PERSON are conceptually continuous, however great we might believe the gulf between the living and the dead: our cognitive system handles the first as a minimal — and perhaps thereby reversible — modification of the second. The slope up which Eurydice struggles with her husband describes a path not between two radically discontinuous domains but — precisely — a *gradient* on which categories blur.

Interlude: Relevance and Communication

Such moments of inferential confusion do not invalidate Boyer's account of magical concepts. But the singular instance suggests a level of complexity elided in the epidemiological picture, concerned as it is with multiple episodes of transmission. In anthropological case-studies, not to mention narrative worlds as complex as Ovid's, magical phenomena only rarely appear as pristine tokens of their conceptual type; far more commonly we are required to loosen the concept in such a way that the phenomenon comes to appear only GHOST-like or ZOMBIE-like. This is partly because the dead seem particularly apt to throw our inference systems into conflict, as we have seen. (Ovid's *Metamorphoses* are of course especially rich in instances of transitional or in-between states.) But it is also a more general consequence of the way, according to Boyer, concepts are transmitted in specific instances of human communication.

In Relevance Theory, the inferential model of communication on which Boyer draws, ad-hoc contextual adjustments form an integral part of utterance interpretation. The reason for this becomes more readily apparent when the inferential model is distinguished from code-models of human communication. On the code model, speakers or writers linguistically encode their intended meaning, and hearers or readers then recover that meaning by decrypting it using an identical copy of the code. In Relevance Theory, the encoded concept (e.g. that indicated by 'umbra' in Ovid's narrative) provides only one clue as to the speaker's overall intention, an approximation of which the hearer will only gain by 'enriching' it according to what Sperber and Wilson call the communicative principle of relevance:

> **Communicative principle of relevance**
> Every ostensive stimulus (e.g. an utterance) conveys a presumption of its own optimal relevance.

This second or communicative principle of relevance follows on from the first or cognitive principle invoked above. Because human beings know that other members of their species are geared to scan their cognitive environment for the most relevant inputs, they are able to manipulate that assumption for communicative ends. More specifically, they are able to make themselves understood as meaning far more than they ever have to say.

Take an everyday example.[20] Jack and Jill are standing in Jill's kitchen. Jill looks at Jack, looks at her washing machine, and utters the following words:

(1) Open it.

In order for Jack to grasp Jill's intended meaning, he has most obviously to perform the task of assigning a referent to the pronoun 'it', made relatively easy by the direction of her gaze. But his task is not finished there. Notice that, in a different way, the meaning of 'open' too is underspecified. The encoded, semantic meaning of the verb is only part of the story; it will not be enough, if he wants to understand Jill, simply to scan a mental dictionary entry for the item 'open' (in which a list of all possible variables of 'x opens y' would in any case have to extend indefinitely).[21] If Jack is a friend inclined to help Jill with her laundry, he will assume her to intend (and to intend that he will interpret her as intending) that he should open the washing-machine door. But if he is a plumber, then 'open it' might be an instruction to remove the casing at the back. How Jack interprets Jill is only partly guided by the encoded meaning of her utterance: the rest he must 'fill out' with reference to the immediate context, and by deciding which of his assumptions (about washing-machines, and about his relationship with Jill) Jill is trying to direct his attention towards. The result of this procedure will be the first contextually derived 'ad-hoc' concept (OPEN*) that satisfies Jack's expectation of relevance.[22] According to Relevance Theory, the construction of ad-hoc concepts is an inevitable part of a communication system in which words encode only a tiny proportion of what it is possible to mean.

The final part of this essay attempts to bring together Boyer's theory of magical concepts and a relevance-theoretic approach to linguistic utterances. The utterance in question here, an early modern variant of Ovid's story, provides a further moment of friction between the anthropological theory and the singular instance. It also raises a question not considered so far: what modes of writing, and writing strategies, does cognitive confusion elicit in the early modern period?

Quasi Phantasma: The Widower's Tale

In 1555 the German poet and scholar Georg Sabinus (1508–1560) published a Latin commentary on the *Metamorphoses*, professing on its title page to elucidate the 'moral, ethical and physical' questions raised by Ovid's poem. When Sabinus arrives at Book X, and the story of Orpheus and Eurydice, he opens immediately with the following narrative:

> I heard a tale [*fabulam*] similar to that of Orpheus, if tale is the right word, since many hold it to be a true account [*historiam*]. A gentleman of Bavaria was badly afflicted by the death of his wife, living alone, and refusing all attempts

at consolation. After many tears and laments his wife appeared to him and told him that having heard his importunate pleas, God had brought her back to life that she might live with him, but only on condition that they be remarried by a priest with solemn rites, and that from now on he should no longer curse or blaspheme as he did before — the reason for her death, and something which would deprive him of her once more if he should return to his bad ways. These formalities completed, the wife took up home with him as before, even bearing children, though she was pale and sad. After many years [*post multos annos*] the husband, being drunk one evening, flew into a rage at a servant, and said many things that contravened his promise. His wife, who had left the room to fetch some apples for him, suddenly vanished leaving her clothes standing without a body, almost/as if a ghost [*quasi phantasma*], beside the fruit box. I heard this from many trustworthy men, who themselves affirm that they were present when the Duke of Bavaria recounted it to the Duke of Saxony. But let us expound the tale of Orpheus... [*Sed Orphei fabulam exponamus...*][23]

This story has received no modern commentary, yet it contains a number of remarkable features, not least its similarities with the Ovidian original. The widower's prayer echoes that of Orpheus among the shades, while the prohibition on 'turning back' is transposed into a moral proviso — that the husband not return to his former violence. But most striking of all is the (un)dead woman at its centre. What is the reader to imagine — that is to say, represent conceptually — when reading her story? Several difficulties arise.

The first concerns the time-frame of the apparition. Sabinus's narrative effectively constructs a counterfactual future for Ovid's tale: Orpheus and Eurydice have reached home and resumed domestic life (here represented in the reference to apples and the fruit-box). This arrangement lasts 'for many years' (*per multos annos*) — a dispensation highly untypical of early modern ghost stories, in which the return of a dead person normally marks only a temporary interruption in the ordinary course of nature. Exceptions of this kind prove disconcerting. Comparison might be made with the biblical passage describing how after Christ's resurrection, 'the graves were opened; and many bodies of the saints which slept arose. And came out of the graves after his resurrection, and went into the holy city, and appeared unto many.' (Matthew 27: 52–53). Early modern commentators such as Jean Calvin and André Valladier followed Augustine in wondering whether these risen men subsequently resumed their former lives or sloped back to their tombs.[24] But Scripture is silent on the matter, and a troubling absence of finality persists.

Can a dead woman who takes up her former life, remarries, and fetches fruit for her husband properly be considered an instance of GHOST? It is not simply the deceased wife's longevity — what one might call in this context her ontological stamina — that seems to contradict our intuitions. That longevity is sealed with a second astonishing feat: that of giving birth to children. In this she seems all but to complete the transition back to the living haltingly begun by her classical precursor. The dead wife returns not just in a body, but one capable of having sex, generating and sustaining life — a phenomenon quite exceptional in pre-modern accounts of the return of the dead. As with Eurydice's limp, only more so, embodiment prompts a marked equivocation between GHOST and PERSON, in which default inferences attached to the latter category begin to reassert themselves.

Certain linguistic markers strengthen this sense of conceptual in-betweenness, notably a sequence of what Relevance theorists term 'procedural' and 'scalar' expressions. Procedurals (other English examples of which include certain uses of 'but', 'so', 'after all', and 'nevertheless') do not themselves encode conceptual representations but serve instead to signal and constrain the relevance of the overall utterance: that is, to point the hearer towards shared ('mutually manifest') assumptions likely to yield a maximally relevant interpretation.[25] The phrase '*even* giving birth to children, *though* pale and sad' contains two procedural markers. In this context 'even' cues the reader's access to an implicated premise (1) and an implicated conclusion (2):

(1) GHOST-like women are usually incapable of childbirth.

(2) This concept is PERSON-like.

'Though pale and sad', for its part, immediately qualifies (2) as its premise, while preserving the original premise as its implicated conclusion:

(3) This concept is GHOST-like (i.e., 'pale and sad' = physically diminished).

(4) GHOST-like women are usually incapable of childbirth.

The procedural markers signal the relevance of both GHOST and PERSON, but in such a way that each partially cancels the default inferences normally triggered by the other. Sabinus prompts us to imagine a conceptual chiasmus: a ghost-woman, or woman-ghost, hovering between the categories with which we organise our mental life.

This contextually adjusted, in-between, representation is further strengthened in the mysterious scalar 'quasi phantasma' — the phrase used to describe the manner in which the returned woman vanishes.[26] The word 'phantasma' is given special salience as the only term in this passage that explicitly names a supernatural phenomenon. But what of 'quasi'? In common with other scalars (examples include 'some', 'most', and 'any'), the force of 'quasi phantasma' arrives not simply via its encoded, dictionary meaning ('like a ghost', 'almost a ghost', 'as if a ghost') but via a process of pragmatic enrichment in which the reader additionally infers 'like [but therefore not identical to] a ghost', 'almost [but therefore not quite] a ghost', 'as if [but not in fact] a ghost'. Even as the wife evaporates into thin air, 'quasi' marks a limit beyond which GHOST inferences fail to carry through. As in the Ovidian original, the ontological category PERSON is lent a strange persistence, like the clothes still standing empty in the pantry.

Apposite Thinking

Any relevance-theoretic reading of Sabinus's story must contend with the author's intention. Why tell it, and why here? Framing devices signal various directions in which its relevance might be sought. Candidates include the author's personal investment in its transmission ('I heard [...] I heard') and in its prior circulation among trusted or authoritative individuals (the Dukes of Bavaria and Saxony); in its status as a true account (*historia*) rather than a purely fictional one (*fabula*); in its potential for moral exposition; and in its similarity with the Ovidian original. Any one of these might be thought sufficient to warrant readers' attention though, as we shall see, the matter is far from simple.

Given the political atmosphere in 1555, it is tempting to seek out Sabinus's motives among his theological commitments. These were far less equivocal than Shakespeare's. He was a prominent Lutheran — first rector of the newly founded Lutheran university of Königsberg, and the son-in-law of Philipp Melanchthon. Lutherans of this period usually discredit ghost narratives as Catholic propaganda in favour of the Popish doctrine of Purgatory. Perhaps the fact that Catholic Bavaria is given the role of storyteller is to be read as a veiled swipe at Papist gullibility; possibly the reference to 'trustworthy men' is intended as ironic. But these elements are subtle, if discernible at all, and would be quite uncharacteristic of a work which generally eschews sectarian polemics. Whatever readers might assume Sabinus's religious allegiances to be, the narrative does not make these assumptions sufficiently manifest to warrant a conclusion of polemical intent.

Attempts to read the story with reference to Sabinus's beliefs run up against a further difficulty: his uncertain commitment to its truth-value. The opening line invokes the familiar historiographical distinction between *fabula* and *historia*. This is usually a means of placing the ensuing narrative on the side of the latter; but here the priority is more equivocal. Superficially 'if tale is the right word' might appear an instance of *correctio* (i.e. 'this — no not this but something else'); and yet 'if' here does not so much cancel the possibility of the fictive as sustain it in a different mode. Likewise, in '*many* hold it to be a true account', 'many' does not simply encode 'a significant proportion' (as it does later in 'many tears and laments', 'many years', 'many things'). Here it also includes a scalar implicature: the reader is expected to infer that 'many [*but not all*] hold it to be true'. We might say that the narrative frame at once invites the reader to credit the ensuing narrative, and leaves the door ajar for a sceptical retreat.[27]

If literal truth cannot be assumed for Sabinus's narrative, then any mention of the higher truths promised by his title — physical, and especially 'moral' and 'ethical' — are just as conspicuously lacking. This absence may appear surprising given that an explanatory scheme lay so near at hand. Accounts analogous to this one multiplied across Europe in the years 1570–1600, at the height of the witch craze, when demonologists routinely interpret them as machinations of the devil. Augustin Lercheimer and Nicolas Rémy both report similar tales, in which the putative wife is in each instance revealed to be a demon who has taken up her corpse.[28] The early seventeenth-century theologian René Du Pont sees the devil's hand in all such cases, noting in addition that any offspring issuing from them are bound also to be 'false' ('des enfans supposez').[29] Du Pont's reference to children strongly suggests that he had read Sabinus's account, as does a reference to Orpheus and Eurydice in which he effectively diabolises the Ovidian fable:

> And what do the philosophers mean to say through their fable of Orpheus's descent into the underworld, to recover his wife, if not that he resurrected her by means of magic arts, conjuring into her inanimate body some devil who made her seem alive (yet the spell was so short-lived, and his curiosity in examining her so great, that immediately he lost her once more.)[30]

It was perhaps in regard to this changing climate that a later editor of Sabinus's commentary includes a shoulder note to the tale of the revenant wife, in which a general admonition is issued against looking back too fondly and, in particular, against nostalgic lust for a dead spouse. Though the note is not explicitly demonological in thrust, it aligns Sabinus's widower with a growing list of demonic dupes and, by doing so, delivers the *interpretatio ethica* promised in the title. In the original 1555 version, by contrast, no such apparatus is on hand to clinch the relevance of the widower's tale.

A final possibility arises: that Sabinus considered the parallels with Ovid sufficient in themselves to warrant the attention of his readers. For all his other equivocations, the author foregrounds these quite explicitly: 'I heard a tale similar to that of Orpheus...' Notice that such parallels are not proffered as a feature of commentary proper. This much is suggested by the procedural phrase marking the transition to the next portion of his text: '*sed* Orphei fabulam exponamus ...' ('*but* let us expound the fable of Orpheus...'). This transition to the 'true' commentary seemingly instates the widower's tale as 'mere' interpolation, an incidental adjunct to the proper business of the work. But it can also be construed more positively. Like 'if' ('*if* tale is the right word...'), 'sed' marks off an enabling limit beyond which he invites us to suspend truth-value, religious, moral or ethical conviction. It prompts the reader to seek relevance not on the vertical axis of exposition — that of word-to-world fit or the allegorical *altior sensus* — but instead on the horizontal plane of pure apposition. The narrative becomes relevant insofar as it is *apposite*.

Apposite thinking was arguably fundamental to Renaissance humanist activity (though not exclusive to it, Plutarch's *Parallel Lives* being one prestigious precursor). Through it scholars of the period established their textual parallels, built up their commonplaces and, in their syncretistic appositions of pagan myth and revealed truth, enabled and enacted the freedom to philosophize. Provisional and experimental, the task of the apposite thinker was not to expound but heuristically suspend propositions, commitments, and beliefs, all the more earnestly where — as was the case with ghosts — the topic appeared strapped to ideological extremes. Sabinus's is only one among a large number of supernatural narratives to share exactly this appositional character. A longer investigation might include any number of kindred instances in Boaistuau and Belleforest's *Histoires prodigieuses*, the *Histoires admirables* of Simon Goulart, or the *diverses leçon* of Pedro Mexía, Antoine Du Verdier, and Louis Guyon. Even some demonology has this flavour, for instance portions of Pierre Le Loyer's compendium of ghost-lore, the *IIII Livres des spectres*.[31] But perhaps Montaigne in his *Essais,* a masterwork of apposite thinking, best sums up the appeal of supernatural tales in 'On the Power of the Imagination':

> So in the study I am making of our behaviour and motives, fabulous testimonies, provided they are possible, serve like true ones. Whether they have happened or no, in Paris or Rome, to John or Peter, they exemplify, at all events, some human potentiality [...][32]

Notes to Chapter 3

1. See Keith Thomas's oft-quoted claim that 'Although it may be a relatively frivolous question today to ask whether or not one believes in ghosts, it was in the sixteenth century a shibboleth which distinguished Protestant from Catholic almost as effectively as belief in the Mass or Papal Supremacy', *Religion and the Decline of Magic: Studies in Popular Beliefs in Sixteenth- and Seventeenth-Century England* (London: Weidenfeld and Nicolson, 1997 [1st ed. 1971]), p. 589.
2. See, for example, Stephen Greenblatt, *Hamlet in Purgatory* (Princeton: Princeton University Press, 2001).
3. This chapter will follow the usual practice in linguistics of capitalising concepts.
4. '[...] umbras erat illa recentes / inter et incessit passu de vulnere tardo', Ovid, *Metamorphoses* X, 48–49. I have used Frank Justus Miller's English translation for the Loeb Classical Library (London: Heinemann, 1968), p. 67.
5. *Metamorphoses* X, 40–44.
6. On drawing swords against ghosts, see Homer, *The Odyssey*, X, 535–37; Virgil, *Aeneid* VI, 260. On the motif of the 'vain embrace', see below pp. 61–62.
7. See Timothy Chesters, *Ghost Stories in Late Renaissance France: Walking by Night* (Oxford: Oxford University Press, 2011).
8. Notably the demonological dialogue of the eleventh-century Byzantine philosopher Michael Psellos; see Chesters, *Ghost Stories*, pp. 175–85.
9. On ghosts in the New World, see Chesters, *Ghost Stories*, pp. 154–63; on the *draugr*, popularised by Saxo Grammaticus in the Middle Ages and later in the cosmography of Olaus Magnus, see Jean-Claude Schmitt, *Ghosts in the Middle Ages: The Living and the Dead in Medieval Society* (Chicago: University of Chicago, 1998), p. 13; on Japanese festivals of the dead, see Claude Guichard, *Funérailles et diverses manieres d'ensevelir des Rommains, Grecs, et autres nations, tant anciennes que modernes* (Lyon: Jean de Tournes, 1581), pp. 395–96.
10. On popular ghost beliefs in pre-modern Europe, see Emmanuel Leroy-Ladurie, *Montaillou: village occitan de 1294 à 1324* (Paris: Gallimard, 1975), ch. 26 ('Folklore et revenants'); Claude Lecouteux, *Fantômes et revenants au Moyen-Âge* (Paris: Imago, 1986).
11. *Demon Lovers: Witchcraft, Sex, and the Crisis of Belief* (Chicago: University of Chicago Press, 2002).
12. Pascal Boyer, *Religion Explained: The Human Instincts that Fashion Gods, Spirits and Ancestors* (London: Basic Books, 2001).
13. Dan Sperber, 'Anthropology and Psychology: Towards an Epidemiology of Representations', *Man*, New Series, 20.1 (1985), 73–89.
14. Boyer, *Religion Explained*, p. 86.
15. For recent introductions to Relevance Theory, see Dan Sperber and Deirdre Wilson, *Meaning and Relevance* (Cambridge: Cambridge University Press, 2012); Robyn Carston, *Thoughts and Utterances* (Oxford: Blackwell, 2002); Yan Huang, *Pragmatics* (Oxford: Oxford University Press, 2007), 181–208; Billy Clark, *Relevance Theory* (Cambridge: Cambridge University Press, 2013).
16. Boyer, *Religion Explained*, pp. 84–85.
17. On source-tagging and decoupling, see Leda Cosmides and John Tooby, 'Consider the Source: The Evolution of Adaptations for Decoupling and Metarepresentation', in *Metarepresentations: A Multidisciplinary Perspective*, ed. by Dan Sperber (Oxford: Oxford University Press, 2000), pp. 53–115; applied to literary immersion, see especially Lisa Zunshine, *Why We Read Fiction* (Columbus, OH: Ohio State University Press, 2006), pp. 47–79.
18. 'ter conatus ibi collo dare bracchia circum; / ter frustra comprensa manus effugit imago, / par levibus ventis volucrique simillima somno'. Virgil, *Aeneid*, trans. by Henry Rushton Fairclough (Cambridge MA: Harvard University Press, 2006), II, 792–94. The episode of Achilles and Patroclus is recounted in Homer, *Iliad* XXIII, 99–101.
19. On the many early modern variants of this trope, in Ronsard, Shakespeare and elsewhere, see Chesters, *Ghost Stories*, pp. 12, 175–85. Early modern psychology would have understood Aeneas's perception in terms of illusory *species*; see Katherine Park, 'The Organic Soul', in *The Cambridge History of Renaissance Philosophy*, ed. by Charles B. Schmitt and Quentin Skinner (Cambridge: Cambridge University Press, 2011), pp. 464–84 (471–72); on sensory illusion see also the contributions of Giglioni and Maus de Rolley to this volume.

20. Adapted from Sperber and Wilson, *Meaning and Relevance*, pp. 32–33.
21. On this point, see John Searle, 'The Background of Meaning', in *Speech-Act Theory and Pragmatics*, ed. by John Searle and Ferenc Kiefer (Dordrecht: Reidel, 1980), pp. 221–32.
22. Jack has here followed the so-called 'relevance-guided comprehension heuristic', which Clark defines as follows: '(i) Follow a path of least effort in deriving cognitive effects: test interpretations (e.g. disambiguations, reference resolutions, implicatures, etc.) in order of accessibility. (ii) Stop when your expectations of relevance are satisfied.'; *Relevance Theory*, p. 119.
23. Georg Sabinus, *Fabularum Ovidii interpretatio* (Vitebergae: haeredes Georgii Rhaw, 1555), sigs Lviii^{r-v}. The English translation is my own.
24. Jean Calvin, *Commentaires de Jehan Calvin sur le Nouveau Testament*, 4 vols (Paris: C. Meyruis, 1854–55), I, 722; André Valladier, *La Saincte Philosophie de l'ame* (Paris: J. du Puys, 1614), p. 692.
25. The procedural/conceptual distinction originates in Diane Blakemore, *Semantic Constraints on Relevance* (Oxford: Blackwell, 1987). For an updated account, see the same author's *Relevance and Linguistic Meaning: The Semantics and Pragmatics of Discourse Markers* (Cambridge: Cambridge University Press, 2002), pp. 89–148.
26. For a recent relevance-theoretic account of scalars, see Robyn Carston, 'Informativeness, Relevance, and Scalar Implicature', in *Relevance Theory: Applications and Implications*, ed. by Robyn Carston and Seiji Uchida (Amsterdam: John Benjamins, 1998), 179–236.
27. Kirsti Sellevold pays similarly literary-critical attention to scalars in her 'Reading Short Forms Cognitively: Mindreading and Procedural Expressions in La Rochefoucauld and La Bruyère', in *Reading Literature Cognitively* (= *Paragraph* 37.1), ed. by Terence Cave, Karin Kukkonen, and Olivia Smith (Edinburgh: Edinburgh University Press, 2014), pp. 96–111.
28. Augustin Lercheimer [= Hermann Witekind], *Christlich bedenken und erinnerung von Zauberey* (Heidelberg: J. Müller and H. Aven, 1585); Nicolaus Remigius [= Nicolas Rémy], *Daemonolatreiae libri tres* (Lyon: ex. off. Vicentii, 1595), p. 189.
29. René Du Pont, *La Philosophie des esprits* (Paris: veuve G. de la Nouë, 1602), sigs Evi^{r-v}.
30. Du Pont, *La Philosophie des esprits*, sigs Ffiiii^{r-v}.
31. (Angers: G. Nepfveu, 1586).
32. Michel de Montaigne, *The Complete Works*, trans. by D. Frame (London: Everyman, 2003), p. 91. For a relevance-theoretic approach to Montaigne's *Essais*, see Kirsti Sellevold, *J'ayme ces mots: expressions linguistiques de doute dans les 'Essais' de Montaigne* (Paris: Champion, 2004).

CHAPTER 4

A World Within: The Devil, Delusions and Early Modern Cognition

Thibaut Maus de Rolley

Thinking Demonic Illusions

The pages of early modern demonological treatises are filled with descriptions of wonders that challenged, for their readers, the boundaries between truth and falsehood, reality and illusion, wakefulness and sleep. They tell, among many things, about ghosts and apparitions, flying witches, nocturnal feasts with the devil, humans taking the shapes of animals, and men suddenly afflicted by sexual impotence, sometimes to the point of being unable to see or feel their own genitals. The authors of these texts — 'demonologists' — did not merely compile dramatic reports of these phenomena. They also tried to determine if such wonders were due to demonic agency or to non-demonic causes (God, nature, or human artifice), and, simultaneously, they sought to ascertain whether each of them had to be deemed real or illusory. As Stuart Clark has shown, these two sets of criteria (demonic and non-demonic; real and illusory) governed and structured demonological debate. Between them, they offered four categories of explanation allowing demonologists to classify any extraordinary event as: (i) real demonic effects; (ii) illusory demonic effects; (iii) real non-demonic effects; or (iv) illusory non-demonic effects.[1]

As this 'grid' makes clear, to classify a phenomenon as an illusion was not to consider it as non-demonic, for an illusion could be wrought by the devil. A demonic illusion — demonologists alternatively used the terms imposture, or 'prestige' (*praestigium*) — could be of two kinds. It could consist in a deception of the external senses (and particularly, but not only, of the eye), or in a deception of the internal senses (a delusion of the 'eye of the mind'). In both cases, the devil's victim perceived something that was not veridical — that did not correspond to reality. I will return in a moment to the mechanics of these illusions, in particular those of internal illusions. The point I would like to make for now is that an 'illusory demonic effect' would not necessarily be thought of by demonologists as imaginary: in other words, as a dream or an hallucination. The devil could, for instance, surround a man with a body made out of air in order to give him the appearance of a wolf. However false and illusory, this ghostly semblance of a beast had enough material existence — enough reality, as it were — to be perceived by the bodily senses. Or the devil could, like a juggler playing a card trick, substitute a wolf for a man in the blink of an eye. In this case, the effect achieved by the devil's sleight of hand was the same — the illusion of metamorphosis — even if the objects perceived by the viewer were in themselves perfectly real: a real man, then a real wolf, both carried through space at prodigious speed.

In some instances, the devil forged illusions so as to exaggerate his powers and make men believe that he could accomplish not only wonders (*mira*), but miracles (*miracula*). For almost all demonologists, true miracles were the preserve of God alone. The devil could not overrule the laws of nature, and achieved most of his effects by manipulating nature and its occult properties. His domain was not that of the supernatural, but of the preternatural: the realm of deviant and prodigious phenomena that were yet within nature. Illusions enabled the devil to blur this fundamental boundary. The purpose of illusory metamorphoses, for instance, was to lead men and women to believe that he had the power to create and alter the substance of things, something actually beyond his reach. In other instances, the devil created illusions in order to mask (and not exaggerate) the extent and the reality of his crimes in the world, by making them appear as the product of purely natural causes. Evidence that witches sometimes merely dreamed about the Sabbath, their nocturnal gathering with the devil, instead of attending it 'in the body', was thus interpreted by many as a demonic ruse, meant to undermine belief in the existence and reality of the Sabbath itself, and to save witches from the stake.[2]

'Thinking with demons' meant, therefore, engaging in a constant and subtle process of discrimination, where boundaries needed to be readjusted for each phenomenon discussed and where all the categories of explanation identified by Clark had to be considered at some point. Very few authors accepted all phenomena suspected of being demonic as being truly demonic, or, alternatively, attributed them entirely to natural causes; and none claimed that demonic effects were *all* real, or *all* illusory. A demonologist could place the Sabbath on the first square of the grid (i: real demonic effects), while presenting werewolves as the product of a demonic illusion (ii: illusory demonic effects), sexual impotence as the natural effect of the power of imagination (iii: real non-demonic effects), and, say, the levitation of demoniacs as a juggler's trick (iv: illusory non-demonic effects). And different explanations could of course be offered for the same phenomenon, sometimes within a single treatise, as was usually the case in discussions about demonic 'transvection' — the witches' flight to the Sabbath.[3]

In order to trace these multiple boundaries between truth and illusion, it was necessary for demonologists to explain how illusions — demonic or not — were produced, and thus to detail the workings of the mind and sensory perception. These authors therefore played a major part in early modern debates about cognition and cognitive confusions. As Clark has shown in *Vanities of the Eye*, demonology significantly advanced the idea that the world might not be what it appears to be, and that the senses — and especially vision — were uncertain and unreliable.[4] The rest of this chapter will focus on two of the most influential demonologists in early modern Europe — Heinrich Kramer and Johann Weyer — and explore some of the different ways in which they conceived of the mind, the mechanisms of internal illusions, and the role played by the devil in the making of such delusions. It will examine, in particular, how these demonological discussions were underpinned by a fundamental analogy between the mind and the physical world — the 'world within' and the 'world without'. Like us, demonologists relied heavily on metaphorical language, and particularly on spatial metaphors, to conceptualise the mind and its malfunctions. The mind was conceived of as a physical space, and cognition as a spatial and dynamic process, dependent on the journeys undertook by the entities inhabiting this inner territory. However, as we shall see, demonologists differ from us in taking spatial metaphors of the mind literally, in more than one respect. The boundary between the figurative and the literal, in discussions of mental activity, is a moving and uncertain one.

The Topographical Mind

One of the most thorough and sophisticated discussions of demonic illusions can be found in the famous *Malleus maleficarum*, or *Hammer of Witches*, published in 1486 by the Dominican inquisitors Heinrich Kramer (or Institoris) and Jacob Sprenger, and most probably written by the former alone.[5] The main purpose of the work was to demonstrate the reality of witchcraft. As such, it repeatedly argued for a reinterpretation of the authoritative *Canon episcopi*, a tenth-century text of canon law, and its claim that nocturnal flights were a delusion induced by the devil: an experience happening in the mind, but never in the body (more on that later). To accept such a view, for Kramer, was to pave the way for the idea that all witchcraft was illusory, and thus excuse the witches from their crimes: 'they [those who deny bodily transportation] claim that all acts of sorcery [...] should be ascribed to [witches] as people who do not harm since these are merely matters relating to an illusion in the imagination'.[6] However, Kramer did not rule out the possibility of such delusions. How could he? The devil was indeed the ultimate deceiver, a master conjurer, keen to trick men — and even his own disciples — with external or internal *praestigia*.[7]

Scattered across several chapters of the treatise, Kramer's discourse on the mechanics of internal illusions was heavily indebted to Thomas Aquinas's discussion of the subject, notably in his *De malo* (16.11) and *Summa theologica* (1.78).[8] Kramer's understanding of internal illusions indeed relied on the scholastic Aristotelian theory of faculties of the mind.[9] According to this model (schematically summarised here), sensory cognition was achieved by the joint operation of the external senses (sight, hearing, smell, taste, touch) and the internal senses (or faculties). As Kramer remarked himself, opinions differed as to the exact number and name of the internal senses. For Aquinas, and thus Kramer, there were four of them: the common sense, imagination (or fantasy), estimation (or cogitation, or reason), and memory.[10] Sensory information received by the external senses was conveyed to the brain by animal spirits circulating along the nerves. The imagination received this data through the common sense and converted it into visual replicas of sense objects: 'sensible *species*', or 'phantasms', also described as similitudes, likenesses, or images.[11]

The imagination stored these images, allowing the mind to continue perceiving them when the external object was for instance out of sight, and transmitted them, again through the agency of animal spirits, to the other faculties: reason and memory, where they were more permanently stored.[12]

This dynamic and physiological conception of mental processes allowed for the construction of a cartography of the mind. Developed from Greek medical theory by early Christian writers such as St Augustine, and still widely accepted throughout the Renaissance, in spite of the challenges posed by the anatomical observations of physicians like Vesalius, the medieval 'cell doctrine' of brain function localised the faculties of the mind in the hollow ventricles (or 'cells', *cellulae*) of the brain.[13] Again, opinions differed, but a frequent view was to place the common sense in the first cell (corresponding to the lateral ventricles of the brain), at the front of the head, usually alongside the imagination. Reason was located in the middle cell (the third ventricle), in the position of the judge, and memory in the third cell (the fourth ventricle), in the posterior part of the brain. Anatomical illustrations offered a mapping of this world within the brain, often in the form of three juxtaposed circles or oblongs, labelled like a crude topographical map.[14] From the tenth century, the three cells, like three communicating caves, appear linked together by open passages, consonant with the dynamic conception of sensory perception.[15]

Kramer's presentation of the faculties and their function was in line with this rough outline. The imagination was 'a place of preservation for forms [*species*] received by perception'[16] — in other words, received through the external senses and the common sense. These forms, or images, explained Kramer, were set in motion by animal spirits and humours. They flowed from one faculty to the other, and were eventually stored in the memory, a 'storehouse of conceptions that are not received by perception'.[17] The common sense was located in the front part of the brain, imagination in the middle, and memory in the third *cellula capitis*, at the back of the head.[18] The devil, Kramer reminded his readers, could forge external or internal deceptions. But to do the latter, he first had to glide into the body of his victim — demonic delusions constituted a form of demonic possession.[19] According to Augustine, quoted by Kramer, the devil tempted and seduced individuals by manipulating their senses:

> This evil creeps in through all avenues of perception. It adopts shapes, it adorns itself in colours, it clings to sounds, it subordinates itself to smells, it suffuses itself with flavours.[20]

But this remark could be taken literally: the external senses provided pathways into the body, and because of his spiritual nature, which made him as malleable and evanescent as air, the devil could easily (but with the permission of God) penetrate these breaches.[21] Women were particularly vulnerable to these attacks, since the female body was considered to be more porous and open than the male body, and thus more easily invaded and possessed.[22]

These were widely shared and accepted ideas about demonic possession. A more problematic one was the localisation of the devil inside the body. Unlike God, the devil occupied a location in space. So where did he go, once he had got past the gates of the external senses? Could he physically occupy the mind? Or did he act on the internal senses from other parts of the body? Because they wanted to 'reserve a privileged space' for God, medieval theologians had tended to confine the presence of invading demons to the debased portions of the body: the bowels, away from the heart and spiritual system.[23] The production of demonic internal illusions, argued Kramer, could not happen unless the devil could take possession of the faculties of the mind; he had to be actually present in the head (and thus in its ventricles).[24] But how could two spirits — the devil and the soul, which God made impenetrable to the devil — be in the same place at the same time? It was true, remarked Kramer, that the centre of the heart was the seat of the soul, but it could also be argued, as did the *De spiritu et anima* (a work then widely attributed to Augustine) that the soul was 'in the entire body and in every part of the body'.[25] Scholastic distinctions enabled Kramer to solve the difficulty, and to conclude that the devil and the soul could indeed cohabit in the head, since there was 'no confusion of their respective workings': 'granting that the soul is in the head, still the devil can work there, for his work is different from the work of the soul.'[26]

When inside the ventricles, the devil could not be perceived by the internal senses. He could not assume an aerial body, and he could not forge new *species* that did not previously exist in the two storehouses of the mind, the memory and the imagination. However, he had the power to hijack, as it were, the images flowing along the nerves or in the cavities of the brain, shifting them from one faculty to another. In particular, he could impress upon the imagination images borrowed from the memory, producing visions of things that were not actually perceived by the external senses:

> The demons can direct and set into motion the internal spirits and humours, so that the images stored in the places of preservation are brought forth from the storehouses to the origins of perception, that is, to the virtues of imagination and fantasy, so that this person can imagine certain things.[27]

Demons could also 'transform' these images by combining them, thus creating chimeras and fantastical mirages that had never been perceived, as such, by their victims, and did not even exist.

All this was well within the powers of the devil. These were natural processes that could actually happen without any demonic intervention, while asleep, under the influence of passions, or because of a humoral imbalance.[28] The devil only had to exercise his power of 'local motion' over material objects. In other words, he had but to act upon bodies and move them through space, as he did notably when transporting witches to the Sabbath, when shaping bodies made out of air, or when performing various *praestigia*. Kramer's descriptions of internal illusions actually echoed his own presentation of the devil as a consummate juggler (*ioculator*), for the trick, here, was fundamentally a feat of legerdemain.[29] It relied on the devil's ability to manipulate objects, to convey them swiftly from one hiding place to another, to substitute one for the other. The devil performed in the ventricles of the brain as if on a juggler's stage, with the eye of the imagination for his sole audience.

The Clouded Mind

In the preface to his influential *De Praestigiis daemonum* (*On the Illusions of Demons*, 1563), the German physician Johann Weyer (or Wier) explained that to address the question of witchcraft was to enter a dark 'labyrinth of enchantments' (*incantamentorum labyrinthus*), full of traps and deceptions, where one risked, at every step, losing the thread of truth by confusing the real and the illusory.[30] In Weyer's view, finding the way out implied that one recognised how much of the phenomena attributed to the agency of demons belonged to the realm of illusion, and how little to that of reality. Against those who, like Kramer, had endeavoured to establish the reality of witchcraft, Weyer argued that the crimes and activities ordinarily imputed to *female* witches — poisoning excepted — were imaginary ones, including the Sabbath, the pact with the devil, and their nocturnal flights. Because of the natural frailty of their sex, women, and especially old women, were all too easily deluded by their own imagination, but also by the internal illusions forged by the devil. The argument, at its core, was no less misogynistic than Kramer's. God, explained Weyer, would not allow the devil to persecute these excessively dumb and weak creatures except by dreams and delusions. To permit other forms of persecution (such as a bodily transportation to the Sabbath) would be to submit them to an excessive and unjust punishment. However, *male* witches — learned magicians in the guise of Faust — were guilty of invoking the devil, colluding with him and committing all sorts of diabolical crimes. Unlike their female counterparts, these male magicians had to be executed.[31]

Weyer insisted on the fact that witches' delusions could be explained by natural causes in ways that did not necessarily entail the intervention of the devil. Women were particularly vulnerable to illusions created by a humoral imbalance, being melancholic by nature (a point hotly disputed by Jean Bodin, Weyer's fiercest opponent). In a chapter on 'the distorted imagination of melancholics' (II, 24 in the first version of the text; III, 7 in the expanded one), Weyer reminds his readers that stirred and overheated humours — and first and foremost, black bile — produce vapours that rise from the abdomen to the brain, infecting the 'abode of the mind' and altering the workings of the imagination. Victims of such melancholic delusions are assailed by chimeral thoughts and fantastical visions in their sleep or, more rarely, while awake.[32]

In the following chapter, Weyer expands on the role of the imagination and how it could be corrupted. His explanations lack the precision and sophistication of Kramer's scholastic psychology. Long quotations borrowed mainly from Marsilio Ficino, Aristotle and the fourth-century neoplatonist Iamblichus introduce rudiments of the theory of the faculties detailed above.[33] According to Iamblichus, the function of the imagination (indifferently designated by Weyer as *phantasia*, *imaginatio*, or *vis imaginativa*) was to receive the information provided by the external senses and shape it into 'likenesses and apparitions' (*similitudines specierum, et apparitiones*), which it would then convey to the other faculties, the 'opinion' and the 'intellect' (there is no mention of the memory in these chapters).[34] The imagination was a 'treasure-house for the forms received through the senses' (a quotation from

Aristotle's *De somno*); these images were carried through the nerves and the mind by animal spirits and vapours.[35]

When excessively hot or abundant, humoral exhalations could confuse the *species* and divert them from their course. They could also contaminate them with their qualities, and therefore transform them. A phlegmatic vapour would cause dreams about water, whereas a 'black and melancholic vapour' would make 'something horrible appear — a demon-image, as it were'.[36] Weyer also insisted that these cognitive confusions could be triggered by the imagination itself, without any external stimulation. Quoting Ficino's discourse on the power of imagination, he presented the imagination as a rebel faculty, a disruptive force that, when under the influence of passions (desire, pleasure, fear, and sorrow), could trick the mind and the body, to the point of altering it by sending the animal spirits, through the nerves, to impress the flesh with images.[37] But even in that case, the process remained essentially the same: *species* and animal spirits manipulated (and corrupted) by vapours, themselves stirred up by passions.

As a physician, Weyer was certainly familiar with the cell doctrine, and would probably have come across illustrations like the often plagiarised drawing of the ventricles published in 1503 by Gregor Reisch in his *Margarita philosophica*, a successful university textbook providing a detailed account of Aristotelian psychology.[38] However, Weyer did not map the workings of the faculties in much detail. He located them in the brain — 'the organ of thoughts and imaginings'[39] — though without giving a clear idea of their respective places within it, nor mentioning the three ventricles: a sign, perhaps, of the influence of Vesalius, who rejected the ventricular localisation of the faculties.[40] Weyer also remained quite vague on the problematic issue of the localisation of the devil within the body. Like Kramer and virtually every demonologist of the period, Weyer believed in the devil's ability and eagerness to invade the human body, which was, according to St Cyprian (quoted in I, 20) comparable to a besieged citadel:

> [The devil] passes around us one by one, and, like an enemy laying siege to closed walls, he explores and tests whether some part of our bodily members be less stable and dependable — an avenue whereby he can penetrate to our inner parts.[41]

The external senses, again, were those breaks in the wall allowing the devil to 'insinuate himself' into his victims' bodies in order to delude them. However, unlike the *Malleus maleficarum*, the *De praestigiis* never makes quite clear whether the devil needed to enter the brain to interfere with his victims' thoughts. In Weyer's descriptions of demonic internal illusions, the starting point of the process is invariably the devil's direct action on humours. The devil, it is repeatedly said, 'stirs up' humours and vapours, which then disturb the course of the animal spirits and *species* in the brain, corrupt them, and affect in turn the internal senses.[42] His place, it seems, is within the black bile. Melancholy, Weyer reminded his readers, was known as the devil's bath (*diaboli balneum*), and the devil took indeed 'great delight in immersing himself in this humour' and mingling in its fumes.[43] Melancholic vapours were a vehicle allowing him to circulate around the body — and possibly enter the brain.

However, what these remarks suggest is that the devil, in Weyer's conception, operated essentially from the recesses of the abdomen — from the spleen, where black bile was secreted. More than a juggler directly manipulating images within the brain, the devil appears here as a physician of sorts (an 'old scheming physician', as Weyer himself put it[44]) regulating, or rather deregulating, the production of humours within the body. This portrayal of the devil as a figure stirring up humours in order to raise storms in the upper regions of the brain also conjures up that of the *tempestarii*, those weather witches who, according to Kramer, were able to provoke hailstorms by stirring water (or urine) in a hole in the ground.[45] Like the weather witch controlling atmospheric phenomena from the ground, Weyer's devil, it seems, acted on the internal senses at a distance, from the lower regions of the body, without necessarily taking physical possession of the cavities of the brain.

According to Weyer's *De praestigiis*, the devil, however, does more than simply agitate or heat humours. Drawing on Aristotle's *De insomniis* and Pseudo-Augustine's *De spiritu et anima*, Weyer argues that the devil had the ability to 'form apparitions' by shaping the vapours of melancholy and cloaking himself in these fumes, thus creating a ballet of ethereal figures within the dark caves of the brain:

> Having obtained from God the power of forming such apparitions [*species*] and impressing them upon physical spirits of the soul, the demons use these forms to portray persons — now joyful, and engaged in eating, drinking, dancing, singing, and sexual intercourse — now sad, and devising or suffering every kind of evil — now human, now bestial, now smothering someone, now flying about.[46]

Witches believed they were flying to and attending the Sabbath, when they were actually watching independently, immobile in their beds, a private ghost show set for the eye of the imagination. In the following chapter, Weyer quotes Augustine and Pseudo-Augustine at length to remind his reader of the devil's ability to make bodies out of air, 'devise phantom-images', and 'transform himself into various appearances and likenesses'.[47] It is actually quite unclear whether the remarks of this chapter apply only to external illusions, or to external and internal illusions. The final paragraphs, which paraphrase the *Canon episcopi* and therefore deal with delusions happening 'in the mind' and during sleep (more on that below), suggest the latter. Thus the devil, in Weyer's view, could once inside the body forge images by shaping and assuming aerial bodies; he did not merely combine existing images brought forth from the memory, like Kramer's Thomistic — and less powerful — demons.

The Metaphorical Mind

The devil infested the two worlds separated by the boundary of the skin, the 'world within' and the 'world without'. In both, he behaved and operated in a similar way, using the same powers and techniques: the power of local motion, sleight of hand, and the ability (at least in Weyer's view) to shape and assume bodies made out of air. There was nothing abstract about these actions, nor, more generally, about the mechanisms of sensory perception these texts described. As Stuart Clark remarks,

'Aristotelian cognitive theory was couched in a particular language of veridicality — a kind of scholastic realism',[48] and this was certainly true for the explanations provided by demonologists. This realism was reinforced in their descriptions of demonic illusions by a language that established a series of analogies between the world within and the world without, and evoked, particularly in Weyer's treatise, an interior landscape within the body. Inside, there were winds, toxic fumes and stormy vapours. In the 'citadel' of the body, there were 'gates', 'cells', 'storehouses' and 'avenues' (the nerves), criss-crossed by 'figures' and 'apparitions' engaged, as we have seen, in scenes halfway between a Sabbath and a joyful banquet. This was not a landscape complete with forests, cities and cabbage planters, like the 'new world' discovered by Alcofribas Nasier, the narrator of Rabelais's *Pantagruel*, inside the giant's mouth.[49] Still, we find here a hint of this motif of the body as an inhabited country, a geographical entity replicating to some extent the features of the exterior world.[50] To demons able to glide through external senses, the cavities of the human brain might very well have appeared like the grotesque and gigantic mouth of Pantagruel.

Underlying these analogies was the conception of the body as a microcosm: a world in miniature reflecting in its structure and elementary composition that of the large world, the universe. Beyond what they suggested about the place of man in creation, these analogies had a cognitive value, explaining the unknown by the known, the invisible by the visible, the abstract by the concrete. The experience of natural phenomena occurring in the macrocosm made it possible to think and make sense of the secret workings of the microcosm. In a passage of the *De insomniis* glossed by Weyer, for example, Aristotle explains the formation of mental images in dreams by comparing them to meteorological phenomena — shape-shifting clouds, and the exhalations that arise when the earth is heated by the sun.[51] This analogical principle underpinned early modern conceptions of the body as a 'weather system' or a hydraulic one, and more generally the various metaphors of human biology employed in the period that reflected changing conceptions of the natural world.[52] But it is also the more fundamental experience of geographical space and motion in space that provided a model for Kramer's and Weyer's conceptualization of cognitive processes. Perception was ultimately a matter of concrete entities (the animal spirits, the sensible *species*) and substances (the vapours of melancholy) moving and interacting in a physical space. It was the product, to a large extent, of journeys undertaken in certain directions by the 'objects' inhabiting this topographical mind.

Modern cognitive sciences shed an interesting light on this mapping of the mind and the analogies between microcosm and macrocosm that support it. Research in cognitive linguistics and the philosophy of the mind suggests that our mental representations of abstract domains are largely built up by analogy with our bodily interactions with our physical environment, and therefore our embodied experience of space. In their seminal book *Metaphors We Live By* (1980), George Lakoff and Mark Johnson claimed that this analogical principle — more precisely, this metaphorical principle — is a fundamental mechanism of the mind. We think in metaphors, and the foundation of much of this metaphorical thinking is provided by spatial metaphors, which are grounded in our physical (but also cultural) experience of the world: 'The structure of our spatial concepts emerges from our constant spatial experience, that is, our interaction with the physical environment.'[53]

Spatial metaphors allow us to think and talk about abstract things that we cannot see or touch: time, for instance, but also thoughts themselves, and the workings of the mind.[54] In his *Philosophy of Symbolic Forms*, Ernst Cassirer had already remarked that the use of 'spatial representations' to express 'spiritual processes' was the clearest example of the 'interpenetration of sensuous and spiritual expression in language'; in other words, that the distinction between the physical world and the mind is a fragile and debatable one, as theorists of the 'embodied mind' would argue today.[55] Cassirer presented this use of spatial metaphors as a universal one, present 'not only in languages of the Indo-Germanic group but in linguistic families far removed from it'.[56] The analysis of metaphors used to describe the brain and the workings of the mind shows indeed that spatial metaphors and 'reification metaphors' (that is to say, metaphors presenting ideas, thoughts, and emotions as objects moving in a physical space) constitute one of the major types of metaphors employed in everyday and scientific language, alongside the metaphor of the brain as a computer, and that of the brain as a person.[57] Like early modern demonologists, we tend to construct a dynamic topography of the mind. We imagine it as a world mirroring the world we live in, with its regions, pathways, gateways, storage units; a landscape in which thoughts, emotions and sensory information move around, flow, wander or are kept in reserve. Those spatial and reification metaphors enable us to conceptualize and express complex cognitive and emotional processes. As the recent Pixar animated film *Inside Out* brilliantly demonstrates, they constitute an extremely efficient tool for visualizing, describing and understanding the workings of the mind.

In spite of the realism of the Aristotelian theory of cognition, demonological discourses on illusions obviously did make use of metaphors, and particularly of spatial metaphors. The metaphorisation of the mind and mental activity pervades the language used by our two demonologists, Latin, a language in which ways of speaking about cognitive processes are 'consistently and coherently structured in terms of movement and position in physical space'.[58] However, the boundary between the figurative and the literal can often be difficult to draw. The entities, substances, motions and places described by demonologists in the 'world within' were not necessarily conceived of as metaphorical ones, even if we are often tempted to understand them as such. The body might not have been considered by demonologists to be a real citadel, but spirits for them did flow; mental images did exist in space; they did move and wander inside the mind. The distinction between the figurative and the literal is an uncertain one in these texts, largely because it is dependent on historical conceptions of the mind and the body. The use of spatial metaphors to conceptualize mental activity might be a universal (or at least widely shared) principle, but that does not mean that these metaphors do not have, as Antonina Harbus puts it, 'significant biographies or past lives' worth exploring.[59] Metaphors are culturally and historically relative. They interact with changing cultural and scientific knowledge — here, beliefs about the human body and the mind. The very definition of what is metaphorical or not thus appears historically contingent: what we spontaneously recognise as a metaphor might not have been interpreted as such in the past. It might be that some of our modern metaphors and ways of talking about mental processes derive from what were originally non-metaphorical representations of the mind, or that these metaphors, in certain contexts and at certain moments of their 'past lives', were invested with a literal meaning — which might actually have imbued them with new life.[60]

The Errant Mind

Repeatedly quoted by Kramer and Weyer alike, the *Canon episcopi*, the crux of the demonological debate on illusion, offers a good example of the pitfalls presented by metaphors of mental activity appearing in discussions of demonic illusions. First found in Regino of Prum's collection of canon law (c. 906), and probably derived from an earlier source, the *Canon episcopi* evoked folk beliefs that cannot be assimilated to the concept of satanic witchcraft which underlay the early modern European witch-hunt. However, the text was interpreted from the fifteenth century as a discussion of witchcraft beliefs, and particularly of the witches' flight to the Sabbath. Indeed, its author famously reported that 'some wicked women',

> perverted by the Devil, seduced by illusions and phantasms of demons, believe and profess themselves, in the hours of night, to ride upon certain beasts with Diana, the goddess of pagans, and an innumerable multitude of women, and in the silence of the dead of night to traverse great spaces of earth, and to obey her commands as of her mistress, and to be summoned to her service on certain nights.[61]

The essential lesson of the *Canon episcopi* was that women who believed in the reality of these supernatural expeditions were deluded by the devil. Their journeys were the product of demonic illusions comparable to 'dreams and nocturnal visions'. The mechanisms of such delusions were not explained in great detail:

> Thus Satan himself, who transfigures himself into an angel of light, when he has captured the mind of a miserable woman and has subjugated her by infidelity and incredulity, immediately transforms himself into the species and similitudes of different personages and deluding the mind which he holds captive and exhibiting things, joyful or mournful, and persons, known or unknown, leads it through devious ways, and while the spirit alone endures this, the faithless mind thinks that these things happen not in the spirit but in the body.[62]

Most of what is said here can be read literally, for the passage describes the concrete operations undertaken by the devil in order to confuse his victim's mind: i) he appears in the guise of an angel so as to lure his victim — in this context, the remark invited a more literal interpretation than in its source, Paul's second epistle to the Corinthians (II Corinthians 11.14); ii) he 'transforms himself' into *species* and similitudes presented to the eye of the mind;[63] and iii) he 'exhibits' forged images of persons and things — again, the context suggests that these visions are presented to the internal senses. The mention of the 'captive' mind is more ambiguous. Is the mind captive because the 'miserable woman', of whom the 'mind' is the metonymy, has become a servant of the devil? Or because the devil has physically invaded the woman's brain, in the literal manner described by Kramer?

The spatial metaphor used by the Canonist a few lines afterwards is equally ambivalent: the devil deludes his victims by leading their minds 'through devious ways' (*per devia quaeque deducit*).[64] The same metaphor appears a couple of sentences before, when the text condemns those who believe in the wicked women's claims: 'for an innumerable multitude, deceived by this false opinion, believe this to be true, and so believing, *wander from the right faith* and are involved in the error of the pagans' (my italics). To be 'in [the] error' — to be cognitively and spiritually confused — is again expressed in terms of spatial motion. It is to be led astray. As we know, the link between cognitive and spatial confusion is embedded in the Latin language, where the same word — *error* — designates both. William Short's analysis of Latin vocabulary of mental activity shows that this common metaphor is part of a unified system of metaphorical expression that systematically equates *ideas* with *locations* and *thinking* with *moving*. If reasoning is following a path, then being mentally confused is wandering from place to place, or wandering away from a fixed location.[65] And conversely, in Antiquity as in the Middle Ages or the Renaissance, the physical act of wandering could be understood as the sign of a mental, emotional or spiritual disturbance.[66]

To what extent was the wandering of the mind metaphorical here? Or rather, to what extent would the wandering of the mind have been understood by demonologists as metaphorical? According to the theories of cognition shared by Kramer and Weyer, the metaphor could indeed have a physiological basis, and thus be interpreted literally. As we have seen, errors of perception could be explained as the result of literal wanderings of spirits and *species* going 'through devious ways' (for example, flowing from memory to the organs of perception, when they were supposed to go in the opposite direction). What we spontaneously accept as a metaphor might therefore have been understood in slightly different terms by early modern demonologists. Besides, the result of the devil's deception, according to the *Canon episcopi*, was precisely to create the illusion of motion in space. To lead the mind 'through devious paths' meant not just to deceive it, but somewhat more literally to give it the illusion of erratic movement. By presenting various and contrasted images of things and persons to the eye of the imagination, the devil indeed led the mind to believe that the senses were confronted with quickly changing objects, and thus that the body was itself in motion — traversing great spaces of the earth together with a company of women. For Weyer, but also for Kramer, it was clear that the illusions referred to in the *Canon* were those of demonic transvection, the Sabbath itself, and other 'wandering excursions and activities' like lycanthropy, which led witches to believe that they were wolves 'roaming far and wide' (the final lines of the *Canon* indeed evoked the question of metamorphosis).[67] The wandering of the mind produced dreams marked with the idea of physical wandering: the wild rides in the train of Diana were, so to speak, the realisation in the spirit — not in the body — of the metaphor of the wandering mind. And this would have been even more keenly felt by witchcraft theorists who interpreted these nocturnal expeditions as demonic transvections — erratic journeys *par excellence*.[68]

According to the *Canon episcopi*, the fact that these journeys took place in the mind and not in the body did not necessarily make them less true. As Walter Stephens points out, 'the crucial distinction drawn by the *Canon episcopi* is not between truth and falsehood, or between waking and dreaming, but rather between *body* and *spirit*'.[69] Its fundamental point is to assert that 'the spirit can have real experiences in which the body does not participate'.[70] St Paul, as the *Canon* later explains, might have known a true ecstatic experience 'in the spirit' without it happening 'in the body': the ecstasy of the mind is not necessarily mirrored by a bodily transportation. Therefore, the witches' minds can be 'led in devious paths' without their bodies physically doing so. The *Canon episcopi* posed immense difficulties for the demonologists who, like Kramer, endeavoured to demonstrate the reality of witches' crimes.[71] Among those were precisely the consequences of its dissociation of the mind and body. If the devil's activities could be confined to the secret world of the mind, without translating into distinct physical signs, they were impossible to trace, and the reality of the witches' collusion with the devil therefore impossible to demonstrate empirically.[72] Unlike Weyer and the Canonist, Kramer needed a physical, literal realisation of the metaphor of the mind 'carried off' by the devil. An extreme literalist, so to speak, he needed the possibility to read not only in bodies, but in the motion of bodies in space, the signs of the cognitive and spiritual confusion induced by the devil. In the same way that he saw the incessant ramblings of lovers, who 'travell[ed] unexpectedly, either by day or night, across a great distance despite the roughness of the journey' (note the echoes of the *Canon episcopi*) as the unmistakable sign of demented minds under demonic influence,[73] Kramer expected the bodies of witches whose minds were led astray by the devil to manifest it through some extraordinary form of spatial motion. Carried away by their desire for the devil himself, witches should wander superlatively, as it were: not 'as if flying' (*quasi volando*), like lustful lovers did, but properly flying.[74] For Kramer and all the demonologists eager to demonstrate the reality of demonic transvection, the witches' flights were the literal physical manifestation of a spiritual wandering.

But again, this is precisely what the *Canon episcopi* denounced. Those who 'wandered in their faith' were those who failed to distinguish not only between dreaming and waking, between mind and body, but also, I would suggest, those who confused the figurative and the literal, and tended to take metaphors of cognitive and spiritual confusion at face value. This is a constant in Kramer's *Malleus maleficarum*. To some extent, it is also true in Weyer's *De praestigiis*. Indeed, the devil who 'led the mind in devious ways' was also for Weyer a roaming force who revelled in physically 'leading travellers astray from the right path',[75] occasionally transporting them from place to place through the air.[76] However, what distinguished Kramer and Weyer was that for the latter, this exact correspondence between demonic cognitive confusions and confusions in spatial motion was reserved for men. As a humanist physician, Weyer was undoubtedly a 'discerner of external signs', 'relying on the outside of the body to know its inside'.[77] However, when it came to women, wandering with the devil was for him confined to the cavities of the brain. The metaphor — 'to be carried away by the devil' — could only materialise in the world within, not in the world without.

Notes to Chapter 4

1. Stuart Clark, 'The scientific status of demonology', in *Occult and Scientific Mentalities in the Renaissance*, ed. by Brian Vickers (Cambridge: Cambridge University Press, 1984), pp. 351-74 (p. 359). I am of course indebted in this chapter, and particularly in these introductory remarks, to the rest of Clark's work on demonology and visual illusions: *Thinking with Demons: The Idea of Witchcraft in Early Modern Europe* (Oxford: Oxford University Press, 1997), in particular Part II ('Science'), pp. 149-312, and *Vanities of the Eye: Vision in Early Modern European Culture* (Oxford: Oxford University Press, 2007). For other studies of the demonological discourse on illusion, see: Walter Stephens, *Demon Lovers: Witchcraft, Sex, and the Crisis of Belief* (Chicago: The University of Chicago Press, 2002); Claudia Swan, 'Eyes wide shut: early modern imagination, demonology, and the visual arts', *Zeitsprünge: Forschungen zur Frühen Neuzeit*, 7 (2003), 560-81; Thibaut Maus de Rolley, 'La part du diable: Jean Wier et la fabrique de l'illusion diabolique', *Tracés. Revue de sciences humaines*, 8 (2005), pp. 29-46 (republished in *Fictions du diable: Démonologie et littérature de saint Augustin à Léo Taxil*, ed. by Françoise Lavocat, Pierre Kapitaniak and Marianne Closson (Geneva: Droz, 2007), pp. 109-30); Rebecca M. Wilkin, *Women, Imagination and the Search for Truth in Early Modern France* (Aldershot: Ashgate, 2008), chapter 1 ('Common sense: Johann Weyer and the Psychology of Witchcraft'), pp. 7-52.
2. Thibaut Maus de Rolley, *Elévations: L'écriture du voyage aérien à la Renaissance* (Geneva: Droz, 2011), p. 467.
3. On the discussion of demonic transvection — one of the most debated questions in early modern demonology — see Stephens, *Demon Lovers*, pp. 125-44, and Maus de Rolley, *Elévations*, chapter 8 ('Vols sous influence: Débats savants sur le transport diabolique'), pp. 413-74.
4. Descartes's 'mauvais génie', this master of deception, owed much to the devil of witchcraft theorists: see Clark, *Vanities of the Eye*, pp. 320-1.
5. On the authorship of the *Malleus maleficarum*, see Christopher Mackay's introduction to his edition of the text: Heinrich Kramer, *The Hammer of Witches: A Complete Translation of the Malleus Maleficarum*, ed. and trans. by Christopher S. Mackay (Cambridge: Cambridge University Press, 2009). All further references to the *Malleus maleficarum* are to this edition. The Latin text I use is: Heinrich Kramer, *Malleus Maleficarum in Tres Divisus Partes* (Frankfurt am Main: apud Nicolaum Bassaeum, 1580).
6. Kramer, *The Hammer of Witches*, Pt. II, Q. 1, Ch. 3, p. 300.
7. See Kramer's discussion of natural and demonic *praestigia* in Pt. I, Q. 9, pp. 194-201.
8. On Kramer's debt to Thomistic demonology, see Christine Pigné, 'Du *De malo* au *Malleus maleficarum*: les conséquences de la démonologie thomiste sur le corps de la sorcière', *Cahiers de Recherches Médiévales*, 13 (2006), 195-219 (on internal illusions, see 209-15). On the mechanics of demonic illusion in Kramer's *Malleus maleficarum*, see also Stephens, *Demon Lovers*, pp. 300-21.
9. For a clear presentation of Aristotelian psychology, see Katharine Park, 'The Organic Soul', in *The Cambridge History of Renaissance Philosophy*, ed. by Charles B. Schmitt and Quentin Skinner (Cambridge: Cambridge University Press, 1988), pp. 464-84. For the medieval theory of internal senses, see: E. Ruth Harvey, *The Inward Wits: Psychological Theory in the Middle Ages and the Renaissance* (London: The Warburg Institute, 1975); Simon Kemp and Garth J. O. Fletcher, 'The Medieval Theory of the Inner Senses', *The American Journal of Psychology*, 106, 4 (1993), 559-76; Robert Pasnau, *Theories of Cognition in the Later Middle Ages* (Cambridge: Cambridge University Press, 1997); Simo Knuuttila and Pekka Kärkkäinen, 'Medieval Theories of Internal Senses', in *Sourcebook for the History of the Philosophy of Mind: Philosophical Psychology from Plato to Kant*, ed. by Simo Knuuttila and Juha Sihvola (Dordrecht: Springer, 2014), pp. 131-45. For the Renaissance tradition, see Lorenzo Casini, 'Renaissance Theories of Internal Senses', in *Sourcebook for the History of the Philosophy of Mind*, pp. 147-56.
10. Kramer, *The Hammer of Witches*, Pt. I, Q. 7, p. 177, and Pt. II, Q. 1, Ch. 7, pp. 324-5.
11. See also Giglioni, this volume, for further discussion of this.
12. In *The Modularity of Mind* (1983), Jerry Fodor labelled as 'horizontal faculty psychology' this school of thought according to which mental processes rely on interactions between the same set of separated mental faculties, which are 'supposed to be invariant from one topic of thought

to the next' — in other words, non-domain-specific (*The Modularity of Mind: An Essay on Faculty Psychology* (Cambridge, Mass.: MIT Press, 1983), pp. 10–12). By contrast with this 'common-sense theory of the mind', the 'vertical tradition' revived by Fodor — whose origins he traces back to Franz Joseph Gall's phrenology — distinguishes faculties not by the effect they have on information (discriminating, storing, etc.), but by the content of information they process. According to this model, faculties (or rather 'modules') are specialised and 'computationally autonomous': they can function independently of one another. For a presentation of modular views of the mind in cognitive psychology, from Fodor and onwards, see Ellen Spolsky, *Gaps in Nature: Literary Interpretation and the Modular Mind* (Albany: State University of New York Press, 1993), chapter 1 ('Minds, Modules, and Models'), pp. 19–42.
13. On the cell doctrine, see Edwin Clarke and Kenneth Dewhurst, *An Illustrated History of the Brain Function* (Oxford: Sandford Publications, 1972), pp. 10–55, and the references above (note 9). On sixteenth-century debates on the localisation of the faculties, see Marie-Luce Demonet, 'Le lieu où l'on pense, ou le désordre des facultés', in *Ordre et désordre dans la civilisation de la Renaissance*, ed. by Gabriel-André Pérouse and Francis Goyet (Saint-Etienne: Publications de l'Université de Saint-Etienne, 1996), pp. 25–47.
14. Clarke and Dewhurst, *An Illustrated History of the Brain Function*, figs. 26–38.
15. Ibid., figs. 39–58. Even if this mapping of the brain relies on a distinctly different conception of the architecture of the mind (see above, note 12), it chimes somewhat with the suggestion made by supporters of a modular view of the mind that cognitive processes are anatomically localised in specific regions of the brain — a topic that has become a thriving field of study with the development, from the late twentieth century, of non-invasive brain imaging techniques. For a review of research on brain mapping in cognitive psychology and cognitive neurosciences, see Pieter van Eijsden et al., 'Neurophysiology of functional imaging', *Neuroimage*, 45.4 (2009), 1047–54. For a critical assessment of these endeavours, see William R. Uttal, *The New Phrenology: The Limits of Localizing Cognitive Processes in the Brain* (Cambridge, Mass.: MIT Press, 2003).
16. Kramer, *The Hammer of Witches*, Pt. I, Q. 7, p. 177.
17. Ibid., Pt. I, Q. 7, p. 177.
18. Ibid., Pt. I, Q. 7, p. 178; Pt. II, Q. 1, Ch. 7, p. 325. In the latter reference, Mackay's translation incorrectly places memory 'in the front part of the head': the Latin text says 'in posteriori parte capitis' (Kramer, *Malleus Maleficarum*, p. 269; see also p. 282: 'in ultima parte capitis').
19. Kramer considered the invasion of the mind by the devil as one among 'various methods of possession' (*The Hammer of Witches*, Pt. II, Q. 1, Ch. 10, p. 343).
20. Augustine, *Eighty-Three Different Questions*, 12. Quoted in *The Hammer of Witches*, Pt. I, Q. 9, p. 196.
21. See Kramer, *The Hammer of Witches*, Pt. I, Q. 7, p. 186. On this conception of the senses as 'entry points', see Nancy Caciola, *Discerning Spirits: Divine and Demonic Possession in the Middle Ages* (Ithaca and London: Cornell University Press, 2003), pp. 188–9.
22. Caciola, *Discerning Spirits*, pp. 140–58 (see in particular the reference to Kramer's *Malleus maleficarum*, p. 147).
23. On the localisation of the devil inside the human body, and more generally, the physiology of spirit possession, see Caciola, *Discerning spirits*, pp. 176-222 (the quotation is p. 207).
24. This question is discussed at length in Pt. II, Q. 1, Ch. 9 ('How demons exist inside bodies and heads without causing harm when they work changes involving conjuring').
25. Kramer, *The Hammer of Witches*, Pt. II, Q. 1, Ch. 9, p. 336.
26. Ibid., Pt. II, Q. 1, Ch. 9, p. 336. On Aquinas's conception of the soul, see Norman Kretzmann, 'Philosophy of Mind', in *The Cambridge Companion to Aquinas*, ed. by Norman Kretzmann and Eleonore Stump (Cambridge: Cambridge University Press, 1993), pp. 128–59.
27. Kramer, *The Hammer of Witches*, Pt. I, Q. 7, p. 178.
28. Kramer discusses these natural illusions in Pt. I, Q. 7, p. 179; Pt. II, Q. 1, Ch. 7, p. 325; Pt. II, Q. 1, Ch. 9, p. 336.
29. Like many demonologists, Kramer explained the 'prestiges' of the devil by comparing them to those wrought by jugglers. If jugglers could achieve wonderful effects by natural and artificial means, *a fortiori* the devil, with his incomparable agility, speed, and knowledge of nature: 'For whatever a human knows how to do by art, a demon can know better' (*The Hammer of Witches*,

Pt. I, Q. 9, p. 198). On the figure of the devil as a juggler, see Clark, *Vanities of the Eye*, pp. 78-83 and 151-2; Thibaut Maus de Rolley, 'Le diable à la foire: jongleurs, bateleurs et *prestigiateurs* dans le discours démonologique à la Renaissance', in *Kunst der Täuschung: über Status und Bedeutung von ästhetischer und dämonischer Illusion in der Frühen Neuzeit (1400-1700) in Italien und Frankreich*, ed. by Kirsten Dickhaut (Wiesbaden: Harrassowitz Verlag, 2016), forthcoming.

30. Johann Weyer, *De Praestigiis daemonum et incantationibus ac venificiis libri V* (Basel: Oporinus, 1563), p. 20. The treatise was expanded in 1568 in a version in six books: *De praestigiis daemonum, et incantationibus ac veneficiis libri sex* (Basel: Oporinus, 1568). The text of the preface is missing from the modern English translation: [Johann Weyer,] *Witches, Devils and Doctors in the Renaissance: Johann Weyer*, De Praestigiis Daemonum, ed. by George Mora *et al.* (Tempe: Center for Medieval and Renaissance Texts and Studies, 1998).
31. See Clark, *Thinking with Demons*, pp. 117-8 and 198-203; Maus de Rolley, *Elévations*, pp. 440-53; Wilkin, *Women, Imagination and the Search for Truth*, pp. 10–18.
32. Weyer, *Witches, Devils, and Doctors*, pp. 183-6.
33. On Iamblichus's and Ficino's views on the imagination, and their use by Weyer, see Guido Giglioni's chapter in this volume. Henri Busson signals that Weyer's knowledge of Ficino's theory of the imagination comes from Pietro Pomponazzi's *De incantationibus* (1556): see Henri Busson, 'Introduction' to Pomponazzi, *Les causes des merveilles de la nature ou les enchantements*, ed. and trans. by Henri Busson (Paris: Rieder, 1930), pp. 67-8.
34. Weyer mentions the *vis memorativa* in III, 17, in a quotation from Della Porta (*Witches, Devils, and Doctors*, p. 225); the *sensus communis* is mentioned in III, 19 (p. 232).
35. Weyer, *Witches, Devils, and Doctors*, pp. 186-9.
36. Ibid., p. 188.
37. Ibid., p. 187.
38. See Clarke and Dewhurst, *An Illustrated History of the Brain Function*, figs. 48-55.
39. Weyer, *Witches, Devils, and Doctors*, p. 285.
40. Weyer did not mention Reisch's *Margarita philosophica* in the *De praestigiis*, nor in his medical treatises. However, he quoted several times Vesalius's *De humani corporis fabrica* (1543), praising him as a peerless physician and anatomist (*Witches, Devils, and Doctors*, p. 229). For Vesalius, the ventricles were 'nothing more than cavities or passages in which air is attracted by inspiration, and the vital spirit, conveyed to them from the heart, is mutated into animal spirit by the power of the substance of the brain itself': Vesalius, 'On the Cerebral Ventricles' (*On the Fabric of the Human Body*), quoted in Marco Catani and Stefano Sandrone, *Brain Renaissance: From Vesalius to Modern Neuroscience* (Oxford: Oxford University Press, 2015), p. 98. On Weyer and Vesalius, see Wilkin, *Women, Imagination and Search for Truth*, pp. 25-36.
41. Weyer, *Witches, Devils, and Doctors*, p. 63. In the third book of his treatise (the fourth in the expanded version), Weyer dismissed several tales of demonic possession as cases of melancholy, or frauds orchestrated by the alleged demoniacs and their priests (see in particular chapters 25-28). However, he accepted many others as authentic. The wonders accompanying these possessions could be denounced as illusions forged by the devil (the presence, for example, of objects inside the body of the possessed), but these possessions were nevertheless presented as real. What Weyer denied was the possibility that possession might be caused by witchcraft. On Weyer and demonic possession, see Brian P. Levack, *The Devil Within: Possession & Exorcism in the Christian West* (New Haven and London: Yale University Press, 2013), pp. 75-7.
42. See for instance (all references to Weyer, *Witches, Devils, and Doctors*): 'he has corrupted their mind with empty images, lulling or *stirring to this task the bodily humours and spirits*' (p. 181, my italics); 'Why then will a crafty spirit like the Devil not be able, with God's permission, to insinuate himself into the organs of sense, and *stir the humours and vapours* suitable for his purposes, or bring his own special air into the organs?' (p. 186, my italics); 'The devil is no less able, being a spirit, to *stir up such humours* and make them receptive to his illusions' (p. 189, my italics); 'it is not difficult for the devil when *he sets in motion the humours and spirits* suitable for these illusions' (p. 193, my italics).
43. Weyer, *Witches, Devils, and Doctors*, pp. 188, 315, 346.
44. Ibid., p. 315.
45. See Kramer, *The Hammer of Witches*, Pt. II, Q. 1, Ch. 15, pp. 380-6, and Pt. II, Q. 1, Ch. 3,

p. 299. Storm-raising is listed by Weyer among the principal beliefs attached to witchcraft (*Witches, Devils, and Doctors*, p. 166). On this motif, see Maus de Rolley, *Elévations*, pp. 437-8.
46. Weyer, *Witches, Devils, and Doctors*, p. 193.
47. Ibid., pp. 189-92.
48. Clark, *Vanities of the Eye*, p. 15.
49. On this episode (*Pantagruel*, chap. 32), and its debt to Ancient and medieval literature, see the classical study of Erich Auerbach, 'The World in Pantagruel's Mouth', *Mimesis: The Representation of Reality in Western Thought* (Princeton: Princeton University Press, 1953), pp. 262-84.
50. Jonathan Sawday points out the 'riot of geographical metaphors' in late sixteenth- and seventeenth-century anatomical discourses, before the rise of the Cartesian metaphor of the body as machine. The anatomist, in these texts, is presented as a 'microcosmic explorer' and the human body as a New World to discover and conquer. See Jonathan Sawday, *The Body Emblazoned: Dissection and the Human Body in Renaissance Culture* (London and New York: Routledge, 1996), pp. 22-32.
51. Weyer, *Witches, Devils, and Doctors*, p. 188.
52. Owsei Temkin, 'Metaphors of Human Biology', in *The Double Face of Janus and Other Essays in the History of Medicine* (Baltimore and London: The Johns Hopkins University Press, 1977), pp. 271-83. The analogy between meteorological phenomena and human physiological processes worked in both directions in Aristotelian thought, as Lisa Taub shows in 'Physiological Analogies and Metaphors in Explanations of the Earth and the Cosmos', in *Blood, Sweat and Tears: The Changing Concepts of Physiology from Antiquity into Early Modern Europe*, ed. by Manfred Horstmanshoff, Helen King and Claus Zittel (Leiden: Brill, 2012), pp. 41-64.
53. George Lakoff and Mark Johnson, *Metaphors We Live By* (Chicago: Chicago University Press, 1980), p. 57. Lakoff and Johnson develop the concept of the embodied mind in *Philosophy in the Flesh: The Embodied Mind and Its Challenge to Western Thought* (New York: Basic Books, 1999).
54. Daniel Casasanto and Roberto Bottini, 'Spatial language and abstract concepts', *WIREs Cognitive Science*, 5 (2013), 139-49; Daniel Casasanto and Lera Boroditsky, 'Time in the mind: Using space to think about time', *Cognition*, 106 (2008), 579-93; Lera Boroditsky, 'Metaphoric structuring: understanding time through spatial metaphors', *Cognition*, 75 (2000), 1-28.
55. Ernst Cassirer, *The Philosophy of Symbolic Forms: Language* (New Haven: Yale University Press, 1952), p. 198. The relevance of Cassirer's remarks to metaphor theory was first pointed out by René Dirven in 'Metaphor as a Basic Means for Extending the Lexicon', in *The Ubiquity of Metaphor: Metaphor in Language and Thought*, ed. by Wolf Paprotté and René Dirven (Amsterdam: John Benjamins, 1985), pp. 85-120 (p. 86).
56. Cassirer, *The Philosophy of Symbolic Forms*, p. 199.
57. Juliana Goschler, 'Metaphors in Cognitive and Neurosciences: Which [sic] impact have metaphors on scientific theories and models?', metaphorik.de, 12 (2007), p. 11: '"Path" and "container" are particularly frequently used source domains: the brain is described as a landscape or a container. Information, signals, memories, thoughts, and the like, are — at least linguistically — treated as "things", concrete objects that move around in "paths" inside the "container".' The online databank of metaphors for the mind built by John Barnden at the University of Birmingham lists similar metaphors, in particular 'Mind as Physical Space' <http://www.cs.bham.ac.uk/~jab/ATT-Meta/Databank/>.
58. William S. Short, 'Thinking Places, Placing Thoughts: Spatial Metaphors of Mental Activity in Roman Culture', *I Quaderni del Ramo d'Oro*, 1 (2008), 106-29 (p. 106).
59. Antonina Harbus, 'Thinking in Metaphors: Figurative Language and Ideas on the Mind', *Sydney Studies in English*, 30 (2004), 3-20 (p. 9). As Harbus points out, a criticism that can be made of the conceptual metaphor theory developed by Lakoff and Johnson is that it tends to overlook the historical and cultural origin of metaphors. For recent examples of diachronic metaphor research, see the volume *Metaphor and Metonymy across Time and Cultures*, ed. by Javier Díaz-Vera (Berlin; Munich; Boston: Walter de Gruyter, 2015), and James J. Mischler, III, *Metaphor across Time and Conceptual Space: The Interplay of Embodiment and Cultural Models* (Amsterdam/Philadelphia: John Benjamins, 2014).
60. This hesitation between the literal and the figurative is also noted by Dominique Brancher in her study of Renaissance metaphors of cognition: Dominique Brancher, '"Un gramme de

pensée": Figures de la cognition chez Montaigne et Rabelais', *Poétique*, 173 (2013), 3-26.
61. I use the English translation of the *Canon episcopi* given in *The Witchcraft Sourcebook*, ed. by Brian P. Levack (New York and London: Routledge, 2004), pp. 34-5.
62. *The Witchcraft Sourcebook*, p. 34.
63. I follow here Clark's reading of the passage: 'The English rendering 'species' is obviously open to ambiguity, and 'image' would be more accurate, since the Latin word used in the *Canon* clearly refers to the Aristotelian theory of *species*.' (*Vanities of the Eye*, p. 326, n. 48.)
64. In his translation of the *Malleus maleficarum*, Mackay translates the expression as 'through all sorts of places off the beaten path' (Kramer, *The Hammer of Witches*, p. 204).
65. Short, 'Thinking Places, Placing Thoughts', pp. 117-8.
66. On the links between the 'art of thinking' and the 'art of travel', in Ancient Greece and in the Renaissance, see the work of Normand Doiron: *L'Art de voyager: Le déplacement à l'époque classique* (Québec: Presses de l'Université Laval; Paris: Klincksieck, 1995); *Errance et méthode: Interpréter le déplacement d'Ulysse à Socrate* (Québec: Presses de l'Université Laval; Paris: Vrin, 2011).
67. Weyer, *Witches, Devils, and Doctors*, p. 193.
68. Grégoire Holtz and Thibaut Maus de Rolley, 'Le diable vagabond', in *Voyager avec le diable: Voyages réels, voyages imaginaires et discours démonologiques (XVe–XVIIe siècles)*, ed. by Grégoire Holtz and Thibaut Maus de Rolley (Paris: Presses Universitaires de Paris-Sorbonne, 2008), pp. 13–23; on the link established between flying and erring in Renaissance literature and knowledge, see Maus de Rolley, *Elévations*.
69. Stephens, *Demon Lovers*, p. 127.
70. Ibid., p. 127.
71. Maus de Rolley, *Elévations*, pp. 432-9.
72. Stephens, *Demon Lovers*, p. 130.
73. Kramer, *The Hammer of Witches*, Pt. I, Q. 7, p. 183. See also Pt. II, Q. 2, Ch. 3, p. 427: 'when [lovers] cannot sleep during the night-time but are so deranged that they have to walk through every trackless area [*per devia quaeque incedere habeant*]...'
74. Ibid., Pt. II, Q. 1, Ch. 6, p. 322.
75. Weyer, *Witches, Devils, and Doctors*, p. 34. On the following page, Weyer associated in the same sentence the physical transportation of bodies and demonic internal illusions: 'It is the habit of the devil to transport bodies in various ways and throw their humours into disorder and disturb the source of the nerves in the brain...'
76. Maus de Rolley, *Elévations*, pp. 444-6.
77. Wilkin, *Women, Imagination and the Search for Truth*, p. 28.

CHAPTER 5

Delusion, Drowsiness and Discernment: Degrees of Awareness in Renaissance Dream Activity

Guido Giglioni

We usually describe the human being as a rational animal, but what do we mean by the adjective 'rational' in this definition? Conventional wisdom has it that humans come with the ability to make decisions and conform their actions to their beliefs; it is also widely accepted that beliefs rely upon the specific contexts in which they develop and that they result from shared traditions and cultural assumptions. This means that the extent to which beliefs and actions match up depends on the normative frameworks which are in place at a particular time, and that, as a result, the dominant criteria of rationality may vary significantly. This has relevant consequences in the parallel domain that is ordinarily qualified by the adjective 'irrational'. It would not be too much of a stretch to say that the adjective 'delusional' is as adaptable and liable to subjective assessment as the adjective 'rational'. Delusions owe their uncanny force of persuasion to expectations that are deeply ingrained in the fabric of our physical and cultural worlds. As physicians from Hippocrates' time onwards recognized, delusions may have a biological basis, but they can also be psychological devices to fulfil otherwise unattainable wishes. The interplay of belief and reality, however, is too complex to be explained through the use of reductive and artificial models (be those models logical, biological or ethical). Nowhere is this more evident than when we fall asleep and begin to dream, or when — alert and eyes wide open — we set out to examine past views about the nature of dreams.

Within any belief system, there are specific ontological, cosmological and social constraints that make one's own experience of dreams consistent with a number of cultural and logical assumptions. This was the case during the sixteenth and seventeenth centuries, when dreams were an integral part of particular philosophical, medical and theological contexts just as it is today. Perhaps we now dream in ways that differ from our ancestors in pre-modern and early modern times, with different expectations and desires. We certainly explain dreams in different ways, applying different philosophical and scientific categories. We should, however, resist the temptation to look at our explanations as more rational than theirs. Ontological, cosmological and social constraints are always at work in all belief systems and they account for similarities and differences, regularities and anomalies. The principal ontological constraint one needs to bear in mind when examining early modern views about dreams is the view that the intellect was not simply the most sophisticated cognitive function, but also the embodiment of the highest degree of reality, where any division between subjectivity and objectivity disappeared. The intelligible order of the universe was characterized as a state of eternal simultaneity, in which all temporal dimensions converged; as a result, the closer dreams got to the truth of things by allowing the imagination to connect with the intellect, the greater their content of foreknowledge. This particular feature in the process of dreaming was intimately linked with a general cosmological framework, for the correspondence between the supra-lunary world of celestial influences and the sublunary universe of physical change saw to it that images matched the reality they represented. From a social point of view, too, the sense of an almost seamless continuity between sleeping and waking in the actions of one's life, with its vital links to hope, future and foreknowledge, justified the moral, political and religious uses of dreams. Through its union with the divine intellect, the dreaming soul could turn the ideal patterns of the intelligible world into productive forces that had the power to change reality in significant ways. As we shall see in this chapter, the ontological, cosmological and social constraints underpinning early modern understanding of dreams were all related to the faculty of the imagination and the delicate role it played in mediating literal and symbolic meanings, the past and the future, fears and hopes. Dream imagination belonged to the vast expanses of imagined reality situated between the phenomenal and the intelligible domains of reality, a territory that the late antique philosopher Synesius (c. 373-c. 414 AD), as I will illustrate more extensively in section three of this chapter, described as life in the state of imagination. The distinction between imaginary and imagined reality (that is, between mental images not anchored in the world and images reliably informed by the senses) was a crucial one, which clearly separated any fleeting appearance of things from a stable vision of the intelligible forms (a distinction that has often, but not always, been encapsulated in the Latin dichotomy of *phantasia* and *imaginatio*). Even today, in our everyday experience, the difference between imaginary and imagined reality is nowhere more evident than in our dreams, when our mind undergoes a great many degrees of cognitive turbulence and the limits of its awareness are incessantly tested.

Against this background of ontological, cosmological and social constraints, the early modern period was still confronted with the ancient paradox that dreams could be more real than instances of phenomenal and empirical reality. These kinds of dreams were called veridical and prophetic. For Descartes, the possibility that a dream could be more real than empirical reality represented a powerful sceptical objection to his view of cognitive certitude. He addressed the problem by resorting to the self-evidence of conscious thought.[1] Today the belief that dreams may be more real than phenomenal reality is no longer perceived as a paradox, but rather as a cultural fossil to be studied by the paleontologists of human thought (historians and anthropologists) or a matter of clinical judgment to be dealt with by the new interpreters of our distressed imaginations (psychiatrists, psychotherapists, cognitive philosophers and so on). The criteria that made the idea of veridical dreams possible — that is, the suddenness of their revelations, the unlikely nature of their representative content, their alleged predictive and practical success (through processes of healing, the establishment of new laws, the creation of religious rituals and the promotion of technological advances), not to mention the level of ascetic probity of the people involved in dream experience — are now amongst the very criteria that discredit them. Although Synesius and Cardano, as we shall see, always recommended that any interpretation of dreams be contextualised within the life of the dreamers and their surrounding reality, the unexpected manifestation of intelligible truths prevailed over any attempt to historicize and rationalize that particular experience. For us today, this approach is an indication of both dogmatism and gullibility. And yet, given their greater scope from a medical, philosophical and theological point of view, early modern attitudes towards dreams demonstrated that a nuanced understanding of cognitive confusion was clearly in place at the time. As I will clarify at the end of this chapter, the defence of an autonomous sphere of dream imagination in Synesius and the glorification of the freedom to dream in Ficino reveals a deep belief in the civilizing effects of dream experience.

1. The Meaning of Dreams

The possibility that dreams may have a meaning, be that meaning related to past events, present circumstances or future developments, remains for us the most disquieting and unsettling aspect of our dream experience. Dreams can be easily explained away as digestive accidents or screensavers for mental interfaces, and yet the possibility of meaningful connections (between our body and our mind, and our mind and the world) lingers on. That dreams may have a meaning is unsettling because they inhabit a liminal space: they signal the presence of a threshold and demonstrate with their existence that the mind is sometimes allowed to cross it. In an even more subtle way, they posit and at the same time question the boundaries between sleep and waking, consciousness and unconsciousness, digestion and indigestion, and finally between the self, the body and the environment. The force behind this tension is the imagination. As Aristotle clearly pointed out in the short treatise on dreams included in his *Parva naturalia*, dreaming as a form of imagination was dangerously close to sensory delusion. Indeed, it was a case of ordinary delusion, a ritual that took place in our mind almost every night. Dreaming was trivial, and yet extraordinary in that it exemplified the great amount of power that the imagination was able to release, in cognitive, imaginal and emotional terms (*De insomniis*, 458b, 460b, 461a-462).

In this chapter, in an attempt to show relevant connections between the universes of early modern philosophy, medicine and theology, I will concentrate on several early modern texts dealing with the nature of dreams, but in particular on works by Marsilio Ficino (1433–1499), Girolamo Cardano (1501–1576) and Francisco Sánchez (c. 1550–1623), more specifically, on Ficino's translations of Iamblichus's *De mysteriis Aegyptiorum* and Synesius's *De insomniis* (1497), Cardano's book on 'Synesian' dreams (1562) and Sanchez's commentary on Aristotle's *De divinatione per somnum*

(1581).[2] Ficino was a Florentine priest and a theologian who saw in the recovery of Platonic wisdom the way to reconnect with the most ancient sources of divine knowledge; Cardano was a Milanese physician who adapted the characteristic Aristotelianism and Galenism he absorbed when he was a student in the Universities of Pavia and Padua to a new world of ideas and discoveries; Sánchez, finally, was a professor of medicine and philosophy at the University of Toulouse who put the most controversial issues in philosophy and science to the test of a severe sceptical doubt. For all their differences, Ficino, Cardano and Sánchez were figures in a world that shared fundamental ontological, cosmological and social assumptions. Cardano often referred to both Ficino's works and his translations of Greek authors; Sanchez criticized Cardano as well as Ficino. And yet, when seen against the general background of sixteenth- and seventeenth-century philosophy, medicine and theology, they all clearly belong to the same cultural milieu.

This is particularly evident in the case of dreams. Ficino's, Cardano's and Sánchez's books are highly representative of a culture — early modern European culture — in which dreams were still perceived as natural and cultural entities that could affect the course of human life. As such, they helped establish definitions of rationality. The conditions and circumstances that connected human dreams to delusional states of mind were acknowledged with certainty, both in their individual and collective aspects. More importantly, though, it was the cognitive — and sometimes ethical and political — import of dreams that was seen as the defining feature of dream activity.[3] In this chapter, I argue that in the pre-modern and early modern periods dreams were generally seen as meaningful events in people's lives, even — and sometimes especially — when they were at their most counterintuitive. They represented a unique situation in which the human mind could experience and observe a most elusive interaction of drowsiness and discernment in its very making.

This chapter is divided into three main sections dealing with the characteristic amalgam of delusion, drowsiness and discernment involved in the production of dreams. In the first section, I explore the time-honoured association between dreams and divination by looking at the imagination as the force that secured the continuity of knowledge and life within the bodily economy of the vital functions. Since antiquity, I shall argue, the interdependence of dreams and divination had formed the basis for both a significant expansion of the faculties of the mind through the power of the imagination and an enlargement of the temporal scope of human experience through the powerful appeal that the future had on human aspirations and ideals. In the second section, I concentrate on the view that certain dreams, because of their clarity and vividness, could be used as antidotes against what was seen by some philosophers as a typical human tendency to fall into a routine of familiar delusions. The third section, finally, looks at the nature and function of dreams in a universe that was thought to be pervaded by waves of imaginative energy at many levels, from inanimate nature to the human mind. It will become apparent, by the end of the chapter, that both considerations of dreams — the prophetic and the cosmological — were symptomatic of a more general way of looking at the imagination as a reliable and productive instrument for understanding reality. The study of dreams had significant consequences for how early modern philosophers, theologians and physicians interpreted awareness and freedom. It showed that human awareness was a cognitive faculty that could be much more articulate in dreams than during momentary episodes of introspective clarity, while freedom was the power of the human mind to overcome the constraints of perceptual immediacy and dogmatic literalism, which was something it did best in dreams.

2. Dreams and Divination

In *De praestigiis daemonum et incantationibus ac veneficiis* ('Illusions of Demons, Enchantments and Poisonings'), a painstaking study of the imagination and of imagining subjects (originally published in 1563), the physician Johann Weyer (1515–1588) described how dreams and imaginations populated the murky area between reason and nature, where the human mind was prone to episodes of self-delusion and demonic seductions. Surprisingly, for all his sceptical impatience with stories of possessions and witchcraft, Weyer had no qualms about referring to the ancient Iamblichus (c. 245–c. 325), the great authority on Platonic theurgy, as someone who could be trusted — both philosophically and theologically — on matters concerning the difference between delusional and reliable imagination, between imaginary and imagined reality.[4] In his work *Master Abammon's Reply to Porphyry's Letter to Anebo*, composed between 280 and 305 AD and conceived of as a riposte to a series of queries on magic and divination submitted to him by the fellow Platonist Porphyry (c. 234–c. 305), Iamblichus had defended the existence of truthful dreams, veridical imaginations and divine epiphanies. The work was translated and paraphrased by Ficino with the title *De mysteriis Aegyptiorum, Chaldaeorum, Assyriorum* ('On the Mysteries of the Egyptians, Chaldeans and Assyrians') and published in Venice in 1497 in a collection of Platonic texts that would become very influential in the following century. Iamblichus's position was used by Weyer to establish the epistemological, ethical and theological criteria that he deemed necessary to discriminate between appearance and reality. As a devout Lutheran physician who believed in the existence of the devil, Weyer was certainly eager to find such criteria.[5]

With the spreading of the Reformation, the possibility of laying the foundations for a trustworthy access to God had become increasingly fraught with difficulties. On the one hand, the emphasis on the self-evident nature of private certainty, implicit in the principle of *sola fide* (according to which divine justification could be granted by faith alone) had conferred greater legitimacy to subjective accounts of reality. The principle of *sola scriptura*, for which the Bible was the only authority on questions of doctrinal and practical nature, had on the other hand narrowed the scope of the authoritative tradition down to the word of the sacred text. In this situation of diffuse uncertainty, prophecy received unprecedented attention. Since prophetic divination could both enlarge and corroborate the means of access to God, debates on the epistemic status of divine dreams and visions gained particular momentum.[6] In many ways, then, Weyer's favourable attitude towards

Iamblichus and his treatment of the imagination had been influenced by theological anxieties.

Weyer read Iamblichus through Ficino. In *De mysteriis Aegyptiorum*, Ficino had translated, paraphrased and in some cases commented upon Iamblichus's treatise. Ficino's work is a typical early modern appropriation of an authoritative text of the past, rather than a close translation. He was particularly interested in the way in which Iamblichus had presented a specific kind of dream as an 'antidote' against the delusions of the senses and the imagination. 'Antidote' was the word used by Iamblichus to refer precisely to the kind of self-evident vision capable of dispelling any uncertainty with respect to both reality and knowledge.[7] Such visions were supposed to come in the form of dreams — sudden, unplanned — and to tell people about future events. Foreknowledge was seen as a sort of experimental confirmation that these visions were unadulterated reflections of eternal truths.

According to Ficino's gloss on Iamblichus, sometimes the divine life of the mind could wake up when we were asleep and act in full spontaneity.[8] True dreams belonged therefore to the category of veridical visions and thoughts. They were waking dreams understood as heightened states of perception and outbursts of mental concentration induced by divine revelations. Like ordinary dreams, they needed to emerge out of a background of shadows and refractions through currents of images in order to be perceived by the human mind. The imagination worked here as the power that dimmed the light of the mind, producing a state of half-consciousness favourable to revelations of intelligible truth. Gods and ideas manifested themselves in the penumbra of the mind.

Before we delve into the 'mysteries' of the Iamblichean and Ficinian dreams of the intellect, however, it is necessary to provide an outline of the medical-philosophical background against which both Iamblichus and Ficino defended their views about veridical dreams. We all agree that the life of human beings is spent waking, sleeping and dreaming. By contrast with today, though, dreams were seen as reliable tokens of both life and knowledge in the pre-modern and early modern periods. Belief in the strong cognitive import of dreams was well attested in the medical tradition, as was the divinatory aspect that allowed practitioners to unify dreams with therapy and healing. In the Hippocratic text *Regimen*, for instance, its author enumerated the advantages of having access to a patient's dreams: 'He who has a precise knowledge of the signs that occur when one is asleep will find out that they have a great power over all things.' The soul could be the true master of itself only when the body was asleep. When the soul was 'at the service of the waking body', it was not entirely in control, but divided itself into countless functions to respond to the information received through the senses as well as to perform all the required vital processes. In the waking condition, in other words, the activity of thinking lacked focus and was unable to reach a state of cognitive self-assurance. By contrast, when the body was in deep sleep, the soul regained possession of its inner life: 'it governs its own sphere and performs by itself all the bodily actions'; it 'knows everything, sees what is visible, hears what can be heard, walks, touches, feels pain, reflects' (IV, LXXXVI). There is something fundamentally positive in the way the Hippocratic collection as a whole looks at dreams. This notion that the soul wakes up when the body is asleep implies that dreams are seen as inherently related to life. For Plato (and Freud, for that matter) the contrary was rather the case: it is the body — that is, the energy of the appetitive drives — that wakes up when reason falls asleep. Plato and Freud shared a biological understanding of dreams that one would struggle to find in the Hippocratic corpus. Hippocrates did distinguish between divine and biological dreams, the former heralding good or evil for individuals and communities, the latter signifying healthy or pathological states of the body (IV, LXXXVII–LXXXVIII), but dreams in general were the realm of the soul rather than the body.

When the physician and philosopher Sánchez, the author of one of the foundational texts of early modern scepticism, *Quod nihil scitur* ('That Nothing Is Known' 1581), recalled these Hippocratic loci, he acknowledged that a limited form of divination could be recognized in the dreamer's activity:

> The nature of our mind is extraordinary, in so much as it seems to be nothing and to be able to do nothing without a body, while in fact it seems to exist and to be able to do things on its own without it, as happens during sleep. It is true that, when awake the mind does not see, hear or think without a body; and yet, when asleep and the body is completely at rest, it seems to crawl through each single part of the body, as if it were released from its external duties, not distracted by the objects coming from outside, entirely devoted to its own dwelling and fully concentrated there. As Hippocrates said, the mind manages its own house and, since the body does not have perceptions when it is asleep, the mind, being awake, knows the body, sees visible things, hears audible things, wanders around, touches, becomes sad, is aware; in sum, whatever the functions of the body or the soul are, the soul carries them out when asleep.[9]

The soul, Sánchez continues, perceives 'either by itself or together with the temperament of the brain'. The same thing occurs in dreams. In this case, the imagination (*phantasia*) takes centre stage by creating a condition of half-awareness that is conducive to all sorts of meaningful exchanges between the soul and the body:

> Through the organs, species (*species* = visual replicas of sense objects) are transmitted from the things that are contained in the body to the imagination, which never falls entirely asleep while at rest; it is in a state of drowsiness, as it were, and is fettered. As if through a cloud, the soul perceives the species it has received and mixes them up. And since it is not entirely master of itself, it conflates true with false images and does not judge and distinguish them in a completely correct way. And yet, it takes them when they are offered to it, and it is stimulated by them and it stimulates the body in turn to avoid harmful things, to acquiesce when things are pleasant and to desire and pursue necessary and useful things.[10]

In the full spirit of Hippocratic divination (*Regimen*, I, XII), Sánchez insists that this correspondence between bodily states and images in dreams is a powerful diagnostic resource for a physician, but is unwilling to enlarge their predictive scope any farther than that: 'In these night visions' (*nocturnae visiones*), he states, 'the soul knows only the present condition of the body, and not in a sufficiently plain and clear way, but through dreams and through a cloud as it were.'[11]

Imaginings, dreams and foreknowledge are essential aspects of everyone's experience. Their intertwinement goes to the very roots of the bond that connects knowledge to physical survival. We tend to look at knowledge in abstract terms as a disembodied function of the mind, but in fact knowledge emerges out of interrelated sequences of cognitive and vital acts. For this reason, it is not always easy to assess the boundaries that separate knowing from being. In very broad terms, the activities of receiving, retaining and discarding external input are central to both cognitive and vital processes. These activities require subtle discernment, both when the input is information and when it is food. Ancient doctors trusted dreams as reliable touchstones to judge how patients transformed food and information. This is one of the major reasons why physical and mental health was significantly related to the way people dreamed. Of the six categories through which physicians, starting with Hippocrates and Galen, shaped the art of preserving human health — categories known in the medical tradition as the 'six non-naturals' (air, food and drink, motion and rest, evacuations, sleeping and the passions) — dreaming disclosed in patients a number of telling interactions between their sleep, their representation of reality and their emotional responses to it.[12] In order to sum up pre-modern and early modern medical and philosophical attitudes to sleeping and dreaming and to show their links with life, desire and knowledge, I will suggest three laws through which one can investigate the relationship between cognitive and vital processes. I would call the first law, particularly influential among physicians, the law of the inverse proportionality between sentient and vegetative life. The more dormant the senses were, the higher, they thought, was the level of activity in the processes of digestion, blood production ('sanguification') and vitalization of the body (also described as a production of spirits: natural, vital and animal). A second law was the one governing the relationship between the operations of the senses and the exercise of thought, a law that was taken quite seriously by philosophers, and those, in particular, belonging to the Platonic tradition. I would call this the law of the inverse proportionality between the senses and the intellect. In this case the mind was supposed to become sharper when the senses were less active. To quote Ficino from his philosophical masterpiece, *Theologia Platonica* ('Platonic Theology', published in 1482), 'external activity is increasingly remitted... internal activity is more and more intensified'.[13] The third law, finally, regulating the relationship between the business of living and knowing was a law of direct proportionality: the more human beings were exposed to the representations of the imagination (its 'phantasms'), the more vigorous their appetites were believed to grow (and these in turn would foster desires that could be either virtuous or unruly). In *The Republic*, Plato had associated this most perilous rapprochement between imagination and desire with the functions of sleeping and dreaming. This is a passage (IX, 571CD) which Ficino was clearly familiar with and which, not surprisingly, he mentions in the *Theologia Platonica*:

> When the rest of the soul is asleep, that is to say, the rational, civilized, controlling side of it, the untamed savage side, full of food or drink, darts about and, when it has shaken off sleep, seeks to go and satisfy its own natural tendencies. You know that in such circumstances it is emboldened to do everything, as it's free and rid of a sense of all shame and intelligence. It does not shrink from trying to have sex with a mother, as it fancies, or with any

other human being, or god, or wild beast; it will commit any kind of blood-thirsty murder, and there is no food it won't touch. In a word, it isn't lacking in any folly or shamelessness.[14]

Although the main differences between the medical and the philosophical traditions had been clearly outlined since antiquity and then institutionalized during the Middle Ages within the scholastic framework of the educational system, for centuries what I have just called the three laws of proportionality between cognitive and vital processes remained part of the received way of looking at the relations between the body and the soul by both physicians and philosophers. This approach continued well into the seventeenth century. The senses, the appetites and the mind were seen as different faculties forced into a difficult cohabitation, and dreams were windows into an otherwise invisible world of tensions and contrasts. The unconscious functions of life, the perception of the senses, the representations of the imagination, the appetitive drives of desire and the crystalline visions of the mind were the counterbalancing forces that held together the complex economy of life and knowledge. According to the anatomy of cognitive processes, the conscious exercise of knowledge was believed to interfere with the production of life; conversely, according to the logic of philosophical asceticism, the fulfilment of vital operations, the perception of the senses and the motions of the appetites hampered true knowledge (i.e. the direct vision of intelligible reality). Judged according to the parameters of philosophical intellectualism, metabolism was not real life, sense was not real knowledge, and desire was not real activity. Real knowledge — or real life, which in this case was the same thing — could only be the intellect, for the intellect was in fact the ultimate and undivided source of being.

Regardless of whether dreams were used to scrutinize the body or the intellect, the fact remained that dreams were instructive, dependable and capable of fine-tuning our waking existence. Seeping through the crevices that separated bodily from mental processes, they bridged the apparent gaps between life, sense and desire. They also filled in the interruptions of waking life during sleep. And this on two levels, for, as Cardano explained very well in his book on dreams, the *Somnia Synesia* mentioned at the beginning of this chapter, there were digestive dreams (the great majority of dreams), but there were also divine, cognitive dreams.[15] In explaining how the imagination governed our everyday behaviour, asleep as well as awake, Ficino had already distinguished between two levels of inner visualization: *phantasia* and *imaginatio*. Through the images they produced, both functions of the imagination constructed the world of external reality and interlaced the functions of sleep and waking while producing dreams. If *phantasia* collected the light pouring from the intellect to initiate the process of mental abstraction, *imaginatio* adjusted the mental images to the senses and the motion of the spirits, the main bodily instrument of the soul. When considered in this way, the representations of the mind were not in a position to distinguish by themselves between dreams and sense impressions. Thinking, memories and bodily processes could all variously affect the dreaming activity enacted by the operations of *phantasia*. This also meant that, while some dreams had a clear digestive significance, others could open the door to real knowledge.[16]

In Ficino's account of human dream life, the boundaries that separated imaginary from perceptual constructs were fluid. Moreover, precisely because the body, the senses and the intellect were intertwined in coordinated sequences of actions and reactions (the three laws regulating the interplay of life and knowledge mentioned above), Ficino stated that prophetic dreams could only occur to people who devoted themselves entirely to the most severe forms of ascetic life, thoroughly purged of the dross contracted during their waking life. Having completely surrendered to God, such people undertook nothing on their own initiative. As a result, their eyes were wide open and cleansed, even more so when they were asleep, for it was in that state that the mind was completely free.[17] The most religious among them — the prophets who were drawn to contemplating God behind the cosmos — perceived the truth as a flood of light, undivided and all-embracing, transcending the limits of the imagination (*phantasia*) and its carousel of familiar images (*consuetae imagines*).[18] Here Ficino referred to a passage in *The Republic* where Plato had described the nocturnal life of the 'healthy and temperate' sage. This, he said, 'does not starve or overindulge the element of desire, but yearns 'for a perception of what it does not know: something of the past, the present or the future'. In such circumstances, Plato concluded, the wise man was able to grasp the truth 'more readily', and the visions appearing in his dreams were at their 'least lawless'.[19] Synesius, the author of a specific treatise on dreams which, as we will see in the next section, became quite popular during the Renaissance, agreed with Plato that those who had an imaginative spirit that was 'pure and well-defined' were able to receive the true representation of things, both when they were awake and when they were asleep (*On Dreams*, X). Dreams were the proof that a soul that preserved itself from the daily assault of external impressions could aspire to wisdom (*On Dreams*, XI).

3. Dreams as Antidotes against Delusion

In metabolizing knowledge, dreams were therefore powerful carriers of meaning. It was a metabolism that acted at various levels and affected the functions of digestion (dreams as bodily symptoms), the processing of sense knowledge (dreams as repositories of images) and, finally, the release of the self from the constraints of the body (dreams as direct visions of the truth). The analysis of prophetic dreams, seen as offering privileged access to intelligible reality and therefore God, is one of the main themes in Ficino's *De mysteriis Aegyptiorum*, one of the peaks in Ficino's lifelong involvement with post-Plotinian Platonism.[20] On the question of divinatory dreams, Iamblichus had rejected in the clearest of terms the position held by Porphyry, who, along the lines of Hippocratic divination, had explained dream predictions as a natural process subject to the laws of change and generation.[21] For Iamblichus, by contrast, a prophetic dream could only be a divine epiphany and as such it bore no resemblance to changeable and temporal phenomenon. It was, rather, an abrupt and unforeseen glimpse into the eternal life of the intellect.

One of Porphyry's queries originally addressed to Iamblichus concerned the question whether human dreams had the power to attain knowledge of future events. In his reply, while defending the reality of prophetic dreams sent by the gods,

Iamblichus ruled out the possibility that, by being capable of producing dreams, the human soul could be seen as an autonomous source of divine foreknowledge. Iamblichus insisted that veridical dreams derived from a transcendent source and therefore had the power to lead the human soul beyond the narrow confines of individual consciousness. Divine dreams were not a product of the human mind, visions emanating 'from thoughts or words stirred up in us', 'from our fantasies, or from everyday concerns of some kind'.[22] As for the way in which divine dreams manifested themselves, Iamblichus confirmed that they occurred between sleep and waking, more specifically, just before falling asleep or right before waking up. They seemed to emerge in the space that separated our consciousness from the vast uncharted territories of unconscious life. In this case, too, divine dreams implied no ordinary perception or attentive state of the mind. To make clear that human intentionality was not involved in the process, Iamblichus also referred to cases in which an 'intangible and incorporeal spirit' surrounded the dreamer's body so that his perception was subsumed under forms of mental awareness that were of a higher order and scope.[23] In his translation, Ficino referred to a cognitive state capable of perceiving in tune with higher levels of awareness.[24]

When reading passages like these, it is easy to assume that both Iamblichus and Ficino regarded divine dreams as forms of heightened perception bearing no resemblance to any specifically human cognitive powers. In this sense, as Iamblichus was ready to acknowledge, they could also manifest themselves when humans were wholly awake and their minds full of vigour. Iamblichus made a list of dream-like conditions that seemed to be favourable to the revelation of superior forms of knowledge: 'dream-sleep'; 'possession of the eyes'; a 'seizure similar to a blackout'; transitional states between sleep and waking; and bouts of sudden reawakening.[25] Ficino summed up this point in very eloquent terms:

> When we receive dreams from the gods, we are not at all asleep; we grasp and perceive in a way that is clearer than we usually do when we are awake. It is above all in this kind of dream that prophecy occurs.[26]

This is for us all the more surprising because Iamblichus's series of mental conditions open to the reception of prophetic dreams could also be read as a list of symptoms identifying a wide range of mental disorders. Indeed, the line between delusion and enlightenment was fine and problematic. For Iamblichus and Ficino, divine dreams, as vehicles of prophetic knowledge, were emanations of unadulterated truth. As such they were capable of dispelling all doubts and obscurity surrounding any ordinary attempt to attain knowledge. Above all, they provided models of discernment that trained dreamers to recognize the difference between appearance and reality. Prophetic dreams appeared to people who practised models of ascetic lifestyle and were in control of their emotions, able to distinguish any human tendency to self-delusion (*phantasia*) from the effort to visualize the realm of intelligible truths (*imaginatio*). In addressing Porphyry's queries about the limits of human foreknowledge, Iamblichus had invoked the 'greatest antidote', mentioned above, also described by Iamblichus as the foundation of divination. For both Iamblichus and Ficino, the antidote against delusional dreams lay in looking at divination as a source of unfamiliar and yet primordial experience, prompted 'neither by bodies nor by bodily conditions, neither by a natural object nor by natural powers, neither by human dispositions nor its related habits'.[27] As I explained in the introduction to this chapter, authors as different as Iamblichus and Ficino, Synesius and Cardano invoked both objective and subjective criteria to distinguish dreams as bodily reactions from dreams as visions of being: on the one hand, they listed the sudden appearance of dreams, their odd and incongruous representation of things and their predictive and practical success (in terms of healings, establishment of new customs and traditions); on the other, they insisted on the moral trustworthiness of the dreamers, their reliance on healthy regimens of life and their willingness to engage in the exercise of intellective knowledge. Divination was, in Iamblichus's words, 'a thing divine, supernatural, sent from heaven; both unbegotten and eternal'.[28] Ficino paraphrased this crucial point in Iamblichus's argument with his usual clarity and concision:

> Prophecy is not caused by any technique, by nature, natural or animal causes or motions, nor is it something subject to change; rather, it is both eternal and sent to us by God.[29]

For Iamblichus prophecy was therefore a genuinely theurgic affair, in that it was a true image, a 'divine work', consisting of divine visions and insights endowed with a sense of absolute certainty.[30] What is more, prophetic dreams as antidotes against delusive perceptions of reality overcame the limited focus of the individual soul and the wavering course of its decision-making. They dramatically expanded the boundaries of what could be perceived through the circumscribed forum of private introspection. For this reason, unintentionality and randomness were their identifying marks. Their scope was cosmological (the divine intellect poured its light everywhere in the universe) as well as practical (the revelation of truth led to the progress of human civilization in the form of customs, laws and rituals). Against all attempts to naturalize divination and prophecy (as made by Porphyry), Iamblichus insisted on the transcendent foundation of foreknowledge: 'how, I ask, can divination be produced from things without a power of divination, and how may a soul be created from bodies without a soul?'[31] Real dreams — that is, dreams that revealed the true nature of things — were the least dependent on our will and imagination, therefore more objective. For Iamblichus, this was further evidence that prophetic dreams could only come from God: 'the fact that the truth in our dreams does not wholly concur with our actions, and often shines forth from itself, shows that divination comes from without, for it is from the gods.'[32] In this case, Ficino felt the need to add a comment:

> Often the perception of future events is given to people who are not looking for it, for if the result of a dream depended on our nature and human will, this would happen every time we look for it.[33]

If that were the case, the product of our dreams, the *somnialis effectus* — that is, the truth — would be created by our will, which for writers like Iamblichus and Ficino, trained in the ontological niceties of Platonic idealism, sounded like an obvious absurdity. On the contrary, Iamblichus explained veridical dreams as the result of an unremitting transmission of prophetic knowledge, occurring at any moment throughout the universe, while Ficino described the same phenomenon as *perpetua praesagii consecutio*, a seamless continuity of foreknowledge.[34]

Within the framework of Platonic ontology, divine reality corresponded to the intelligible order of the universe. Every time divine intellects enlightened the soul, the soul would attain a firm contemplation of the causes of real beings and would know beforehand future events as they were supposed to take place in tune with the intelligible harmony of the universe. Dreaming was defined by Iamblichus as a kind of 'liberated activity' through which the soul received 'the truest plenitudes of intellection'.[35] Freedom from the illusions of the senses meant an expansion of activity. From this point of view, the most interesting outcome of Iamblichus's and Ficino's interpretation of prophetic visions through dreams was the practical consequences they drew from it. Iamblichus maintained that, because of their high epistemic value, divine dreams could also imbue the soul with the power to change material reality in a number of different ways, for they were manifestations of knowledge, but also of power. Through dreams, Iamblichus pointed out, '[the soul] heals sick bodies, and re-arranges many things that were discordant and disorderly among human beings, and also it often transmits the discovery of human skills, legal regulations, and the establishment of customs'. Indeed, 'the medical arts arise from sacred dreams'.[36]

In translating and interpreting this part of Iamblichus's text, Ficino put even more emphasis on the transformative power of the imagination as a mediator between the seminal forms in nature and the ideas in the realm of intelligible reality. He introduced a clause that was not in the original text, albeit in line with Iamblichus's argument: 'ideo anima his [i.e., the ideas which are in the gods] coniuncta', which is to say, by means of dreams and the imagination, the human soul could join the gods. Of course, not all kinds of dreams or imagination were up to the task, but the awakening of the mind prompted by divine dreams could certainly bring about the purification of the imagination and make it ready to perceive the truth of the intelligible realm. As clarified by Ficino, since the soul was endowed with the ideal patterns that governed the production of changeable beings and, to a certain extent, participated in their power, both in a productive and a cognitive sense, contemplation of divine forms turned into a most productive experience:

> when it reaches its union with the gods, the soul actualizes the forms it has within itself. This is the most important act of knowledge, which occurs according to the order of divine providence. And through providence and the forms the soul thinks over past, future and all temporal things, and their actions and passions, the remedies for the passions, the cures for diseases and mental ills, the laws and the arts necessary to humankind.[37]

Even more emphatically than Iamblichus, Ficino thus stated that divine dreams and the imaginations that produced them were the conduits through which divine energy could be channelled and made into a force capable of shaping both natural and social reality: healing, reconciliation of divisions, technological advancements and creation of customs. Far from being delusions, these dreams were considered to be constitutive of reality. They were so real that they produced new reality: health, laws, oracles and inventions.

4. Dreaming as a Cosmological Function

Regardless of the opinion that philosophers might have about atomism and its ontological implications, Democritus's doctrine of knowledge, described as a process in which countless effluvia of films were constantly being released from all objects in nature, certainly had an enormous appeal for natural philosophers and physicians, from antiquity to the early modern period. This is also the case when we approach the history of theorizations about dreams. In Synesius's *On Dreams*, the physics and cosmology of dreams was of a Democritean kind. When humans dreamt, he argued, they simply surrendered to the unremitting flow of the imagination. It was a flow of images that occurred at any moment in nature and in every corner of it; their effects, however, were not always perceived in a conscious way (*On Dreams*, XV). Reality and imagination thus coalesced into one substance which Synesius called the reality of the imagination. In this sense, as humans shared in the universal flow of the imagination, they — together with demons, animals, plants, even inanimate beings — were in the process of dreaming at each moment of their life. Three ontological assumptions underlay Synesius's views on dreams: the idea that phenomenal reality resulted from a continuum of pneumatic matter capable of undergoing infinite degrees of condensation and rarefaction; the belief that the representations of the imagination (both *idola* and *phantasmata*) were the elements that made up the fabric of reality and allowed shifts of energy among sensations, memories and intellections; and, finally, the thesis that dream imagination had important temporal dimensions which were always associated with its divinatory character (as discussed in the previous sections). Dream imagination rested therefore on an account of reality as thoroughly fluid and pliant, in terms of matter, knowledge and time. As aptly summed up by Synesius (*On Dreams*, XIX), the imagination had the power of making room for and embracing everything.

The close association between the activities of dreaming and imagining, and the description of reality as a seamless flow of vital and cognitive energy were the most original aspects in Synesius's analysis: the mind contained the 'forms of beings', it communicated them to the soul through the imagination and the imagination was at its most effective when human beings were asleep (*On Dreams*, III). Accordingly, to imagine and to dream were two instantiations of the same activity:

> This seems to be a life that is just below the surface and is of a very specific nature. The powers of the senses can be found in it. We see colours, we hear noises, we get the most subtle perception of touch, while the organs of the body are at rest. It could even be that this kind of perception is more sacred, for it is through it that often we come into contact with the gods (*On Dreams*, IV).

This is what Synesius called life in the state of imagination, by which he meant a condition of cognitive openness to sudden manifestations of intelligible truths, a condition that he viewed as natural for human beings, though often obfuscated by the daily impressions of the senses. In Synesius's opinion, the path to the highest visions of being could only pass through dream imagination (*On Dreams*, IV and V). More importantly, while clear and unambiguous access to this reality was not granted to everyone, dream imagination was open to all human beings. Dreams revealed that 'a life according to the imagination' was sometimes better, sometimes worse than 'life in the middle' (i.e. between the intellect and nature), and it was a life that depended on 'the state of health or illness of the spirit' (*On Dreams*, XVIII). It was by virtue of its special link with the *pneuma* ('spirit') that the imagination was 'the sense of senses', for the imaginative spirit was 'the most common sensory organ' and 'the first body of the soul' (*On Dreams*, V). Imagination understood as a form of 'being' was therefore a direct and unmediated perception of intelligible realities; its sheer representative energy was conveyed by the *pneuma*, described by Synesius as an imaginal borderland, in which reason and unreason, lack of matter and body are able to meet and coexist for a limited amount of time (*On Dreams*, VI, IX). Countless films, capable of representing the objects from which they were peeling off, are incessantly being formed in the intermediate regions of penumbra. Here the transition from intellectual vision to scattered materiality occurs through the blending of infinite shades of light and darkness. This is therefore a reality that is always pregnant with meaning, laden with echoes of previous events and ready to burst into new life. In the eternal presence of being, past, present and future converge in concentrated moments of intelligible clarity. Above all, nothing is lost: 'All that is possessed by nature, be that present, past and future (for this, too, is a mode of being), flows with images' (*On Dreams*, XV). Through the representative continuum of the spirit, images herald future events. At this most critical juncture, Synesius resorts to metaphoric descriptions; these are 'waves of a present that is about to happen and the blossoming of an undeveloped nature, like riddles that burst and leap forth from seeds that had been previously stored away' (*On Dreams*, XV). It was for this reason that for Synesius — anticipating objections that Sánchez would reiterate in the sixteenth century — there could even be images of things that had ceased to exist and of things that were not in existence yet.

In his treatise on dreams inspired by Synesius, Cardano adopted the theory that the universe was constantly signalling imminent developments and events which were shaping up from a more distant future. This phenomenon was part of the very essence of nature, for nature liked to provide anticipations of its own operations. In this respect, the human desire to know the future was fully legitimate. This also applied to dreams, as Cardano made clear in his own exercise in 'Synesian' imaginations: 'dreams signify in a natural way, regardless of what their meanings are'; 'the meanings of dreams are natural, devoid of any necessity, and yet connected to natural causes.'[38] Unsurprisingly, great changes of fortune and customs or exceptional circumstances were often announced by dreams, for God had created nature in such a way that what was about to happen always impressed an image on the souls that were well-disposed to receive it.[39] Among the requisites that made a mind open to receive truthful dreams, Cardano — like Iamblichus, Synesius and Ficino before him — listed a transparent and strong soul, freedom from cares and a natural disposition to self-restraint.[40]

Sánchez, who, as we have already seen, was highly sceptical of this model of all-encompassing divinatory meaningfulness, criticized both Synesius and Cardano, rebutting their main ontological assumptions one by one, that is to say, the incessant flow of images, the pneumatic make-up of reality and the confluence of temporal dimensions into one condition of eternal presence. He began his criticism by summing up the received view of dream divination:

> Democritus, and Synesius the Platonist with him, believed that certain *idola* and images (*simulachra*) were always flowing from all things — past, present and future. They strike the imaginative spirit (*spiritus phantasticus*), which is their mirror, as it were, and in doing so they stimulate both this spirit and the mind to self-contemplation. This is the way in which divination occurs. Therefore the *idola* present themselves and cause people who are asleep — and not those who are awake — to divine. They do the same with those who undergo ecstasy and with common people rather than wise men, at night rather than during the day, for the mind is free from cares when asleep, in bouts of ecstasy and among ordinary people, and the air is calm at night and during sleep hours.[41]

Crucially, Sanchez denied that there was any true likeness (*verisimilitudo*) between reality and the images flowing in the universe.[42] 'What was in the past does not exist now; what is about to be does not exist yet; what exists now has only an instant of its existence':

> Therefore, if past, present and future things send forth *idola* and effluvia made up of them, do those *idola* retain the character of time that was impressed at the time when the thing occurs or will occur? For, if they do not retain that character, we will take the past for the future. If they do retain it, they are not *idola*, for an *idolum* is a mere depiction of a thing without any indication of time.[43]

For Sánchez, however, the most puzzling among Synesius's and Cardano's theses was the idea that there could be effluvia 'not only of permanent things, but also of thoughts, actions and words'. The result would be the most absurd and unmanageable chaos of things, works, images, words and thoughts, for all would be filled with 'the effluvia of every possible thing'. What mind, Sánchez insisted, could ever be able 'to perceive, foresee or discern among so many and so various, different, indeed, even disparate, opposite and contradictory things?'[44] The idea of the infinitely fungible nature of images (*eidólon* in Greek) and their entering the composition of dreams — the spirit (*pneuma/spiritus*) — was the recurrent motif in both Synesius's and Cardano's explanations. Sánchez rejected this assumption in the most decisive of terms: his *idola* were visual and spatial replicas of things, inert and passive, which for this reason could not convey such abstract entities as the passing of time, the intentions behind human actions and the meanings of thoughts and words.

5. Conclusion: the Blurred Focus of the Dreaming Mind

When the activity of dreaming is set against the background of pre-modern and early modern cosmology, as I have been doing in this chapter in relation to Democritus, Iamblichus, Synesius, Ficino, Sánchez, Cardano and Weyer, the seemingly irreconcilable states of drowsiness, delusion and discernment become in fact different degrees of clarity within one unremitting flow of conscious perception. Marks of reliability and trustworthiness are not always easy to identify in this characteristic situation of cognitive confusion. Dreams show that, besides the state of full alertness, the mind may undergo various stages of epistemological discernment, ranging from drowsiness to delusion, which all have to do with what it means to be 'conscious'. The simple fact of falling asleep testifies to the very ambivalence of the somnolent state of mind: it may be the condition that is preliminary to the disintegration of the self or the condition of heightened imagination that prepares the mind to be flooded with the light of the intellect. This ambivalence is accentuated by the work of the imagination and memory, for they can notoriously smudge the outlines of things. It is an effect that, as everyone knows, is enhanced during the process of sleep. When we fall asleep and begin to dream, the boundaries dividing immediate and remote surroundings, old and recent memories, mental states and the self fade and can, at times, disappear.

One can understand, then, the reason that, within the continuum of knowledge and life represented by dream imagination, Cardano was keen on distinguishing among several degrees of consciousness. He identified five of these degrees:

> Five are the orders in our mind if we examine them according to the act of understanding: we know that we are awake; we understand that we are sleeping; we think we are awake when in fact we are asleep; we simply dream; we are deep asleep.[45]

A state of profound sleep was still a degree of mental life for Cardano. The most critical boundary, however, among the many set in place by the activity of dreaming was the threshold separating sleep from waking. In an original way, Cardano interpreted the experience of ecstatic alienation as a vision of reality that was very close to the act of dreaming: 'There are some dreams that belong to the category of ecstasy, where someone sees certain things, but he is not sure whether he sees such things while awake or when asleep.' Cardano called this condition drowsy waking. This was deemed to be the opposite of the sleeping state in which the mind remained alert, a situation that today is known as 'lucid dream', when someone who is asleep is aware that he is sleeping.[46]

The stratification of the dreaming mind had its counterpart in the multi-layered meaningfulness of dreams. In laying down his directions for interpreting dreams, Cardano describes how everyone is always in the process of selecting several plausible meanings from an infinite reservoir of different interpretations.[47] This was precisely the chaotic farrago criticized by Sánchez. For this reason, to avoid confusion and most of all the risk of ushering in episodes of self-delusion, interpretations of dreams needed to be contextualized from both an individual and a social point of view, for the same things did not have the same meaning for everyone.[48] In addition, particular images might have more than one meaning.[49] Synesius had presented the art of interpreting dreams as the ability to understand meanings within contexts of increasing complexity: from letters to words to sentences to whole books (*On Dreams*, 2). In doing so, he had compared dreams to texts. In line with the principles of his Synesian philosophy of dreams, Cardano, too, described dreams as complex textual artefacts in which one could explore 'the very nature of things' — that is, the soul and its visions — in its infinite permutations.[50] An interpreter of dreams was therefore supposed to be valiantly open to the possibility of multiple significance and to the inevitable ambiguity of images and words, especially when they happened to coalesce.⁵¹

This was particularly evident in those dreams in which one seemed to see and do contradictory things. Here more than in any other situation, dream imagination demonstrated its power to heighten and expand the possibilities of perception and the scope of awareness. Cardano called these kinds of dreams 'dreams that go beyond thought', such as 'to be in two places simultaneously' or 'to be and not to be something at once'. When the mind is awake, he continued, it 'cannot think of those things that it conceives of while asleep'.⁵² Synesius had defended the possibility of stretching the boundaries of thinkable reality by discussing the characteristic tension between words and images in dreams. The best rhetorician, he argued, was the one who was able to adapt speech (*lógos*) to visions (*phantasmata*), not only when awake, but especially when asleep (*On Dreams*, XIX). In doing so, the imagination expanded its power to the point of removing things from and introducing them into being, altering the very limits of the credible and the conceivable. I have already referred to the particularly pithy sentence by Synesius: 'the imagination makes room for everything.' And yet Synesius did not hesitate to ask how words could 'make such room'. He addressed this question by describing the imagination as a force that was able to articulate infinite possibilities into words, transcending the very limits of visual representability. This level of expressiveness and freedom could be reached by the imagination precisely in the state of a dream: 'There is no Adrastian law that forbids someone who is sleeping from hovering above the earth more happily than Icarus.' When this happened, Synesius added, it became easy to say 'what before was difficult to express'. Quoting Homer (*Odyssey*, VII, 201; XVI, 161), he exalted the vivid reliability of the imagination's account: 'the gods manifest themselves in a clear way' (*On Dreams*, XIX).

As in many other cases of Platonic transmission during the Renaissance, it was Ficino above all who was largely responsible for fostering knowledge of Synesius's philosophy among his contemporaries. His translation appeared in 1497, in the same collection of Platonic texts where Iamblichus had clarified the meaning of prophetic dreams. In his treatise on dreams Synesius had granted a sphere of cognitive autonomy to the activity of dreaming (*On Dreams*, 19), a key phrase which Ficino significantly rendered with *somniorum licentia*, 'dreaming licence'.⁵³ By championing the autonomy of dream imagination, Synesius defended a view of meaningfulness in which dreams were supposed to contribute to the expansion of rationality, civilization and freedom. Once again, in dealing with the topic of dreams in the early modern period, we need to stress their link with issues of cosmology, divination and prophecy (and the related questions of discernment and reliable knowledge). In their unique manner of activating the force of the imagination, dreams brought to the fore uneasiness with the present, expectations about the future and confusion concerning the past. In the end, though, as we have seen in the case of Iamblichus and Ficino, it was the future that prevailed over the present and the past in the definition of dreams. In other words, hope was a more powerful motive than fear, as Synesius had more than once explained in his treatise on dreams. The interplay of foreknowledge and hope confirmed the existence of a virtuous circle in the many aspects of dream divination, which could not be simply reduced to an unconscious desire to fulfil a wish unattainable in the reality of waking experience. What is more, beyond the immediate gratification of short-term predictions, the interplay of foreknowledge and hope allowed the soul to become more aware of its spontaneous and irrepressible nature. This also meant that freedom was especially empowered by dream imagination. Belief in the meaning of dreams rested on the liberating power of the future: human beings 'hold the future to be more trustworthy than the present' (*On Dreams*, XIII).[54]

As noted in the previous section, Cardano had associated the inexhaustible meaningfulness of dreams to the original spontaneity of nature's activity. He did not rule out the possibility that dreams might act as sources of immediate wish-fulfilment: 'Every dream, even the most revolting one, since it occurs according to a wish, can be good, as when someone who is looking for revenge sees a sun stained with blood.'[55] Fulfilling a desire through a dream, however, was no flight from the principle of reality. Rather, for Cardano it was part of an irrepressible striving towards greater clarity and freedom. As we have just seen, Synesius had spoken in positive terms of the force of dream imagination because it was a power that could break the law of necessity, thus allowing the mind to think the unthinkable (*On Dreams*, XIX). Of all the gifts donated by dreams, freedom was perhaps the most important. Cardano shared with Synesius the glorification of divination as one of the noblest disciplines cultivated by human beings. More than medicine, astrology, agriculture and navigation, dream divination was useful, pious, affordable and democratic; everyone could practise divination through dreams for everyone was able to dream. Above all, since it relied on the absolutely gratuitous intervention of God, dream divination was spontaneous, disinterested and free: 'Not even the laws of a mistrustful state forbid divination through dreams; even if they wished to, they would not be able to do so, for there would be no evidence against their practitioners. Would we perhaps violate the law by sleeping? No tyrant could prevent us from having dreams, unless he bans sleeping from his kingdom' (Synesius, *On Dreams*, XII). Which amounts to saying: I sleep, therefore I am free.[56]

Notes to Chapter 5

1. René Descartes, *Oeuvres*, ed. by Charles Adam and Paul Tannery, 11 vols (Paris: Vrin, 1964–1974), VII, pp. 19–20.
2. Marsilio Ficino, translations of Iamblichus, *De mysteriis Aegyptiorum* and Synesius, *De somniis* (Venice: Aldo Manuzio, 1497), sigs a1^v-f1^r; L^r-M6^v; Girolamo Cardano, *Somniorum Synesiorum omnis generis insomnia explicantes libri quatuor* (Basel: Sebastian Henric Petri, 1562); Francisco Sánchez, *De divinatione per somnum ad Aristotelem*, in *Opera medica. His iuncti sunt tractatus quidam philosophici non insubtiles*, 2 vols (Toulouse: Pierre Bosc, 1636), II, pp. 43–76. In this chapter, I will quote from the following editions: Marsilio Ficino *Opera omnia* (Basel: Officina Henricpetrina, 1576); Girolamo Cardano, *Somniorum Synesiorum libri quatuor*, ed. by Jean-Yves Boriaud, 2 vols (Florence: Olschki, 2008); Francisco Sánchez, *Tutte le opere filosofiche*, ed. by Claudio Buccolini and Ettore Lojacono, with Claudia Montuschi (Milan: Bompiani, 2011). Unless otherwise specified, all English translations from other languages are mine. In the interests of accessibility (and economy), and in keeping with the other chapters in this volume, I have kept ancient Greek and Latin glosses of words to a minimum and provided page or textual references instead of original Greek and Latin excerpts.

3. On dreams in the Renaissance, see: *Le songe à la Renaissance*, ed. by Françoise Charpentier (Saint-Étienne: Institut d'Études de la Renaissance et de l'Âge Classique, 1990); Florence Dumora, *L'oeuvre nocturne: Songe et représentation au XVIIe siècle* (Paris: Honoré Champion, 2005); Sylviane Bokdam, *Métamorphoses de Morphée: Théories du rêve et songes poétiques à la Renaissance, en France* (Paris: Honoré Champion, 2012); Guido Giglioni, 'Phantasms of Reason and Shadows of Matter: Averroes's Notion of the Imagination and Its Renaissance Interpreters', in *Renaissance Averroism and Its Aftermath: Arabic Philosophy in Early Modern Europe* (Dordrecht: Springer, 2013), pp. 173–93. On dreams in in the pre-modern period, see: *I sogni nel Medioevo*, ed. by Tullio Gregory (Rome: Edizioni dell'Ateneo, 1985); William V. Harris, *Dreams and Experience in Classical Antiquity* (Cambridge: Harvard University Press, 2009); Philip J. Van der Eijk and Maithe Hulskamp, 'Stages in the Reception of Aristotle's Works on Sleep and Dreams in Hellenistic and Imperial Philosophical and Medical Thought', in *Les* Parva naturalia *d'Aristote: Fortune antique et médiévale*, ed. by Christophe Grellard and Pierre-Marie Morel (Paris: Publications de la Sorbonne, 2010), pp. 47–75.
4. Johann Weyer, *De praestigiis daemonum et incantationibus ac veneficiis*, in *Opera omnia* (Amsterdam: Peter van den Berge, 1660), pp. 121 and 251. On Weyer's treatment of the imagination, see Guido Giglioni, '*Phantastica Mutatio*: Johann Weyer's Critique of the Imagination as a Principle of Natural Metamorphosis', in *Transformative Change in Western Thought: A History of Metamorphosis from Homer to Hollywood*, ed. by Ingo Gildenhard and Andrew Zissos (London: Legenda, 2013), pp. 307–30. On the meaning of theurgy and Iamblichus's views about it, see E. R. Dodds, *The Greeks and the Irrational* (Berkeley: University of California Press, 1951), pp. 283–311; Emma C. Clarke, *Iamblichus'* De Mysteriis: *A Manifesto of the Miraculous* (Aldershot: Ashgate, 2001).
5. On the importance of Ficino's translation of Iamblichus and on Weyer's critique of the imagination, see Guido Giglioni, 'Theurgy and Philosophy in Marsilio Ficino's Paraphrase of Iamblichus's De Mysteriis Aegyptiorum', *Rinascimento*, 52 (2012), 3–36.
6. On the early modern revival of prophecy against a background of theological uncertainty, see Stuart Clark, *Vanities of the Eye: Vision in Early Modern Culture* (Oxford: Oxford University Press, 2007); Susan E. Schreiner, *Are You Alone Wise? The Search for Certainty in the Early Modern Era* (Oxford: Oxford University Press, 2011).
7. Iamblichus, *On the Mysteries*, ed. by Emma C. Clarke, John M. Dillon, and Jackson P. Hershbell (Atlanta: Society of Biblical Literature, 2003), p. 119. The 'antidote' is also expressed in the form of a 'correct rule' and as a 'first principle' that warns 'never to derive divination of the future from those things that have no foreknowledge as such, but to derive it from the gods, who in themselves possess the limits of all knowledge of existing things, from whom the mantic power is distributed throughout the whole cosmos'. See Iamblichus, *On the Mysteries*, pp. 120–21, translated in Ficino, *De mysteriis Aegyptiorum*, p. 1882.
8. Ficino, *De mysteriis Aegyptiorum*, in *Opera omnia*, p. 1883. See Iamblichus, *On the Mysteries*, p. 124.
9. Sanchez, *De divinatione per somnum, ad Aristotelem*, in *Tutte le opere filosofiche*, p. 346 (my translation).
10. Ibid., p. 350.
11. Ibid., p. 352.
12. On the doctrine of the 'six non-naturals' in the medical tradition and the Renaissance, see Sandra Cavallo and Tessa Storey, *Healthy Living in Late Renaissance Italy* (Oxford: Oxford University Press, 2013).
13. Ficino, *Platonic Theology*, ed. by Michael J. B. Allen and James Hankins, 6 vols (Cambridge, MA: Harvard University Press, 2001–2006), IV, pp. 150–51. On Ficino's view on dreams, see Robert Klein, 'L'imagination comme vêtement de l'âme chez Marsile Ficin et Giordano Bruno', in *La forme et l'intelligible: Ecrits sur la Renaissance et l'art moderne* (Paris: Gallimard 1970), pp. 65–88; Cesare Vasoli, 'Ficino e la rivelazione onirica', *Accademia*, 1 (1999), 67–75.
14. Plato, *Republic*, IX, 571CD, ed. and tr. by Chris Emlyn-Jones and William Preddy, 2 vols (Cambridge, MA: Harvard University Press, 2013), II, p. 309.
15. Girolamo Cardano, *Somniorum Synesiorum libri quatuor*, I, p. 26.
16. Ficino, *Platonic Theology*, IV, pp. 150–52.
17. Ibid., pp. 154–55.
18. Ibid., pp. 158–59.

19. Plato, *Republic*, IX, 571D-572A, II, pp. 308-11.
20. On Ficino's Platonism see Michael J. B. Allen, *The Platonism of Marsilio Ficino: A Study of His Phaedrus Commentary, its Sources and Genesis* (Berkeley: University of California Press, 1984); Michael J. B. Allen, *Synoptic Art: Marsilio Ficino on the History of Platonic Interpretation* (Florence: Olschki, 2008); Christopher S. Celenza, 'Late Antiquity and Florentine Platonism: The 'Post-Plotinian' Ficino', in *Marsilio Ficino: His Theology, His Philosophy, His Legacy*, ed. by Michael J. B. Allen and Valery Rees, with Martin Davies (Leiden: Brill, 2002), pp. 71-97.
21. Porphyry, *Lettre à Anébon l'Égyptien*, ed. by Henri Dominique Saffrey and Alain-Philippe Segonds (Paris: Les Belles Lettres, 2012), pp. 21, 32.
22. Iamblichus, *On the Mysteries*, pp. 120-21. See Ficino, *De mysteriis Aegyptiorum*, p. 1883.
23. Iamblichus, *On the Mysteries*, p. 122.
24. Ficino, *De mysteriis Aegyptiorum*, p. 1883.
25. Iamblichus, *On the Mysteries*, p. 122; Ficino, *De mysteriis Aegyptiorum*, p. 1883.
26. Ficino, *De mysteriis Aegyptiorum*, p. 1883.
27. Iamblichus, *On the Mysteries*, p. 119; Ficino, *De mysteriis Aegyptiorum*, p. 1882.
28. Iamblichus, *On the Mysteries*, p. 119; Ficino, *De mysteriis Aegyptiorum*, p. 1882.
29. Ficino, *De mysteriis Aegyptiorum*, p. 1882.
30. Iamblichus, *On the Mysteries*, p. 119; Ficino, *De mysteriis Aegyptiorum*, p. 1882.
31. Iamblichus, *On the Mysteries*, p. 174.
32. Iamblichus, *On the Mysteries*, p. 177.
33. Ficino, *De mysteriis Aegyptiorum*, p. 1889: 'saepe id [i.e., *praesagium*] non quaerentibus datur, quod si somnialis effectus esset ex nostra natura arbitrioque humano, nobis ad hoc providentibus eveniret'.
34. Iamblichus, *On the Mysteries*, p. 120; Ficino, *De mysteriis Aegyptiorum*, p. 1882.
35. Iamblichus, *On the Mysteries*, p. 126; Ficino, *De mysteriis Aegyptiorum*, p. 1883.
36. Iamblichus, *On the Mysteries*, p. 126. On epiphany dreams of a healing nature, see Harris, *Dreams and Experience*, p. 31.
37. Ficino, *De mysteriis Aegyptiorum*, p. 1883.
38. Cardano, *Somniorum Synesiorum libri quatuor*, I, p. 6. On the complex relationship between dream activity and *Fatum*, see ibid., I, pp. 24.
39. Ibid., I, pp. 40-42; II, 400; 452.
40. Ibid., II, p. 406. On Cardano's views on dream, see Alice Browne, 'Girolamo Cardano's *Somniorum Synesiorum Libri IIII*', *Bibliothèque d'Humanisme et Renaissance*, 41 (1979), 123-35; Guido Giglioni, 'Synesian Dreams: Girolamo Cardano on Dreams as Means of Prophetic Communication', *Bruniana et Campanelliana* 16 (2010), 575-84; Nancy Siraisi, *The Clock and the Mirror: Girolamo Cardano and Renaissance Medicine* (Princeton: Princeton University Press, 1997), pp. 174-91.
41. Francisco Sánchez, *De divinatione per somnum*, p. 284.
42. Ibid., p. 284.
43. Ibid., pp. 286-88.
44. Ibid., p. 288.
45. Cardano, *Somniorum Synesiorum libri quatuor*, II, p. 424.
46. On this point see Evan Thompson, *Waking, Dreaming, Being: Self and Consciousness in Neuroscience, Meditation, and Philosophy* (New York: Columbia University Press), 2015.
47. Cardano, *Somniorum Synesiorum libri quatuor*, II, 550.
48. Ibid., I, p. 54.
49. Ibid., I, p. 78.
50. Ibid., II, pp. 390 and 392.
51. Ibid., II, p. 392.
52. Ibid., II, p. 436.
53. Ficino, *Opera omnia*, p. 1978.
54. Ibid., p. 1974.
55. Cardano, *Somniorum Synesiorum libri quatuor*, p. 104.
56. Which is also the reason sleep deprivation is one of the easiest and more diffused ways of practising torture.

CHAPTER 6

Others' Dreams, Others' Minds in Descartes's *Meditations*

James Helgeson

On the night of 10–11 November 1619, Descartes, it seems, slept badly, assailed by an 'evil spirit'. Baillet, in his 1691 paraphrase of the fragments of an early (c. 1620), no longer extant, Latin treatise by Descartes, the *Olympica* (AT X 179–205), recounts a trio of dreams written out by the young philosopher. The first evokes an intense wind carrying the young man off ('un vent impétueux [...] l'emportant dans une espèce de tourbillon'), causing him to take refuge in a college on his path. In his manuscript, Descartes had apparently written: 'a malo Spiritu ad Templum propellebar' ('I was being propelled towards the Temple by an evil spirit'). On reaching the college chapel he received the gift of a melon from a certain Monsieur N. In the second dream, Descartes heard a terrifying, sharp noise, like a thunderclap, from which he immediately awoke to his own, defamiliarised room, filled with fiery sparks. The third dream, less frightening, involves books, in particular, an encyclopaedia and an anthology of poetry placed upon a table. Descartes was given a fragment of Latin verse, identified as coming from Ausonius, by an unidentified man, to whom he replied that the poem in question, from the *Idylls*, was also in the anthology on the table; the incipit was 'est et non', which Descartes took as a reference to Pythagoras ('yes' and 'no' were, for the Greek philosopher, the words that required the most thought).[1] Baillet tells how Descartes's fatigued mind subsequently fell into an extended state of inspired excitement ('enthousiasme') that was the spur for his life's work.[2]

So Descartes, or rather Baillet, tells us that Descartes's philosophy begins in dreams, or more specifically in the consideration of philosophical argument in, and from, dreams and delusional states. Many will take the story with a grain of salt (and perhaps with less psychoanalysis than was once popular). These dream states are central to the *Meditations on First Philosophy*. What follows is a reading of several passages from Descartes that bring up the availability of others' mental, and, in particular, dream states. The spur for these reflections was a reading of the very end of the First Meditation, which has been somewhat overlooked by commentators.[3] The reading of the final sentences of the First Meditation, which here stands as the endpoint of my analysis, is preceded by related readings from the Meditations as well as the Objections and Responses.[4] Throughout, my idea is not to separate the philosophy from its rhetorical and 'literary' presentation, but to examine how that rhetorical presentation interacts with philosophical argument, since social interaction is always present even when the Meditator flirts with solipsism.[5]

I

How do we understand the dream-states of others? The idea that we might be able to access the content of others' mental states through the general application of a 'theory of mind' is familiar to twenty-first-century readers. The philosophy of consciousness of the last century, whether phenomenological or 'analytic', placed the thinking subject 'in situation' in a populated world, deriving solitary mental life from social interaction. Contemporary cognitive research suggests that human theories of mind develop, when we are children, according to recognisable patterns. Much recent work in cognition and theory of mind has centred on the capacities humans have to read others' mental states from their actions, gestures, facial expressions, and even from words. People are assumed to have minds like our own and are expected to come to conclusions about the world that are analogous, though not necessarily identical, to our own. (We are surprised, in simple cognitive tests measuring, say, the sense of object constancy, when this is not the case.[6]) Computers can to some extent simulate this sense of mind, but in general not so that they can convince human subjects that they are human in sustained interaction.[7] We assume that some things we encounter in the world (e.g. boulders) do not have minds in any sense. Other phenomena that we encounter in our peregrinations (llamas, for example, or, more so, locusts) are more indeterminate with regards to theory of mind.

Such contemporary distinctions in what is often called 'mindreading' have a long prehistory.[8] Descartes is, of course, an important part of this story, although in a curious sense: in his most famous thought experiment, he affects to remove other minds from the picture entirely, arriving at the existence of the external world through God, and not through the experiences of social life. In the *Meditations*, Descartes postulates, briefly, that his (Meditator's) mind is, in fact, the only 'thinking thing' in the world. When, in the Third Meditation, the Meditator discovers that he is 'not alone in the world' ('*hinc neccessario sequi, non me solum esse in mundo*'), his company is God, not other minds, nor the things of the world (AT VII 42).

Dreams are a curious case as far as mindreading is concerned, one that much occupied the early modern imagination. The question of the dreams of other minds arises explicitly in the Sixth Objections to Descartes's Meditations. Descartes's correspondents suggest, in their third point, that dogs dream of pursuing hares; they seem indeed to be conscious of the experience, real or dreamed, of running and barking. Although we do not have direct access to their animal minds, nor they to ours, it is nonetheless possible that they, like us, make judgements about internal mental states, even those of humans (AT VII 218–19). The observation may remind the reader of Montaigne's famous musings about his cat, in the 'Apology for Raymond Sebond' (*Essais*, II, 12).[9] Descartes's response is very different from Montaigne's thought experiment: the author of the *Meditations* makes short shrift of the possibility of animal minds, affirming a rigorous distinction between humans and animals and denying that the latter have minds at all (AT VII 229–30).

Nevertheless, Descartes's Meditator always proceeds on the assumption that what dreams are is perspicuous to his reader. Moreover, the reader can understand what it would be like to experience the dreams of others. It is this sense of other minds, implicit in Descartes's argument from the beginning of the *Meditations*, that will occupy us in the following sections.

II

The first-person stance in the *Meditations* is peculiar, not the least because it tends to slip between singular and plural.[10] In Latin, and indeed in French, the first person plural may convey a singular meaning in many cases, running from modesty to majesty, but this slippage also betrays the difficulty of maintaining a rigorously sceptical first-person focus throughout works that are rhetorical constructions, aimed at convincing a reader by scripting a set of actions and reactions.[11]

In linguistic terms, the distinction between 'conceptual' and 'procedural' expressions in recent cognitive pragmatics, proposed initially by Diane Blakemore[12] and developed by, for example, Deirdre Wilson and Dan Sperber, may be useful in understanding not only the content of Descartes's argument but also its rhetorical strategies.[13] A 'conceptual' expression is one that encodes concepts constituting the truth-value of a given expression, e.g. 'tree', 'panda', 'essay'.[14] Others, 'procedurals' (for example: 'but', 'so', 'however', 'also', 'unfortunately', deictic expressions such as 'now' and 'yesterday', pronouns), are expressions used to constrain the kinds of inferences that can be made from utterances, or in other words to 'guide the *inferential comprehension process* by imposing [...] constraints on the construction of *contexts* and/or *cognitive effects*.'[15] Pronouns and morphologically marked verbal person both count as procedurals; they are involved simultaneously in the truth-value of utterances *and* in the channelling of the inferences of their audience.[16] It is this double, quasi-conceptual and rhetorical, function, and the way it strengthens the persuasive force of Descartes's argumentation, that will concern us in what follows.[17]

There are eddies of first-person-plural usage throughout the *Meditations*, even places where singular gives way rather insistently to plural. These very often occur at the beginnings and in particular the ends of sections (and, not surprisingly, throughout the Responses to Objections and in the introductory, justifying letter to the Theological Faculty of the University of Paris). The first person plural occurs also, for example, at that moment, in the Second Meditation, where Descartes's Meditator sums up his experiment with melting wax in such a way that the reader is implicated in the action and encouraged to imitate it:

> Miror verò interim quàm prona sit mea mens in errores; nam quamvis haec apud me tacitus & sine voce considerem, haereo tamen in verbis ipsis, & fere decipior ab ipso usu loquendi. **Dicimus** enim **nos** videre ceram ipsammet, si adsit, non ex colore vel figurâ eam adesse judicare. (AT VII 31–32, emphasis mine)

> [But as I reach this conclusion], I am amazed at how prone to error my mind is: for although I am thinking about these matters within myself, silently and without speaking, nonetheless the actual words bring me up short, and I am almost tricked by ordinary ways of talking. **We say that we see the wax itself,**

if it is present, not that we judge it to be there from its colour and shape[.] (Descartes 1996, p. 21)

The accusative-infinitive construction is lodged in a sentence in the first person plural; in the 1647 French, the incidence of the first person plural is doubled ('**nous** disons que **nous** voyons la même cire, si on **nous** la présente, et non pas que **nous** jugeons que c'est la même'). Such emphatic repetition is not entirely betrayal, since the notion of linguistic convention (the ordinary use of language 'almost' [*fere*] leads him astray; it does not in fact do so) suggests social, not solipsistic, experience.[18]

Descartes's Meditator tries to pull in his audience by the use of the first person plural at the end of the Third Meditation, inviting the reader to join him in a moment of contemplation of the divine majesty:

> Sed priusquam hoc diligentius examinem, simulque in alias veritates quae inde colligi possunt inquiram, placet hîc aliquandiu in ipsius Dei contemplatione immorari, ejus attributa apud me expendere, & immensi hujus luminis pulchritudinem, quantum caligantis ingenii mei acies ferre poterit, intueri, admirari, adorare. Ut enim in hac solâ divinae majestatis contemplatione summam alterius vitae foelicitatem consistere fide **credimus**, ita etiam jam ex eâdem, licet multo minus perfectâ, maximam, cujus in hac vitâ capaces **simus**, voluptatem percipi posse **experimur**. (AT VII 52, emphasis mine)

> [But before examining this point more carefully and investigating other truths which may be derived from it, I should like to pause here and spend some time in the contemplation of God; to reflect on his attributes, and to gaze with wonder and adoration on the beauty of this immense light, so far as the eye of my darkened intellect can bear it. For just as **we believe through faith** that the supreme happiness of the next life consists solely in the contemplation of the divine majesty, so **experience tells us** that this same contemplation, albeit much less perfect, enables us to know the greatest joy of which **we are** capable in this life.] (Descartes 1996, p. 35–36)

The passage addresses the reader's religious feeling. It does this in a sentence that contains a trio of first-person-plural verbs, wherein 'we' are invited to join in the felicity of contemplation in this and the other life. Unlike in Montaigne (who also speaks in the first person plural about such matters: 'Il n'y a point de fin en nos inquisitions; nostre fin est en l'autre monde' ('There is no end in our enquiries: our end is in the other world'),[19] 'we' are already privy to information about the world to come. Just as 'we believe' that the contentment provided in the afterlife consists in contemplation, so by comparison, the contemplation of God in this life is the highest contentment we can hope for here below. Descartes thus ties together reader and Meditator in a common confessional act. The truths of the faith are presented by assertion; indeed, assertions about the experiences proper to the world-to-come might, reasonably, seem less 'clear and distinct' than many others presented by the philosopher as truths. Certainly it is easier to melt wax than to contemplate God himself and the activities of the afterlife.

In both of these cases, the Meditator pulls in the reader by inviting her, in part through the slippery use of procedurals, to identify with the mental experience of another, by including her in the experience of contemplation, as if the limits of the mind were for a moment suspended.

III

Divine contemplation is not the only felicity; sleep is perhaps another one. Let us suppose, then, with the narrator of the First Meditation, that we are asleep:

> Age ergo **somniemus**, nec particularia ista vera sint, **nos** oculos aperire, caput movere, manus extendere, nec forte etiam **nos** habere tales manus, nec tale totum corpus; tamen profecto fatendum est visa per quietem esse veluti quasdam pictas imagines, quae non nisi ad similitudinem rerum verarum fingi potuerunt; ideoque saltem generalia haec, oculos, caput, manus, totumque corpus, res quasdam non imaginarias, sed veras existere. (AT VII 19, emphasis mine.)

> [Suppose, then, that **we are dreaming**, and that these particulars — the opening of eyes, the moving of the head, the stretching out of the arms — are not true ones. Perhaps, indeed, **we** do not even have such hands or such a body at all. Nonetheless, it must surely be admitted that the visions which come in sleep are like paintings, which must have been fashioned in the likeness of things that are real, and hence that at least these general kinds of things — eyes, hands, and the body as a whole — are things which are not imaginary but are real and exist.] (Descartes 1996, p. 13)[20]

Descartes's Meditator here suggests a new thought experiment. He pulls his reader in, at first, by assertions with a Scholastic flavour. What is in our head is a representation of things that exist outside: 'picta[e] imagines.' The argument is representationalist: the suggestion is that perceptions give rise to internal pictures, the likenesses of things that we believe we perceive. The argument will go on to call into question the reality of external objects even in such cases where 'we' are awake. But initially it is presented through an appeal to common experience, that is, to the assumption that we understand by analogy the characteristics of the waking life — and indeed of the dream experiences — of others.

The Meditator returns to this commonality of cognitive experience in the last paragraph of the final, Sixth Meditation, where he affirms the reliability of his senses in most cases and raises again the problem of dreaming. Having (he hopes) convinced the reader that God is reliable, and that it is reasonable to believe in the existence of the external world, he points again, in his closing gesture, to a marked difference between the ways objects appear to him in waking states and in dreams. When objects appear, they emerge in such a way that he can make a narrative connection between their entrance at a particular moment, and the other parts of life taken as a whole:

> Praesertim summa illa de somno, quem a vigiliâ non distinguebam; nunc enim adverto permagnum inter utrumque esse discrimen, in eo quòd nunquam insomnia cum reliquis omnibus actionibus vitae a memoriâ conjungantur, ut ea quae vigilanti occurrunt; nam sane, si quis, dum vigilo, mihi derepente appareret, statimque postea dispareret, ut fit in somnis, ita scilicet ut nec unde venisset, nec quo abiret, viderem, non immerito spectrum potius, aut phantasma in cerebro meo effictum, quàm verum hominem esse judicarem. Cùm verò eae res occurrunt, quas distincte, unde, ubi, & quando mihi adveniant, adverto, earumque perceptionem absque ullâ interruptione cum totâ reliquâ vitâ connecto, plane certus sum, non in somnis, sed vigilanti occurrere.

Nec de ipsarum veritate debeo vel minimum dubitare, si, postquam omnes sensus, memoriam & intellectum ad illas examinandas convocavi, nihil mihi, quod cum caeteris pugnet, ab ullo ex his nuntietur. Ex eo enim quòd Deus non sit fallax, sequitur omnino in talibus me non falli. Sed quia rerum agendarum necessitas non semper tam accurati examinis moram concedit, fatendum est humanam vitam circa res particulares saepe erroribus esse obnoxiam, & naturae nostrae infirmitas est agnoscenda. (AT VII 89–90)

[This applies especially to [the principal reason for doubt, namely] my inability to distinguish between being asleep and being awake. For I now notice that there is a vast difference between the two, in that dreams are never linked by memory with all the other actions of life as waking experiences are. If, while I am awake, anyone were suddenly to appear to me and then disappear immediately, as happens in sleep, so that I could not see where he had come from or where he had gone to, it would not be unreasonable for me to judge that he was a ghost, or a vision created in my brain, rather than a real man. But when I distinctly see where things come from and where and when they come to me, and when I can connect my perceptions of them with the whole of the rest of my life without a break, then I am quite certain that when I encounter these things I am not asleep but awake. And I ought not to have even the slightest doubt of their reality if, after calling upon all the senses as well as my memory and my intellect in order to check them, I receive no conflicting reports from any of these sources. For from the fact that God is not a deceiver it follows that in cases like these I am completely free from error. But since the pressure of things to be done does not always allow us to stop and make such a meticulous check, it must be admitted that in this human life we are often liable to make mistakes about particular things, and we must acknowledge the weakness of our nature.] (Descartes 1996, pp. 61–62)

Sight stands in here for the senses as a whole; narrative continuity in perception is paramount. Here the idea that a man or an object might flicker in and out of perception, without him being able to trace its path in and out, would be a sure sign that that object was in fact a mental figment formed in the mind (or indeed brain: *in cerebro meo*) and not something existing in the world. This, for the Meditator, distinguishes sleep from wakefulness: coherent narratives suggest themselves about the relationship between perceptions at particular moments and those that precede and follow them. The idea is not only that a momentary story is apparent, but also that perception connects to the 'whole of the rest of life' (*cum totâ reliquâ vitâ*). One might well object that the Meditator does not here address the question of how that connection with the 'rest of life' can be made (for example, how are the nightly interruptions of sleep to be understood in terms of the continuity of the 'rest of life'?). But the Meditator in fact suggests that moments of perception can be connected to those parts of his life when he is conscious, which he distinguishes from times when he is asleep and objects do not appear to his perception at all. There is a distinction, not made explicit, between the causes of pseudo-perceptions in dreams (they happen in the mind), and the causes of perceptions in wakefulness (they are objects intruding into his perceptual field). It is on the basis of narrative coherence in visual evidence, then, that the senses can be trusted in most cases. Since the Meditator has come to the conclusion that God is no deceiver (*quòd Deus non sit fallax*), he claims that he is not deceived about when he is dreaming and when he is awake.

As if fearing that his reader might be less than convinced, Descartes proceeds immediately to close the debate: it is indeed common to be mistaken about the answers to particular questions since human capacities are limited. Here the Meditator moves from the first person singular — what I see when I look at objects when I am awake, as opposed to what I appear to see when I dream about objects — to a more general reference to the fallibility of human life (*fatendum est humanam vitam circa res particulares saepe erroribus esse obnoxiam*) and finally to an inclusive statement about human weakness, formulated as a general affirmation about the need to acknowledge the weak nature of 'our nature' (*fatendum est [...] naturae nostrae infirmitas est agnoscenda*).

In the passages we have examined in this section, the movement from particular experience, to the assumption of shared experience between reader and Meditator, and finally to a series of general statements about the nature of human weakness, explicitly generalises the thinking experience of the Meditator. It is in this light that the closing gesture of the First Meditation is particularly illuminating.

IV

Crucially, Descartes refers to dreams that are neither his own nor those of the reader, as at the end of the First Meditation:

> Supponam igitur non optimum Deum, fontem veritatis, sed genium aliquem malignum, eundemque summe potentem & callidum, omnem suam industriam in eo posuisse, ut me falleret: putabo coelum, aërem, terram, colores, figuras, sonos, cunctaque externa nihil aliud esse quàm ludificationes somniorum, quibus insidias credulitati meae tetendit: considerabo meipsum tanquam manus non habentem, non oculos, non carnem, non sanguinem, non aliquem sensum, sed haec omnia me habere falsò opinantem: manebo obstinate in hac meditatione defixus, atque ita, siquidem non in potestate meâ sit aliquid veri cognoscere, at certe hoc quod in me est, ne falsis assentiar, nec mihi quidquam iste deceptor, quantumvis potens, quantumvis callidus, possit imponere, obfirmatâ mente cavebo.// Sed laboriosum est hoc institutum, & desidia quaedam ad consuetudinem vitae me reducit.// Nec aliter quàm captivus, qui forte imaginariâ libertate fruebatur in somnis, cùm postea suspicari incipit se dormire, timet excitari, blandisque illusionibus lente connivet: sic sponte relabor in veteres opiniones, vereorque expergisci, ne placidae quieti laboriosa vigilia succedens, non in aliquâ luce, sed inter inextricabiles jam motarum difficultatum tenebras, in posterum sit degenda. (AT VII 23, divisions marked with // are mine)

> [I will suppose therefore that not God, who is supremely good and the source of truth, but rather some malicious demon of the utmost power and cunning has employed all his energies in order to deceive me; I shall think that the sky, the air, the earth, colours, shapes, sounds, and all external things are merely the delusions of dreams which he has devised to ensnare my judgement; I shall consider myself as not having hands or eyes, or flesh, or blood, or senses, but as falsely believing that I have all of these things; I shall stubbornly and firmly

persist in this meditation, and, even if it is not in my power to know any truth, I shall at least do what is in my power, that is, resolutely guard against assenting to any falsehoods, so that the deceiver, however powerful and cunning he may be, will not be able to impose on me in the slightest degree.// But this is an arduous undertaking, and a kind of laziness brings be back to normal life.// I am like a prisoner who is enjoying an imaginary freedom while asleep; as he begins to suspect that he is asleep, he dreads being woken up, and conspires with the pleasant illusion as long as he can; in the same way, I happily slide back into my old opinions and dread being shaken out of them, for fear that my peaceful sleep may be followed by hard labour when I wake, and that I shall have to toil not in the light, but amid the inextricable darkness of the problems I have now raised.][21] (Descartes 1996, p. 15)

The effect of this passage comes from the contrast between two extended periods that pack their cognitive reward at the end, and one pithy one, sandwiched between them. The best-known feature of this passage is the 'malicious demon' evoked at the beginning. This rogue is Descartes's most famous character; he will reappear in the Second Meditation and is, still today, endlessly productive of brains in vats, the Matrix, and suchlike. His origin, is, perhaps, distantly the *malus spiritus* of Descartes's youthful dream. Because of the artificial nature of this first-person narrative, the trembling fear on the precipice of doubt with which the passage ends — a rhetorical cliff-hanger — may seem a bit contrived.

The last sentence of this passage presents two thorny philosophical problems: the question of lucid self-deception ('conniving' with dreams), and interpersonal identification with the dream states of other people. Striking in this sentence is the comparison to the sleeping 'captive', or 'prisoner'. The word *captivus* is translated, already in 1647, as 'esclave' (slave), although in classical Latin it has no suggestion of this legal status (to be sure, captives were often slaves).[22] The final sentence is structured according to an elaborate epic simile in which the captive, who dreams of freedom and 'conspires' with the dream, is compared to the narrating philosopher with whom the reader is encouraged to identify.

The question of falling back into old opinions anticipates in miniature the structure of the Meditations as a whole, which are a voyage into doubt and back (to borrow Freud's story of the child who hides and retrieves a toy, without its psychoanalytic trappings, the Meditations are a variety of 'fort-da' game played with the world). In the end we return to the beginning: we as readers are invited to reassume the place of the captive — the habits of daily life — but to know that place for the first time. The opposition here is between habit (*consuetudo*) and active investigation; for the moment, although I know that I, the Meditator, need to continue with the investigation, 'I' fall back on habit (which relapse, as we see, in the Sixth Meditation, is justified). On the one hand we have the depiction of vigorous investigation, on the other, that of habitual understanding (on the one hand a fiction of highly active, searching cognition, on the other automatism).

The claimed laboriousness of the task is of course rhetorically determined; it supports the fiction of a six-day meditation (on the seventh one rests), telling the reader 'it is fine to stop here for the moment'. In the *Discours de la méthode* (1637), also in six parts, Descartes tells us that if we can't read the whole thing together in one sitting, we should read it in six. He wants, seemingly, to guard against cognitive fatigue, against lapses in attention.[23]

The oppositions here are between the first person (the Meditator) and the third person (the captive): I do this, the captive does that, yet I am not other than the captive (*nec aliter quam captivus*). There is also the implicit comparison between the first person of the Meditator and the second person of the reader, or, in short, a complicated set of interpersonal similarities: 'I' am like the captive; and, more implicitly, you are both like me (in that you can repeat the exercise I have already carried out) and also like the captive.

Most interesting, perhaps, is again the problem of retrieving, or simulating, the dreaming experience of other minds: or, in this case, the question of making sense of what it would be like to conspire (*connive[re]*) with a dream in order not to wake.[24] Note how the vocabulary of conniving and conspiracy fits with the topos of the captive; it is redolent of slave-like sedition. One might suggest that it makes sense to 'connive with dreams' — that many people have done something like this — but that seems uncertain (because of the difficulty of remembering dreams). One could certainly have problems grasping what it would be like to be in the state of lucid dreaming.

The middle sentence is strikingly short, by comparison with the long ones that frame it. (In some printings, including the first 1641 edition, this sentence is attached to the final one; John Veitch, the nineteenth-century translator of Descartes, joins them with a semi-colon.) Here *desidia* (idleness, inactivity, laziness, indolence, sloth) becomes the subject of a verb, *reducit* (leads back), whose object is 'me'. The first sentence is elaborately structured, based on a series of parallel clauses which all start with a first person verb in the future indicative active ('*supponam*', '*putabo*', '*considerabo*', '*manebo*'), except the last one, which ends with one ('*cavebo*'). The first three of these also repeat the same grammatical device, namely accusative/infinitive constructions, such that the change in grammatical structure after the fourth verb, *manebo*, catches the reader's attention for a grammatically much more complicated 'if not x, then at least y' sub-clause. Finally, '*cavebo*', the cognitive payback of the long sentence, here certainly means something like 'I will prevent, or guard against', although it is worth noting that another, perhaps more common, meaning of this verb is 'I will fear'. So both the first and last sentences end with at least an adumbration of fear, not inappropriate in a paragraph that features a malicious demon so prominently.

The striking recourse to the dream of the captive evokes an experience which, presumably, neither Descartes nor his reader shares; indeed Descartes has been taken to task for his blindness, even his complicity, with colonial ideologies and brutal 'subject'-ion (Reiss 2002). Nonetheless, in Descartes's defence, one might well note that, unlike many Renaissance Aristotelians, he does not eject his 'captive' (not, in fact, his 'slave') here from full membership in humanity, and indeed Descartes's rhetorical strategy depends on the possibility of full identification with the 'captive'.

V

In the second of his trenchant and amusing ripostes to Descartes (in the Third Objections), Thomas Hobbes suggests that if one says that 'I am thinking, therefore I am a thought' (which he feigns to understand Descartes to be saying), one might as well say that 'I am walking, therefore I am a walk' (AT VII 172: 'sum ambulans, ergo sum ambulatio'). By the same token, one might say that 'I am dreaming, therefore I am a dream'. Descartes's Meditator is not tempted by this option: the Meditator may be a dreamer, but he is not a dream. Indeed, although the question of whether one can know if one is dreaming or awake preoccupies him, he never suggests that the distinction is unintelligible or that it can be collapsed.

Nor is it problematic to understand, and indeed to inhabit vicariously, the dream states of others. Baillet's account of the origin of Descartes's philosophical project involves a dream told and retold, translated from the first person to the third person. The reader is expected to be able to inhabit these dreams as if from the inside. In the *Meditations*, as well, the evocation of others' dream-states adds texture to, complicates, perhaps at times weakens, the argument from first-person experience. Nevertheless, the experience of others' dreaming is always taken as intelligible.

Of course, the *Meditations* are a highly self-conscious construction, presenting a series of mental, or spiritual, exercises that the reader is invited to take on and repeat. They have little of the spontaneity of dreams. They display a metaleptic structure: flickering back and forth between whole and part, between the experience of following the argument as it progresses and the understanding that the argument exists before the reader begins to read it. Descartes sees the whole landscape as it were at a glance while the reader is still stumbling through it.[25] In short, Descartes assumes that his reader knows what dreams are, although he disagrees with his interlocutors about, for example, whether animals can dream. He also assumes that the reader can identify what is going on in other minds ('mindreading' is presupposed) even at those points in the argument where, ostensibly, the Meditator and the reader are not supposed to be sure that such minds exist.

The slippery use of procedurals contributes considerably to the persuasive force of the argument. Descartes plays on the ambiguity of singular and plural in first-person expressions; this is both a matter of the truth of experience (I and we can be seen to have recognisably similar experiences) and a matter of rhetorical strategy (the use of the first person plural seduces the reader into an assent that she might not have easily given). The constraining function of pronouns (their ability to pick out referents) does not simply help the reader derive the correct implications, following the argument to its conclusion. It is also persuasive (and moreover there is a link between pronouns' constraining and persuasive qualities).[26] In other words, first-person-plural usage, curious in a text based so strongly in first-person-singular experience, pulls the reader into the argument. Sleep and dreams in particular are evoked in such a way that the reader is expected to identify with the mental states evoked (most strikingly when Descartes presupposes that the reader will be able to identify with the dreams of a sleeping captive). In the end, for all their impulse towards solitary experience, the *Meditations* are in fact full of invitations to inhabit a world in which the reader is situated, and identify with the people in it and their mental experiences. Such invitations betray the porousness of thought, and indeed, its non-private, social nature.[27]

The trajectory of this chapter reflects in miniature that of the present volume. The essay moves from Descartes's early dream interpretation, inflected with notions of prophecy, Neoplatonic in flavour, towards the use of dreams to spark readers' intuitions about other minds and the world. Descartes passes from the mysteries of oneiric revelation — that is, from flashes of inspiration that set the philosopher's thought in motion — to relatively unproblematised assumptions about the availability of others' mental experiences such as dreams, experiences taken to be analogous to that of the Meditator. Ultimately, however, the Meditator shares with the reader not just assumptions about the content and structure of mental experience, but also a set of theological beliefs, 'known' by revelation and taken to be — in the divine light — clearly and distinctly self-evident. Although the dreams Descartes evokes in the Meditations are not prophetic ones, the Meditator and the reader have not left behind a world of divine revelation that Descartes's early dream-accounts no doubt inhabit more fully.

Notes to Chapter 6

1. Geneviève Rodis-Lewis suggests that the account of the dreams is Edenic. Descartes had dreamed of becoming 'like the Gods in knowledge' (note the plural), after which he awoke with a sharp pain in his left side. But if the story suggests Genesis, albeit somewhat obliquely, it is also residually Neoplatonic: what was perhaps simply a moment of indigestion is converted into divine inspiration, ultimately into Descartes's Christian philosophical vocation. I discuss these dreams in greater detail in a longer version of this material, in preparation. See Geneviève Rodis-Lewis, 'Descartes: the development of his philosophy', in *The Cambridge Companion to Descartes*, ed. by John Cottingham (Cambridge: Cambridge University Press, 1991), pp. 21–57 (p. 31).

2. I cite, throughout, the text of Adam and Tannery, *Oeuvres de Descartes*, 11 vols (Paris: Vrin, 1983 [reprint]), henceforward AT, retaining the post-classical diacritical marks. The English translations are those of John Cottingham, in René Descartes, *Meditations on First Philosophy, with Selections from the Objections and Replies*. Translated by John Cottingham, with an introductory essay by Bernard Williams and a new introduction by John Cottingham (Cambridge: Cambridge University Press, 1996). I have on occasion modified Cottingham's punctuation (and, rarely, his choice of words), generally without comment, in order to recapture some of the cumulative swell of Descartes's sentences. (When translations are offered without attribution, they are mine.) The French and English texts of the *Meditations* are also available in a useful trilingual HTML Edition, edited by David B. Manley and Charles S. Taylor [1996/2013] <http://www.wright.edu/~charles.taylor/descartes/> [consulted 1 May 2016]. This website contains John Veitch's nineteenth-century translation of the work, which, though not as careful as Cottingham's, perhaps gives a better sense of the text's rhythm and rhetorical construction.

3. The passage does not detain Harry Frankfurt, for example, in his exhaustive close reading of that Meditation, nor Bernard Williams in his classic study of Descartes. An exception is Timothy J. Reiss, 'Descartes's Silences on Slavery and Race', in Andrew Valls, *Race and Racism in Modern Philosophy* (Ithaca: Cornell University Press, 2005), pp. 16–42. See Harry Frankfurt's classic *Dreams, Dreamers and Madmen: The Defense of Reason in Descartes's Meditations* (first edition) (Indianapolis and New York: Bobbs-Merrill, 1970); revised edition consulted for this essay (Princeton: Princeton University Press, 2008). Bernard Williams, *Descartes: the Project of Pure Enquiry* (London: Routledge, 2005, first edition London: Penguin, 1978). An English translation of Baillet's paraphrase by John F. Benton is provided as an appendix to W. T. Jones's article on

Descartes's dreams, 'Somnio ergo sum: Descartes's three dreams', *Philosophy and Literature*, 4.2 (1980), pp. 145–62 (the appendix is on pp. 162–66 of the same journal volume).
4. Descartes circulated his Latin philosophical treatise, *Meditations on First Philosophy* (subtitled *In which the existence of God and the immortality of the soul are demonstrated*), to philosophers, theologians, and logicians. Their Objections were included in the first publication of the *Meditations* in 1641, together with Descartes's Replies.
5. There has been considerable recent interest in Descartes's rhetoric. See, for example, David Cunning, *Argument and Persuasion in Descartes' Meditations* (Oxford: Oxford University Press, 2010), and Jean-Pierre Cavaillé, *Descartes, la fable du monde* (Paris: Vrin, 1991). Emma Gilby is preparing a book-length study on Descartes's argument and rhetorical and poetic theory; Shizuka Kubota has recently defended *Descartes et l'éloquence de la vérité. Les héritages jésuite et humaniste* (doctoral thesis, University of Paris-IV, 2012).
6. Object constancy is the sense, developed in early childhood, that objects continue to exist when they are hidden from view.
7. The question of animal minds is a burning ethical one, as well as one concerning the particularities of cognition: Animals seem to have 'minds' of various complexities: a great many seem to have a sense of object constancy, some indeed have linguistic capacities. Chimpanzees can be taught human sign languages and also can teach them to each other.
8. From antiquity, Aristotelian philosophers distinguished between types of souls (vegetative, sensitive, and rational), recognising that animals with the power of locomotion were alive in ways different from plants as well as from humans. (It is the highest of these, the 'rational soul', that might seem to correspond to 'mind', although the distinction between 'rational' and 'sensitive' is not really tenable for our purposes: how animals and people move can tell us much about what they might be thinking.)
9. Montaigne, *Essais* (II.12): '(c) Quand je me joue à ma chatte, qui sçait si elle passe son temps de moy plus que je ne fay d'elle.' Michel de Montaigne, *Les Essais*, ed. by P. Villey and V. L. Saulnier (Paris: Presses Universitaires de France, 1965), p. 452. All subsequent references to Montaigne in the original French are to this edition. [[c] 'When I play with my cat, who knows if I am not a pastime to her more than she is to me?']. Michel de Montaigne, *The Complete Essays of Montaigne*, trans. by Donald Frame (Stanford: Stanford University Press, 1958 & reprints), p. 331. The example of the dreaming dog given by Descartes's correspondent no doubt comes from Lucretius via Montaigne. *Essais*, II.12, p. 482 [English translation, p. 355].
10. The *Discours de la méthode* (1637) is marked by a similar slippage between singular and plural. Unlike the *Discours*, which was published in French, the *Meditations* appeared in Latin in 1641 and then in 1647 in a French translation by the Duc de Luynes. Clerselier translated the objections and responses for publication.
11. 'Nous' is indeed somewhat more salient in the French translation than in the Latin (where the first person plural is, for the most part, marked by conjugation and not pronouns). See the discussion of procedurals below in note 13.
12. Diane Blakemore, *Semantic Constraints on Relevance*. Oxford: Blackwell, 1987, p. 144.
13. I am grateful to Kirsti Sellevold for encouraging me to explore the category of 'procedurals', which she has used fruitfully in her close readings of Montaigne and to which she returns in her article in this volume. Deirdre Wilson has recently characterised this distinction in the following way:

> 'The conceptual/procedural distinction **cross-cuts** the TC/Non-TC distinction.
> [...] Some *non-truth-conditional* adverbials (e.g. *unfortunately, seriously*) encode concepts.
> [...] Some *truth-conditional* items (e.g. *I, she, now, then*) don't encode full-fledged concepts.
> [...] Some *non-truth-conditional* items (e.g. mood indicators, particles, interjections, intonation) encode procedural constraints on *speech-act, propositional-attitude or affective-attitude* information (analysed in terms of *higher-order explicatures* rather than implicatures).'

'Semantics, pragmatics and the conceptual-procedural distinction'. Paper given at the University of Ghent in November 2012 <http://www.gist.ugent.be/file/378> [accessed 1 May 2016].
14. For example, the concept PANDA makes a difference to the (likely negative) truth-value of the utterance 'The panda is green', just as the necessarily non-full-fledged concept 'I' makes a difference to the (also negative) truth-value of the utterance 'I am green'.

15. Wilson, *ibid.*
16. The conceptual-procedural distinction might be thought reducible to the more familiar distinction between truth-conditional and non-truth-conditional items, a distinction that it in fact crosscuts. Pronouns are procedurals, since they do not encode full-fledged concepts, yet they remain truth-conditional, that is, they make a difference to the truth-value of utterances containing them. See the examples in note 13.
17. To speak only of pronouns here in all cases would be, of course, misleading. It would also be useful to know whether morphologically marked plurals differed in their cognitive effect from pronominally marked ones; my guiding hypothesis here is that they fall into the same procedural category but that pronouns are more emphatic. We do not have native Latin speakers, or even early modern readers schooled in Latin, of course, on whom to test this hypothesis directly, but Italian and Spanish, for example, work much the same way as Latin as far as morphological marking of verbal person is concerned, and so that is a good place to start examining this hypothesis critically.
18. On Descartes's recourse to 'usus loquendi', see my comments in *The Lying Mirror* (Geneva: Droz, 2012), ch. 1, pp. 61–62.
19. Montaigne 1965 (III.13), p. 1068.
20. In the first sentence of this quotation, Cottingham has substituted the first-person-singular pronoun for the first-person-plural one. I have revised his translation accordingly, rewriting the first sentence.
21. Note that there is some divergence in the division of this passage into sentences and indeed paragraphs. (Descartes was apparently unhappy about the paragraph divisions in the first Latin edition.) Early modern punctuation is protean, and in fact, the last two sentences are often linked in seventeenth-century printings, including the 1641 first edition. I have, for the sake of clarity, divided the passage into three parts, using //, both in the original Latin and in the English translation. I have revised Cottingham's punctuation — his translation often cuts up Descartes's long sentences into shorter, more easily digestible ones — in the hope of transmitting some of the rhetorical sweep of the original.
22. On Descartes's slave/captive, see Reiss 2002, p. 22. At least one contemporary dictionary places 'slave' and 'captive' in close proximity: 'esclave, captif, detenu en servitude. Captivus servus, Captivus servitutem serviens.' 'Servuus, -a -um', in Philibert Monet, *Invantaire des deus langues, françoise et latine: assorti des plus utiles curiosités des deux idiomes* (Lyon: C. Obert, 1636), p. 335.
23. The argument that Descartes is particularly concerned with memory has been attacked, most famously by Frankfurt (see Frankfurt 1970/2008, in particular pp. 92, 105–06, and 215–34). Matthew L. Jones, for example, has since suggested plausibly that memory is more central than Frankfurt allows it to be. See, for example, his 'Descartes's Geometry as Spiritual Exercise', *Critical Inquiry*, 28.1 (2001), pp. 40–71.
24. According to Baillet, Descartes claimed that, in his third dream, he was aware that he was dreaming before it was over and indeed started to interpret the dream before waking.
25. In this interpretation, I differ somewhat from Harry Frankfurt's understanding of the temporality of the *Meditations*, which I take as simultaneously occupying the state of having been completed, taking place, and being still to be undertaken by the reader. Compare, however, Frankfurt's intriguing suggestion: 'There is no need, then, to maintain categorically either that Descartes empties his mind before he presents his sceptical arguments or that he introduces these arguments in order to accomplish the overthrow of his beliefs. When a person makes the resolution that rids his mind of all his opinions, his situation is like that of the smoker who decides to give up his habit: it remains to be seen whether the resolution is actually tantamount to bringing about the intended result. Descartes makes his resolution before he begins to review and criticize his beliefs; he overthrows his opinions, in this sense, at the very start of his meditations. From that point on he is committed to conducting his inquiry without assuming any of the beliefs he has overthrown. His resolution is not adequately reinforced or confirmed, however, until he has provided himself with reasons for doubting the overthrown beliefs. In this sense, his effort to empty his mind is not complete until, at the end of the First Meditation, he has developed arguments that systematically undermine his former opinions.' (Frankfurt 2008, 30)
26. I am grateful to Kirsti Sellevold for the formulation in this sentence and the previous one.

27. I wish to thank Terence Cave, Katherine Ibbett, Nicholas Hammond, Ita Mac Carthy, Joseph Pearson, Kirsti Sellevold, and Olivia Smith for their very helpful comments on a draft of this chapter.

CHAPTER 7

Fiction, Vision, Dream, Revelation: D'Aubigné's *Tragiques* and the Ocean episode[1]

Kathryn Banks

Introduction

Agrippa d'Aubigné's *Tragiques* (1616) raises questions about the scope and limits of diverse sources of knowledge — such as vision or revelation or fiction — and about the relationships between these sources. The poem, written by an ardent Calvinist during the late sixteenth and early seventeenth centuries, presents the French Wars of Religion within a providential perspective, beginning with the Wars and finishing with the Apocalypse which will conclude human history. As such, it contains much historical and biblical material. At the same time, it includes both obvious fictions and also visions which the poet himself claims to have had. This juxtaposition of fictions and visions with historical events and a biblical framework means that questions about their status are critical. Moreover, at some points in the poem, readers are clearly invited to reflect on such questions. This is nowhere more true than in the much analysed 'vision' of 'Ocean', which confronts the reader with a particularly complex account of the status and sources of the poem's knowledge. The episode draws attention to a number of such sources and, at the same time, silently makes use of a hitherto unacknowledged source in the form of a passage from the Book of Revelation and, in addition, at a key juncture calls on the discourse of prodigies, in a way also hitherto unacknowledged. To explore the issues raised, I shall employ insights into human knowing from the cognitive sciences: first, into metarepresentations; second, into embodied cognition. My aim is twofold: first, to offer a new understanding of the Ocean episode and of d'Aubigné's poem; and second, to make a case for how literary scholars can utilize knowledge about metarepresentations and sensorimotor resonance in producing new readings of texts.

The Ocean episode represents a key juncture in the poem because it is situated at the end of the fifth book and the poem's focus will shift significantly in the final two books which follow. Whereas the first five books foreground the trials and tribulations of the Protestants, the final two books — 'Vengeance' and 'Jugement' — focus on divine justice. The final two books are also more prophetic in tone,

Mais premier que d'entrer au prevoir, et descrire
Tes derniers jugements, les arrests de ton ire:
Il faut faire une pause, et finir ces discours
Par une vision, qui couronne ces jours:
1445 L'esprit aiant encor congé par son extase
De ne suivre escrivant du vulgaire la phrase.
   L'Ocean donc estoit tranquille et sommeillant
Au bout du sein breton, qui s'enfle en recueillant
Tous les fleuves françois, la tournoyante Seine,
1450 La Gironde, Charente, et Loire, et la Vilaine:
Ce viellard refoulloit ses cheveux gris et blonds
Sur un lict relevé dans son paisible fonds,
Marqueté de coral, et d'unions exquises:
Les sachets d'ambre gris: dessous ses tresses grises:
1455 Les vents, les plus discrets, luy chatouilloient le dos,
Les limphes de leurs mains avoient faict ce repos,
La paillasse de mousse, et les matras d'esponge:
Mais ce profond sommeil fut resveillé d'un songe:
La lame de la mer estant comme du laict,
1460 Les nids des alcyons y nageoient à souhait:
Entre les flots sallez, et les ondes de terre
S'esmeut par accidens une subite guerre:
Le dormant pense ouir un contraste de vents
Qui du haut de la mer jusqu'aux sables mouvants
1465 Troubloient tout son royaume et sans qu'il y consente
Vouloient à son deceu ordonner la tourmente.
Comment? (dit le viellard) l'air volage et leger
Ne sera il jamais lassé de m'outrager,
De ravager ainsy mes provinces profondes?
1470 Les ondes font les vents, comme les vents les ondes,
Ou bien l'air pour le moins ne s'anime en fureurs
Sans le consentement des corps superieurs:
Je pousse les vapeurs causes de la tourmente,
L'air soit content de l'air, l'eau de l'eau est contente.
1475 Le songe le trompoit, comme quand nous voions
Un soldat s'affuster, aussy tost nous oions
Le bruict d'une fenestre, ou celuy d'une porte
Quand l'esprit va devant les sens: en mesme sorte
Le songeur prit les sons de ces flots mutinez,
1480 Encontre d'autres flots jappans enfellonnez,
Pour le trouble de l'air, et le bruit de tempeste,
Il esleve en frottant sa venerable teste,
Premier un fer poinctu paroist, et puis le front,
Ses cheveux regrissez par la colere en rond,
1485 Deux testes de dauphins, et les deux balais sortent
Qui nagent à fleur d'eau, et sur leur dos le portent:
Il trouva cas nouveau, lorsque son poil tout blanc
Ensanglanta sa main: puis voyant à son flanc
Que l'onde refuiant laissoit sa peau rougie:

	But before entering into foreseeing, and describing
	Your last judgements, the sentences of your wrath:
	I must pause, and finish these discourses
	With a vision, which crowns these days:
1445	My soul again given leave by its ecstasy
	Not to follow, when writing, the everyday mode of expression.
	Ocean, then, was calm and sleeping
	At the end of the Breton bay, that swells as it receives
	All the French rivers, the winding Seine,
1450	The Gironde, Charente, and Loire, and Vilaine:
	This old man was making flow out behind him his grey and blond hair
	On a bed set up in its peaceful depths,
	Inlaid with coral, and exquisite large pearls:
	The cushions of ambergris: beneath his grey tresses:
1455	The gentlest winds were caressing his back,
	The waters with their hands had made this resting place,
	The bed of moss, and the mattresses of sponge:
	But this deep sleep was disturbed by a dream:
	The waves of the sea being like milk,
1460	The nests of the halcyons were floating there freely:
	Between the salty waters, and the earth's waves
	There breaks out owing to circumstances a sudden war:
	The sleeper thinks he hears warring winds
	Which from the top of the sea to the shifting sands
1465	Were disturbing his entire kingdom and without his consent
	Wanted unbeknown to him to marshal a tempest.
	What? (says the old man) will the fickle and inconstant air
	Never be tired of wronging me,
	Of ravaging in this way my deep provinces?
1470	The waves make the winds, like the winds the waves,
	Or at least the air is not working itself into a frenzy
	Without the consent of the higher bodies:
	I drive off the vapours which cause the tempest,
	Let the air be content with the air, water is content with water.
1475	The dream was deceiving him, as when we see
	A soldier ready himself, as soon as we hear
	The noise of a window, or that of a door
	When the mind runs ahead of the senses: in the same way
	The dreamer took the noise of these waves become tempestuous,
1480	Towards other waves which were raging and grown fierce,
	For the disturbance of the air, and the sound of storm,
	He raises his venerable head, rubbing it,
	First a pointed shaft appears, and then his brow,
	His hair standing on end around his head from anger,
1485	The heads of two dolphins, and the two tails emerge
	As they skim along the water, and carry him on their backs:
	He discovered a novel matter [/ cause for complaint; 'cas']³, when his completely white hairs
	Bloodied his hand: then seeing on his side
	That the passing wave was leaving his skin reddened:

```
1490   A moy, (dit-il) à moy, pour me charger d'envie,
       A moy: qui dans mon sein ne souffre point les morts,
       La charongne, l'ordure, ains la jette à mes bords:
       Bastardes de la terre, et non filles des nües,
       Fiebvres de la nature: allons testes cornües
1495   De mes beliers armez, repoussez-les, heurtez
       Qu'ils s'en aillent ailleurs purger leurs cruautez.
            Ainsy la mer alloit faisant changer de course
       Des gros fleuves à mont vers la coulpable sourse
       D'où sortoit par leurs bords un deluge de sang
1500   A la teste des siens: l'Ocean au chef blanc
       Vid les cieux s'entrouvrir, et les anges à troupes
       Fondre de l'air en bas, ayants en main des coupes
       De precieux rubis, qui plongez dedans l'eau,
       En chantant rapportoient quelque present nouveau,
1505   Ces messagers aislez, ces anges de lumiere
       Trioient le sang meurtry d'avec l'onde meurtriere
       Dans leurs vases remplis qui prenoient, heureux, lieu
       Aux plus beaux cabinets du palais du grand Dieu:
       Le soleil qui avoit mis un espais nuage
1510   Entre le vilain meurtre, et son plaisant visage,
       Ores de chauds rayons exhale à soy le sang
       Qu'il faut qu'en rouge pluie il renvoye à son rang:
       L'Ocean du soleil, et du troupeau qui vole
       Ayant prins sa leçon change advis et parolle.
1515        Venez enfants du ciel (s'escria le viellard)
       Heritiers du royaume, à qui le ciel despart
       Son champ pour cimetiere: ô Saincts que je repousse!
       Pour vous non contre vous, juste, je me courrouce,
       Il s'avance dans Loire, il rencontre les bords,
1520   Les sablons cramoisis bien tapissez de morts:
       Curieux il assemble, il enleve, il endure
       Cette chere despouille au rebours de nature:
       Ayant tout arrangé, il tourne avec les yeux
       Et le front serené ces parolles aux cieux.
1525   Je garderay ceux-cy tant que Dieu me commande
       Que les filz du bon-heur à leur bon-heur je rende,
       Il n'i a rien d'infect, ils sont purs, ils sont nets:
       Voicy les parements de mes beaux cabinets:
       Terre qui les trahis, tu estois trop impure
1530   Pour des saincts et des purs estre la sepulture.
       A tant il plonge au fond: l'eau rid en mille rais,
       Puis aiant faict cent ronds, crache le sable apres.
            (V, 1441–1532)
```

	To me, (he said) to me, to burden me with hatred,
1490	To me, (he said) to me, to burden me with hatred,
	To me, I who in my bosom do not suffer the dead,
	Rotting flesh, filth, but throw it onto my shores:
	Bastards of the earth, and not daughters of the clouds,
	Suppurations of nature: come horned heads
1495	Of my armed rams, drive them back, strike
	That they depart elsewhere to purge their violence.
	Thus the sea was flowing and changing the course
	Of the great rivers upstream towards the guilty source
	Whence was emerging on their shores a deluge of blood
1500	At their head: white-headed Ocean
	Saw the heavens part, and throngs of angels
	Stream down from the air to below, holding in their hands goblets
	Of precious rubies, [angels] who, having plunged into the water,
	While singing were bringing back a new offering,
1505	These winged messengers, these angels of light
	Were separating the murdered blood from the murdering water
	Into their filled vases which, blessed, were taking their place
	In the most beautiful cabinets of the palace of the great God:
	The sun which had put a thick cloud
1510	Between the ugly murders, and its charming face,
	Now with hot rays breathes up to itself the blood
	Which it must as red rain send back to its place:
	The Ocean from the sun, and from the flying flock
	Having learned his lesson changes opinion and speech.
1515	Come children of heaven (cried out the old man)
	Heirs of the kingdom, to whom heaven accords
	Its terrain for a cemetery: O Saints whom I drive back!
	For you, not with you, just [/justifiably], I am angry,
	He advances in the Loire, he reaches the shores,
1520	The crimson sands well carpeted with the dead:
	Diligently he collects, he picks up, he endures
	These dear corpses contrary to nature:
	Having arranged everything, he directs with his gaze
	And becalmed brow these words to the heavens.
1525	I shall keep these until God commands me
	To render the sons of felicity to their felicity,
	There is nothing in them which is corrupt, they are pure, they are clean:
	They shall be the adornments of my beautiful cabinets:
	Earth who betrayed them, you were too impure
1530	To be the tomb of the saints and the pure.
	Thereupon he plunges into the depths: the water smiles in a thousand rays,
	Then having made many ripples, spits out the sand after him.[4]

more dominated by a concern with revelation. The fifth book concludes with the story of Ocean (except that a further thirty lines set up the theme of the following book, 'Vengeance', by lamenting the fallen honour of France before appealing to foreigners to avenge the faithful French and reminding the reader that God himself seeks revenge). Moreover the poet himself says of the Ocean episode that it is intended to 'crown' the preceding books, suggesting that it constitutes some sort of conclusion to everything which has preceded it.[2]

Sources of Knowledge

i. Vision

The poem describes the episode as a 'vision' (l. 1444). The reader may well imagine, therefore, that it will contain truths.[5] Marguerite Soulié notes that we should take the word 'vision' seriously, since d'Aubigné never attaches negative associations to it.[6] Furthermore, the word 'vision' will be used repeatedly in the prayer which opens the following book and which reflects on the Old Testament prophet Joel's claim that, as God warns the Israelites of his forthcoming judgement, 'your old men shall dream dreams, / your young men shall see *visions*';[7] thus it suggests a similarity between the Ocean episode and the insights which follow in the sixth book, which are inspired by the Old Testament and by the history of the early Church as well as more recent history (VI, 141–1122). Furthermore, although the term 'vision' does not appear previously in the fifth book, much of the book (V, 250–1190) has been composed of what might easily be described as visions: scenes which the poet claims to have witnessed painted on the heavens when, badly injured after being attacked at Beauce in the aftermath of the St. Bartholomew's Day Massacre of 1572, he was in an 'ecstatic' state of 'enthusiasm'.[8] Although the paratextual 'Avis au lecteur' defends the presentation of these scenes as 'celestial tableaux' with reference to the 'inventions' of epic poets,[9] the tableaux depict past historical events rather than fictions. In addition, the poet's angelic guide even briefly deciphers for him a dazzling celestial display representing future events (V, 1239–1416). The final 'crowning vision' of Ocean follows these insights directly. Furthermore, it is experienced in a state of 'ecstasy' (1445), and we are told this just fifteen lines after the angel's intervention has reminded us that the earlier insights were similarly achieved by the 'ecstatic' separation of the poet's soul from his body.[10] However, it immediately becomes clear that this final 'vision' is very different from those which have preceded it, as well as from those which follow it in the sixth book.

ii. (Prophetic?) Poetic fiction

The central character of the 'vision' is Ocean, personified as in Greek mythology. In other words, this is a fiction characteristic of poetry. Such an extended focus on a figure from Greco-Roman mythology is very unusual, indeed unique, in the *Tragiques*, and so draws attention to itself. The passage also signals its status as poetry through intertextual reference to Vergil and more loosely to other epics, and through an ornate and descriptive style which evokes the Pléiade or indeed Vergil.[11] Moreover, as well as using poetic fiction ostensively, the passage also invites us to consider the possibility of poetic inspiration. As Jean-Raymond Fanlo has observed, d'Aubigné's evocation of Ocean's 'kingdom' ('royaume', l. 1465) recalls Ocean's palace in Ronsard's famous 'Ode à Michel de l'Hôpital, where Jupiter explains to the Muses that poetry stems from divine fury.[12] Furthermore, in the *Tragiques* Ocean's waters become bloodied and full of corpses, reminding readers of the bloodied and bone-strewn waters of poetic inspiration depicted in the first book of d'Aubigné's poem.[13] This raises questions about whether d'Aubigné's poetic fiction might be inspired and prophetic, a vehicle of divinely-inspired truth. It is worth recalling here that in France in the latter decades of the sixteenth century it was Calvinists who seemed most committed to alignments of poetry and prophecy, and the notion of poetic inspiration seems to have held a special appeal for them. Furthermore, it was epic poetry — evoked by the Ocean passage and more broadly by the *Tragiques* as a whole — which was in particular considered prophetic: Homer was the paradigmatic prophetic poet in the sixteenth century, and it was in their editions of Homer in particular that the Calvinists Jean de Sponde and Henri Estienne promoted a prophetic vision of poetry.[14]

iii. Ocean's dream and vision

From the outset, then, the passage draws attention to itself as both a vision and a fiction, while at the same time pointing to questions about the degree to which fiction might itself be inspired and thus by implication similar in status to vision. To complicate things further, parts of the passage are attributed to dreams or visions experienced (within the poet's own vision) by Ocean. Ocean experiences a dream which, we are told, misleads him (l. 1475), giving him the false impression that the air is attacking his water. Subsequently he has a vision ('l'Ocean au chef blanc / Vid ...', ll. 1499–1500) of the heavens opening, angels descending to collect blood from the water to be displayed in God's palace, and the sun breathing in the blood for subsequent use as blood rain.

iv. History

Another source for the episode is recent history. Ocean initially blames the disturbance on the winds, in an imitation from the *Aeneid*;[15] however, when he apprehends the bloodied water, his initial interpretation does not seem to fit and the episode becomes less like poetic fiction. The contemporary reader would have understood that the blood had come from the Protestant bodies which were cast into rivers after the St Bartholomew's Day Massacre of 1572 which had been presented at length in the 'celestial tableaux' (V, 705–1200). Indeed the bloodying of the waterways by the Protestant corpses is treated only 350 lines before the Ocean episode (V, 1081–1092). Furthermore, the notion of Ocean's horror at the blood can be traced to other contemporary poetic accounts of the same event. A poem by Jean Dorat first published in 1573 had suggested that even Ocean, who usually washes away all stains, rejected the corpses of the sacrilegious Protestants.[16] Another poem, collected by Simon Goulart in the *Memoires de l'Estat de France sous Charles IX*, noted simply that the blood horrified the 'venerable Ocean'.[17] D'Aubigné thus builds on and rewrites other historical accounts written in poetic form. Once the bloody bodies emerge in Ocean's realm, it becomes clear that there is a greater link to the earlier visions of book V than initially seemed to be the case: while one source for the Ocean episode is ostensive fiction, another is history.

v. Prodigy literature

The way in which readers are invited to understand the bodies and blood has yet another source: the discourse of prodigies, which flourished in France during the Wars of Religion, as evidenced in particular by the frequent reprinting of the *Histoires prodigieuses*.[18] Critics have noted that the 'rouge pluie' which the heavens will send (l. 1512) resembles prodigies recorded in the sixteenth century. However, the influence of prodigy culture is far more important to the episode than this. It emerges at the decisive juncture when Ocean first encounters the blood, because the expression 'cas nouveau' (l. 1487) acts as a pointer to the reader to understand the bloody water as a prodigy. The term *cas* was used frequently to refer to prodigies in volume III of the *Histoires prodigieuses* and also reasonably often in volume V.[19] It was accompanied by an adjective, sometimes *nouveau*, the adjective used by d'Aubigné, or often other adjectives which similarly suggest that what is important about prodigies is that they are novel or go beyond the usual order of things.[20] Furthermore, the use of the adjective *nouveau* alongside *cas* to signify a prodigy is not restricted to the *Histoires prodigieuses*: translating Plutarch's description in the *Lives* of the prodigies witnessed at the time of Hannibal's victories in Italy, George de Selve had referred to '*cas nouveaulx* et estranges, et contraires à tout ordre ou raison de nature'.[21] In addition, d'Aubigné will tell us that the 'cas nouveau' of the corpses — or Ocean's response to them — goes against nature ('au rebours de nature', l. 1522), recalling an idea central not only to the *Histoires prodigieuses* but also to medieval writing on prodigies, which employed the common formula that prodigies are produced 'contra naturam' ('against nature').[22]

Ocean's discovery of a 'cas nouveau' is the turning point which sets in motion the chain of events which lead to his 'vision'. It is made more striking by enjambement and by the placing of the shocking word 'ensanglanta' in a prominent position at the start of the ensuing line: Ocean 'trouva cas nouveau, lorsque son poil tout blanc / Ensanglanta sa main' (ll. 1487–8). At this key moment, the expression 'cas nouveau' highlights for the reader the sense that the emphasis is shifting from poetic discourse to the real. Indeed the hair on Ocean's head is at this point 'en rond' not because it is crowned by the laurels of poetic glory but rather because it is sticking up in anger (l. 1484), and furthermore Ocean's hair ('poil') is covered in blood (l. 1487). Moreover, 'cas nouveau' signals a real which is not that of history alone but also that of divine justice. The well-established tradition of prodigies inherited from both the Bible and Greco-Roman paganism treated prodigies as divine messages and signs of things to come, and similarly almost all sixteenth-century authors saw prodigies as divine signs.[23] Indeed the term 'cas', while often used to describe a novel occurrence in itself, was also employed to describe its conjunction with that which it signified.[24] At the beginning of the first volume of the *Histoires prodigieuses*, Pierre Boaistuau's prefatory address to Jean de Rieux explains that prodigies reveal God's anger so that we sense the violence of his justice.[25] In the third, fourth and fifth volumes of the *Histoires* — published between 1575 and 1582 at the height of the Wars of Religion — an increasingly apocalyptic tenor becomes clear. For example, recent prodigies including a river turned to blood are explained with reference to a lesson drawn from Scripture that prodigies indicate universal divine punishment, and readers are informed that they should not doubt that the recent prodigies discussed indicate that the end of the world and Last Judgement are approaching and indeed are already here.[26] Therefore, in the *Tragiques* 'cas nouveau' suggests to the reader that — like prodigies in the Bible — the blood and bodies constitute a sign, most probably of divine justice and quite possibly of the proximity of the Last Judgement. Ocean himself will discover this as the episode progresses: he realises that the 'cas nouveau' he experiences is to be understood in relation to the Last Judgement, and thus interprets it within an apocalyptic framework, much as the *Tragiques* as a whole understands history from a providential perspective.

vi. The Book of Revelation

A final — and absolutely crucial — unnamed source is a passage from the Book of Revelation, the New Testament account of apocalypse which profoundly influenced d'Aubigné's providential conception of history.[27] As critics have noted, when the sun breathes in the blood for subsequent use as blood rain, this blood rain is presumably that predicted by Revelation. Indeed, in Revelation 16 the blood rain bloodies the sea 'as if from a corpse', a little as the blood rain in the *Tragiques* follows the bloodying of Ocean by actual corpses.[28] Much more importantly, though, it seems to me without doubt that the conclusion of the episode — when Ocean declares to the heavens that he will keep the bodies 'until such a time as God commands him to give them up to their bliss' (ll. 1523–6) — is a creative gloss on Revelation 20. 13, which suggests that for the Last Judgement the sea will give up the bodies contained within it: '*And the sea gave up the dead which were in it; and death and hell delivered up the dead which were in them: and they were judged every man according to their works*'.[29] When Ocean decides to store the dead bodies until the Last Judgement, he is playing the role prophesied for him in the Book of Revelation. (A much earlier passage from the *Tragiques* provides further evidence of a connection between the Ocean episode and Revelation 20. 13 because it shares key themes with the Ocean episode and also cites Revelation 20. 13 more directly).[30] The connection between Revelation 20. 13 and the conclusion of the Ocean episode is not noted in the extensive indices of biblical echoes compiled by Elliott Forsyth and Marguerite Soulié,[31] nor, to my knowledge, in any other analysis of d'Aubigné's poem. However, it seems to me very likely that many sixteenth- and early seventeenth-century readers would have recognized it, given the centrality of the Bible at this time and also the interest in apocalypse (especially among some Calvinists).

* * * * *

So the passage has a wide array of sources, in some cases tagged explicitly as such or otherwise drawing attention to their role: it is labelled as a vision, it contains a dream, and it also draws on poetic fiction, the Bible, contemporary history, and prodigy culture. The multiplicity of sources embedded within each other becomes confusing for the reader, at least on a first reading: within a vision experienced by the poet, the fictional character Ocean has an experience grounded in history and recalling prodigy literature, a dream which misleads him, and a vision containing material derived from the Book of Revelation. Indeed, Ocean's own initial cognitive confusion (when he is misled by his dream) arguably reflects a cognitive confusion which, at first at least, the reader is likely to experience concerning the status of the knowledge with which the poem presents her. Thus the passage raises particularly acutely two questions which are also posed by the *Tragiques* as a whole. First, what are the implications of the multiple and diverse sources of knowledge embedded one within the other? Second, what are the scope and limits of fiction, and what is its relation to divinely inspired sources of knowledge?

D'Aubigné critics (and in particular Fanlo in his excellent monograph[32]) have paid considerable attention to the second of these two questions, while the first has been addressed only indirectly and insofar as it relates to the second. I shall begin by addressing the first question but shall then proceed also to offer a new answer to the second. To do so, I shall make use of research into metarepresentations and, more specifically, the notions of the scope problem, scope syntax and source tagging proposed by evolutionary psychologists Leda Cosmides and John Tooby.

'Source Tagging' and Metarepresentational Structures

Metarepresentations are mental representations of mental representations, higher order representations with lower order representations embedded within them, for example 'John believes that it will rain'. They have been of interest to scholars in psychology, philosophy, linguistics, and primate cognition, and are widely recognised as fundamental to human cognition, as well as to linguistic communication.[33] Research into metarepresentation has focused on so-called 'mindreading' or Theory of Mind, our human predisposition to infer (albeit imperfectly) the mental states of other people, their beliefs, desires, emotions, and intentions. In cognitive literary studies, too, metarepresentation has been analysed predominantly in the form of mindreading. In particular, Lisa Zunshine has argued that we read fiction because it 'engages, in a variety of particularly focused ways, our Theory of Mind'.[34] However, according to Cosmides and Tooby at least, metarepresentational abilities serve not only mindreading but also our more general need to know the scope of applicability of any particular item of knowledge.[35]

This need arises, Cosmides and Tooby argue, from a distinctive aspect of human evolution, namely our entry into the so-called 'cognitive niche': whereas other animals can respond to only those features of their environment present widely enough in space and time to have produced adaptations through evolution, human beings can exploit information that is local, transient and contingent, enabling us to improvise behaviour tailored to particular conditions. This peculiarly human ability exponentially increases the information at our disposal but also creates the risk of its misapplication: particular information may be useful under certain conditions, but false, misleading, or harmful outside of the scope of those conditions. To deal with this 'scope problem', Cosmides and Tooby suggest, 'the scope of applicability of the information that the individual human acquires and represents became paramount in the design and evolution of the human cognitive architecture' (p. 59), which 'ceaselessly locates, monitors, updates, and represents the conditional and mutable boundaries within which each set of representations remains useful' (p. 105), regulating their scope of applicability through so-called 'scope syntax'.

Cosmides and Tooby are working with a computational model of the brain, controversial within the cognitive sciences as well as the humanities, and often called into question in favour of more embodied views of human cognition, which certainly seem more convincing to me. However, the idea that we monitor the scope of representations, as Cosmides and Tooby put it, does seem very plausible, and various features of language point towards some kind of 'tagging'. Thus Dan Sperber and colleagues have proposed the concept of 'epistemic vigilance', a different approach to questions also addressed by the notion of scope monitoring; and scholars working on monitoring of, or vigilance towards, fiction specifically, have explored ideas of 'distancing' or 'decoupling'.[36] Attention has also been paid to linguistic devices which play a role in epistemic vigilance mechanisms, such as logical connectives and indicators of epistemic modality and evidentiality.[37] So, there is more than one model which might help us approach a text containing complex information about the status and sources of its knowledge. However, as we shall see, Cosmides and Tooby's idea of source 'tagging', and their discussion of our responses to complex metarepresentational structures, work particularly well for the multiple and embedded sources of knowledge in the Ocean episode. Furthermore, these insights can be helpfully deployed without any need to adopt wholesale the model of human cognition in which Cosmides and Tooby position them.

So, according to Cosmides and Tooby, our need to understand the scope of applicability of information can make sense of our use of metarepresentations. Cosmides and Tooby take as an example 'the statement is false that anthropology is a science'. They suggest that 'the statement is false that' constitutes a 'scope operator' which restricts the scope of the 'scope-representation' 'anthropology is a science'. It is of particular relevance to my concerns that these so-called scope operators often tag sources of information, such as another person, one's vision, or one's episodic memory (pp. 69–72). Furthermore, while the simple example above contains only one proposition in its scope-representation, sets of propositions can be bundled together and 'might become so elaborated, and relatively independent from other data structures, that they might conveniently be called worlds' (p. 61), a description with applicability to fictions or indeed visions. Moreover, propositions can also exist in 'tree structures' of subordinated and parallel relations, which Cosmides and Tooby represent as indented levels. For example:

> Chagnon was under the impression that
>   Clifford has claimed that
>   most anthropologists believe that
>   the statement is false that
>   anthropology is a science. [and]
>   quantum physicists have demonstrated that:
>   science is only an observer-dependent set of arbitrary subjective
>   opinions. (pp. 62–69)

A similarly complex 'tree structure' might be identified in the Ocean episode: the 'poet has a vision that Ocean has a dream that [...]', and so on. The episode is saturated with scope operators and in particular source tags. Some source tags are explicit ('une vision', 'un songe'). Others are evident for intertextual reasons: as discussed earlier, the figure of Ocean indicates fiction, and events in the latter part of the episode point to Revelation. In addition, questions are raised about the value of some sources, as we have seen, and the episode contains implicit indicators of the reliability or importance of sources or the knowledge they provide. For example, 'le dormant *pense* ouir' (l. 1463, my italics) marks the epistemic value of what Ocean hears as uncertain, and the procedural expression 'mais' (l. 1441) suggests that what follows is argumentatively stronger than what precedes it, thus arguably working together with the explicit tagging of content as a 'vision' which 'crowns these days'.[38]

The length and branching contingencies of tree structures are, Cosmides and Tooby suggest, restricted in practice by 'performance limitations' of the cognitive system: structures may be 'too elaborate to be placed, in their entirety, into the workspace' (p. 68). Indeed, experiments suggest that we have great difficulty keeping track of more than five levels of attribution.[39] We can make mistakes: our 'cognitive firewalls' are 'no doubt, far from perfect'.[40] These insights make it unsurprising if — faced with the 'tree structure' in the Ocean episode — we have to exert considerable effort to keep track of its multiple branches, or (at least on a first reading) become confused or make mistakes in following it. But the important question is surely *why* the tree structure in this passage is so complex. One possible answer is offered by Cosmides and Tooby themselves. Rejecting the hypothesis that the arts are simply a by-product of evolution (Steven Pinker's 'arts as cheesecake for the mind' argument)[41], they argue that 'many behaviours which have no obvious evolutionary purpose, including child's play and fiction, may be designed to 'construct the adaptation', or 'organize' it into its 'mature form'.[42] In other words, fiction enables us to exercise the cognitive architecture designed to solve the scope problem. It is this possibility which Zunshine explores in her argument that we read fiction because it constitutes a 'cognitive workout' (p. 159) for our Theory of Mind. In similar vein, d'Aubigné's complex 'tree structure' arguably provides an excellent 'workout' for cognitive capacities relating to source tagging. However, while the general question of how our human cognitive capacities might explain our reading tastes is a fascinating one, I am more interested here in how — armed with insights into, and questions about, human cognition — we might read particular texts differently. While evolved human cognitive capacities are stable across vast swathes of evolutionary time, they can be manipulated in ways which do particular work in particular cultures and in particular texts. So, what work is performed by the complex tree structure of source tags in d'Aubigné's *Tragiques*?

The difficulty of keeping track of the 'tree structure' in the Ocean episode means, it seems to me, that readers are very much on their guard, concerned about the status of the 'knowledge' which the poem offers. As we have seen, Cosmides and Tooby argue that we are cognitively predisposed ceaselessly to monitor and update the scope of applicability of any set of representations. In the Ocean episode, the multiplicity of source tags creates a strong sense of cognitive uncertainty, which is further intensified when attention is drawn to sources or their value, so that our concern with the scope of the knowledge they provide is likely to be the object of monitoring which is conscious as well as unconscious. In particular, as we have seen, the ostensive use of fiction and evocation of poetic inspiration invite questions about the scope of fiction and the status of the knowledge with which it provides us, prompting us to wonder whether the fiction with which we are presented really is inspired and thus a carrier of divine truth, or whether it might instead, like Ocean's dream, constitute delusion. The risk of error is thematized when Ocean — unaware of the source tag 'Ocean dreams that' — makes a mistake about the perturbation around him. As Cosmides and Tooby's model would predict, this sense of cognitive uncertainty operates, I think, to make readers especially watchful for any new information which could support or undermine the episode's knowledge.[43]

Therefore, readers would have been particularly likely to spot the use of Revelation 20. 13, alert to the implicit support lent to the poet's vision at the conclusion of the episode by the much more reliable source of the Bible. If we notice the use of Revelation 20. 13, then it offers us independent verification of important knowledge in the story, so that this knowledge no longer requires the source tag 'the vision or fiction of Ocean asserts that'. The sense of cognitive uncertainty created by the multiple source tags and the ostensive foregrounding of fiction is in large part resolved once the episode concludes with a biblical truth, once the strangeness of the poetic fiction spun from history is given biblical grounding. Therefore, the 'branching tree structure' creates a sense of cognitive risk which makes readers feel relieved when they spot the biblical source: the uncertainty serves to make readers experience all the more the comfort of the Bible as anchor, as source tag to be trusted.

Fiction: Revelation and Embodiment

But, to return to the second of the two questions posed earlier, what about the scope and limits of fiction, and its relation to divinely inspired sources of knowledge? Fanlo strongly emphasises a distinction between the fictional and poetic character of the Ocean episode and more broadly of book V, on the one hand, and the prophetic and apocalyptic revelation of books VI and VII, on the other.[44] However, since the fiction of Ocean ultimately gives rise to information predicted by Revelation 20. 13, in my view we cannot contrast it too sharply with prophetic or apocalyptic revelation. While of course no part of d'Aubigné's poem can have the same status as biblical prophecy or revelation themselves, the Ocean episode does share something with apocalyptic revelation. This strengthens the aforementioned sense ('(Prophetic?) Poetic Fiction', pp. 130–31) that the episode invites us to reflect on the potential of fiction to contain divine truth.

Furthermore, according to Cosmides and Tooby, we are cognitively predisposed not only to update our information on the scope of applicability of sets of representations but also to monitor for further information about their sources: 'source tags are very useful, because often, with contingent information, one may not have direct evidence about its truth, but may acquire information about the reliability of a source. If the sources of pieces of information are maintained with the information, then subsequent information about the source can be used to change the assigned truth-status of the information either upwards or downwards' (p. 69). It is also worth noting that research into epistemic vigilance mechanisms suggests that these mechanisms fall into two broad groups, one of which assesses the reliability of content and the other that of sources.[45] Developmental psychology is also suggestive: Paul L. Harris argues that children are predisposed to monitor closely the reliability of sources of information.[46]

These insights imply that readers are likely to be alert to implications in the Ocean episode of new information about poetic fiction as source of knowledge. Therefore, when events in the fiction turn out to be part of the Book of Revelation, we update our knowledge of the source (poetic fiction), as Cosmides and Tooby would put it. In other words, we learn that, despite poetic fiction's pretences such as the personification of Ocean, it can be the source of fundamental truths. Thus, while the episode's resolution of its cognitive uncertainties is typically Protestant insofar as it depends on the authority of the Bible (Revelation 20. 13), it also points to a view of fiction which is not so typically Protestant. Fiction gives rise to knowledge which already bears the source tag 'the Bible predicts that' and which therefore, for a sixteenth- or early seventeenth-century reader, barely needed a source tag at all. As such, I would argue that the episode points to the *scope* of fiction more than to its limits.

The episode also suggests that fiction has a particular connection with embodied or sensory knowledge, and raises questions about the scope of this knowledge. At the outset, Ocean snoozes in his peaceful watery bed, amid the scents of his perfumed cushions, with gentle winds caressing his back, and his bed of moss and sponge shaped by the hands of water nymphs. As critics have observed, these details are evocative of a particular type of poetic discourse, so that sensory experience seems central to poetic fiction. We are also reminded that the sensory, or our interpretation of it, can deceive us. Ocean, whose experiences have been so dominated by physical sensation, fails initially to perceive the celestial nature of the corpses. Moreover, when he is misled by his dream, this is compared to a soldier who misinterprets the sound of a banging window or door, his 'mind running ahead of his senses'.[47] Thus the episode raises questions about the value of fiction's sensory knowledge.

For Fanlo, the sensory knowledge of fiction is therefore to be contrasted with celestial insight and prophecy, grounding Fanlo's opposition between fiction and prophecy in a further opposition between embodied knowledge and disembodied voice (the prophet 'n'est que le lieu de passage d'une Voix'). According to Fanlo, when Ocean gains celestial insight, poetic fiction is given a new spiritual perspective instead of its usual sensual one: fiction contains celestial signification thanks to the rejection of sensation and natural knowledge.[48] However, to my mind, any sharp distinction between fiction and prophecy in terms of sensory knowledge is problematic because prophecy in the Book of Revelation — the example of biblical prophecy which implicitly surfaces in the episode,[49] as in the case of many Old

Testament prophets — is embodied and sensory, operating as much through concrete terms as abstract ones. More importantly, I am not convinced that d'Aubigné's Ocean episode invites us to reject sensory knowledge or to contrast it sharply with spiritual insight. Indeed sensory knowledge, while potentially problematic, also seems to be deeply connected to the scope of fiction to reveal.

A striking sensory experience occurs at the turning point of the episode, enabling Ocean to recognise the real source of the disturbance and ultimately leading to his spiritual insights. Ocean awakes to find blood in his white hair and to see the waves leaving his skin covered in blood, an experience underlined by enjambement and the positioning of 'ensanglanta', as I noted above. This nightmarish bloody awakening is all the more striking for the gentle and pleasant sensory experiences which have preceded it, when Ocean snoozed amid the scent of ambergris and the gentle touch of waters and winds. In sharp contrast with the pleasurable dozing evoked there, here we are invited to imagine an intimate bodily encounter with the blood of others — blood which has seeped from the corpses of massacre victims — to imagine waking to find blood in our hair, and waves depositing blood on our skin. The reason that the sensory nature of this depiction matters, I think, is that its implications for the role of sensory knowledge in fiction are very different from those foregrounded by Fanlo.

Recent research suggests that we ought to pay careful attention to unusual sensorimotor experiences in literature because they are central to the experience of readers. Cognition — and hence reading — is fundamentally embodied: as the philosopher Shaun Gallagher puts it, 'the broad argument about the importance of embodiment for understanding cognition has already been made in numerous ways, and there is growing consensus across a variety of disciplines that this basic fact is inescapable'.[50] One aspect of embodied cognition, which has recently been fruitfully mobilised in literary studies, is sensorimotor resonance. A growing body of scientific research suggests that when we observe the sensorimotor experience of another, we access our embodied kinaesthetic memory in order to retrieve a simulation of that experience, and so our brains respond in a way similar to if we ourselves experienced it. Furthermore, this motor resonance functions not only when we witness a sensorimotor experience visually but also when we read verbal descriptions of such an experience. Moreover, there is considerable evidence that our cognitive deployment of sensorimotor systems is greater when the description of sensorimotor experience in question is unfamiliar.[51] Therefore, the literary scholar Guillemette Bolens has argued convincingly that literature is a privileged discourse precisely because the unpredictable and surprising nature of its sensorimotor configurations has a greater impact on sensorimotor understanding than other discourses do.[52] In other words, the nightmarish awakening to find our skin and hair drenched in the blood of others is likely to make particularly strong calls on our bodily cognition.

The question of how pre-conscious sensorimotor resonance relates to conscious bodily experience is of course an acutely difficult one but, nonetheless, the neuroimaging research is suggestive. More importantly, in the particular case of the Ocean episode, we are primed in a number of ways to reflect *consciously* on the bodily aspects of our reading experience, on our embodied cognition: as we have seen, sensory knowledge has been omnipresent throughout the episode; it is bound up with the discourse of poetic fiction which is foregrounded ostensively; and the mistakes it can induce have been thematised. In other words, it is particularly likely that our bodily responses will not simply be pre-reflective but also cross into conscious reflection,[53] and furthermore that that conscious reflection will be bound up with questions of the utility and reliability of embodied insights in fiction.

Therefore, it is of central importance that Ocean's sensory experience of being drenched in blood appears to motivate the conclusion of the episode and Ocean's new spiritual insights: it sets Ocean off on his frantic quest to rid himself of the corpses, which creates a 'deluge' of blood (1499) and is followed by the angels collecting the blood and the sun breathing it in, enabling Ocean to attain his new understanding of the blood and bodies. Crucially, the new spiritual perspective gained by Ocean seems to be grounded in sensory experience, so that readers might reflect that sensory experience can play some role in spiritual insight. Moreover, the reader's own new perspective is, it seems to me, fundamentally dependent on sensorimotor inference: the bodily depiction of being drenched in blood brings home to readers, in an embodied way, what is so counter-intuitive or unnatural in the revelation Ocean experiences, that is, what it means to treasure the blood and dead bodies of others. So, while sensory experience can mislead, as an earlier part of the passage shows, it also seems crucial to what fiction does: sensory experience contributes to the scope of fiction to reveal.

Indeed, while fiction cannot be contrasted in absolute terms with Revelation on the grounds of sensory experience, it does appear to make a more pronounced use of it. Ocean's experience echoes yet also differs from Revelation: in Revelation 16, blood appears '*as if* of a dead man' ('*comme* d'une charongne') but in the Ocean episode, rather than an 'as if' (a 'comme'), there is an *actual* close embodied encounter with the *real* blood of *real* dead people. The passage concerning Ocean similarly differs from one found four hundred lines earlier in the *Tragiques* among the more historical and less fictionalised 'visions' of book V, the 'tableaux célestes', and which echoes Revelation 16 more closely than the Ocean episode does:

> Voilà Tournon, Viviers, et Vienne et Valance,
> Poussant avec terreur de Lyon l'insolence,
> Troublez de mille corps, qu'ils eslongnent, et puis
> Arles qui n'a chez soy ne fontaines ne puits
> Souffrit mourir de soif, quand du sang le passage
> Dix jours leur deffendit du Rhosne le breuvage:
> *Icy l'ange troisiesme espandit à son rang*
> *Au Rhosne sa fiole et ce fleuve fut sang:*
> *Icy l'ange des eaux cria. Dieu qu'on adore,*
> *Qui es, qui as esté, et qui seras encore:*
> *Icy tu as le droict pour tes saincts exercé*
> *Versant du sang à boire à ceux qui l'ont versé.*[54]

Cf. Et le second Ange versa sa phiole en la mer, laquelle deveint sang comme d'une charongne, et toute ame vivante mourut. Et *le troisieme Ange versa sa phiole sur les fleuves*, et sur les fontaines des eaux, *et elles devindrent sang. Et j'ouy l'Ange des eaux, disant, Seigneur, tu es juste: Qui es, et qui estois, et sainct, pource que tu as jugé ces choses. Pourtant qu'ils ont espandu le sang des saincts et des Prophetes, tu leur as aussi baillé du sang à boire: car ils en sont dignes* (Revelation 16. 3–6, my italics).[55]

In this passage of the *Tragiques*, more directly imitated from Revelation, we are told that the rivers are full of blood but we are not invited to imagine any close encounter with it; indeed the pollution of the water means precisely that people avoid it. The more fictionalised passage, by contrast, recasts ideas from the Book of Revelation in much more embodied ways, which arguably enable us to experience or know in an embodied way the content of Ocean's revelation, that is, what it might mean to treasure dead bodies.

Conclusion

This essay has demonstrated that the Ocean episode silently makes important use of a hitherto unacknowledged source, Revelation 20. 13, and also calls on the discourse of prodigies in a way hitherto unacknowledged. We can see why this matters if we situate it in relation to the episode's complex 'tree structure' of metarepresentations, that is, its multiple and diverse embedded sources of knowledge, some of which are labelled or otherwise highlighted in ways which invite us to question their status and that of the knowledge they provide. I have argued that the cognitive uncertainties created by this structure make readers particularly alert to the implicit support lent to the poet's vision at the conclusion of the episode by the reliable source of a biblical text, and therefore particularly likely not only to spot the use of Revelation 20. 13 but also to experience it as an especially comforting cognitive anchor. The use of Revelation 20.13 also points to the scope of poetic fiction, which can give rise to something like the knowledge of biblical prophecy. At the same time, fiction seems to have a connection with embodied knowledge even stronger than that of biblical prophecy, and which is deeply connected to its 'revelatory' possibilities.

What impact might this reading of the Ocean episode have upon analyses of the *Tragiques* as a whole? First, it seems to me promising to analyse the specificity of the knowledge provided by the striking embodied language of the *Tragiques* with reference to both period conceptions of sources of knowledge (such as fiction or revelation) and also modern insights into embodied cognition. More importantly, I would advocate examining from the perspective outlined in this essay the multiplicity of diverse embedded sources of knowledge in the poem, considering how it might create cognitive uncertainties, promote the search for further support for (or discrediting of) knowledge and its sources (including vision, fiction, and others), and motivate the locating by readers of additional sources which are *not* flagged up and which might therefore have been missed by critics or at least considered much less important than those which are overtly proclaimed.

Notes to Chapter 7

1. I would like to thank Terence Cave, Kirsti Sellevold and Wes Williams for their insightful comments and responses to earlier versions of this paper. I am also grateful to the editors of this volume for their helpful thoughts and assistance.
2. 'couronne ces jours', *Les Tragiques*, ed. Jean-Raymond Fanlo (Paris: Champion, 2006), book V,

1. 1444. All citations from the *Tragiques* will be from this edition. All translations are my own, unless otherwise specified.
3. See Cotgrave entry for *cas*, as well as the sense of the Latin *casus*. See also the discussion below (on pp. 132–33 above) of *cas* in prodigy literature.
4. The translation is my own. Given the likely audience of this essay, I have followed the French in a fairly word-for-word fashion so that readers can follow the French alongside the English. However, I have benefited greatly from consulting Valerie Worth-Stylianou's translation (forthcoming with AMS Press, Inc, New York) and am very grateful to her for sharing it with me.
5. Michel Jeanneret, 'Les Tableaux spirituels d'Agrippa d'Aubigné', *Bibliothèque d'humanisme et renaissance*, 35 (1973), pp. 233–45 (241).
6. 'Aucune connotation dépréciative ne marque ce mot dans le texte des *Tragiques*, et il se trouve lié, à une exception près, au don de la prophétie'. Soulié, 'Songe et Vision dans les *Tragiques* d'Agrippa d'Aubigné', in *Le Songe à la Renaissance*, Université de Saint-Étienne, 1990, p. 204. In addition to its use in this passage, *vision* appears in the following lines: II, 1178; VI, 16; VI, 39; VI, 66; VI, 88; VI, 89; VI, 817.
7. Joel II. 28–29, my italics; *Tragiques*, VI, 16, 39, 66, 88, 89.
8. 'Parmy ces aspres temps *l'esprit* ayant laissé / Aux assassins mon corps en divers lieux percé, / Par l'ange consolant mes ameres blessures, / Bien qu'impur *fut mené dans les regions pures*, / *Sept heures luy parut le celeste pourpris* / *Pour voir les beaux secrets et tableaux que j'ecris*: / Soit qu'un songe au matin m'ait donné ces images, / Soit qu'en la pasmoison l'esprit fit ces voyages, / Ne t'enquiers (mon lecteur) comment il vid et fit / Mais donne gloire à Dieu en faisant ton profit, / Et cependant qu'en luy *extatic je me pasme* / Tourne à bien les chaleurs de mon *entousiasme*' (V, 1195–1206, my italics).
9. 'Rapin, un des plus excellens esprits de son siecle, blasma l'invention des tableaux celestes, disant que nul n'avoit jamais entrepris de peindre les affaires de la terre au ciel, bien les celestes en terre, l'autheur se deffendoit par les inventions d'Homere, de Virgille, et de nouveau du Tasse qui ont feinct les conseils tenus au ciel, les brigues et partialitez des celestes sur les affaires des Grecs, des Romains, et depuis des Chrestiens' (ed. Fanlo, pp. 227–28).
10. The lines cited in n. 8 (V, 1195–1206) refer explicitly to the poet's 'ecstasy' and 'enthusiasm', as well as to his 'esprit' being guided by an angel into the 'regions pures' in order to witness the celestial tableaux. Following the celestial tableaux and preceding the Ocean episode (V, 1417–1430), the angel's words refer to the return of the poet's soul to his body and therefore remind us the intervening celestial tableaux were witnessed thanks to his ecstatic experience.
11. Fanlo, 219–21; Perrine Galand-Hallyn, *Les yeux de l'éloquence: poétiques humanistes de l'évidence* (Orléans: Paradigme, 1995), pp. 174–75; 'Enargeia maniériste, enargeia visionnaire. Des prophéties du Tibre au songe d'Océan', *Bibliothèque d'Humanisme et Renaissance*, 53 (1991), pp. 305–29 (pp. 324–25). André Baïche, 'Ovide chez d'Aubigné', *Cahiers de l'Europe classique et néolatine* I (1981), pp. 79–122 (87–88); Frank Lestringant, *Agrippa d'Aubigné: Les Tragiques* (Paris: Presses Universitaires de France, 1986), pp. 33–34; and updated edition reprinted with the collaboration of Jean-Charles Monferran as *Lire 'Les Tragiques' d'Agrippa d'Aubigné* (Paris: Classiques Garnier, 2013), p. 34. The style has been described as 'maniériste' (Galand-Hallyn, *Les Yeux*, pp. 175–78; 'Enargeia maniériste', pp. 324–28) and as 'teinté d'alexandrinisme' (for example, Lestringant, 1986, p. 33; 2013, p. 34).
12. 'Chasteau / De l'Ocean', ll. 124–25; Jupiter on inspiration, ll. 379–510, 'Ode à Michel de l'Hospital', in Pierre de Ronsard, *Oeuvres complètes*, ed. by Paul Laumonier (Paris: Libraire Hachette, 1921), III, pp. 118–63. Fanlo, *Tracés, Ruptures: La Composition instable des "Tragiques"* (Geneva: Slatkine, 1990), p. 221.
13. 'Ces ruisselets d'argent, que les Grecs nous feignoient, / Où leurs poëtes vains beuvoient et se baignoient, / Ne courent plus icy: mais les ondes si claires / Qui eurent les saphyrs et les perles contraires, / Sont rouges de noz morts: le doux bruit de leurs flots / Leur murmure plaisant hurte contre des os' (I, 59–64).
14. Jean Lecointe, *L'Idéal et la Différence: la perception de la personnalité littéraire à la Renaissance* (Geneva: Droz, 1993), pp. 351–53, 368–69. Lecointe suggests that Homer and poetic inspiration had particular appeal for Calvinists thanks to assimilations of Homeric destiny to Calvinist predestination, and of poetic inspiration to grace.

15. *Tragiques* V, 1467–74; *Aeneid* I, 132–41.
16. *Poematum liber quartus*, ed. 1586, p. 293, 'In alios Haereticos cum ipso interfectos', cited by Soulié, *L'Inspiration biblique dans la poésie religieuse d'Agrippa d'Aubigné* (Paris: Klincksieck, 1977), p. 365, n. 136.
17. Cited by Fanlo in his edition of the *Tragiques*, p. 657, note to lines 1447–32 (sic). In addition, Du Bartas's *Cantique d'Yvry* depicts a river complaining about the corpses which pollute it. *The Works of Guillaume De Salluste Sieur Du Bartas*, ed. by Urban Tigner Holmes Jr. and others (Chapel Hill: The University of North Carolina Press, 1940), III, p. 500, ll. 323–34.
18. Jean Céard, *La Nature et les Prodiges* (Geneva: Droz, 1996; first published in 1977) pp. 252–72, 317–35, 460–79; Lorraine Daston and Katharine Park, *Wonders and the Order of Nature* (New York: Zone Books; Cambridge, Mass.: Distributed by the MIT Press, 1998), p. 189.
19. Vol. III was compiled by François Belleforest. Vol. V was translated into French by Belleforest from a Latin text by Arnaud Sorbin.
20. According to Sorbin's preface at the beginning of volume V, France at present seems to produce 'de jour à autre quelque *cas de nouveau*' (*Histoires prodigieuses*, Antwerp: Guislain Ianssens, 1594, p. 628, my italics). *Cas* is also accompanied in the *Histoires prodigieuses* by adjectives including *merveilleux, extraordinaire, estrange, rare, nouveau, prodigieux, monstrueux, portentueux, effroyable, admirable*, as well as expressions such as 'qui surpasse l'ordre commun' or 'digne de (grand) merveille' or 'servant d'advertissement de notre desastre'. These highlight the novelty of the prodigy, that it is unnatural and goes beyond the usual order of things, that it causes fear or wonder, and that it signifies something about the future.
21. In his translation of eight of Plutarch's *Lives*, Paris: Michel de Vascosan, 1543, f. 46v (Life of Fabius Maximus, ff. 46r-59v); my italics. De Selve's translation was republished in Paris in 1547 by Arnoul l'Angelier and again in Lyon in 1548 by Jean de Tournes.
22. For example, 'telles apparitions, comme elles ne sont point du cours de la nature, aussi signifient-elles quelque cas extraordinaire en icelle, et des menaces aux hommes' (1594 ed. cit., p. 455). See also n. 20. Daston and Park, p. 50. Note also that the disturbance in the *Tragiques* episode is said to occur 'par accidens' (l. 1462) and thus is implicitly opposed to that which might occur 'par nature'.
23. Céard, *La Nature et les Prodiges*.
24. For example: 'Or est ce ung cas notable et digne d'admiration que du temps mesme que nasquit ce monstre composé de forme humaine et chienne né en Albanie, la cité de Montauban en Quercy fut deschiree [...] par les enragées morsures et abboix pestilentieux des heretiques Albigeois' (1594 ed. cit., pp. 661–62 ; book V, ch. 5).
25. 1594 ed. cit., f. A2r.
26. Vol. IV, ch. 9; ed. cit. 1594, pp. 617–21.
27. Richard L. Regosin, 'Protestant Apocalypse', in *The Poetry of Inspiration: Agrippa d'Aubigné's 'Les Tragiques'* (Chapel Hill: The University of North Carolina Press, 1970), pp. 55–78.
28. 'Et le second Ange versa sa phiole en *la mer, laquelle deveint sang comme d'une charongne*, et toute ame vivante mourut. Et le troisieme Ange versa sa phiole sur les fleuves, et sur les fontaines des eaux, et elles devindrent sang' (Revelation 16. 3–6, 1562 Geneva Bible, f. 98r, my italics; edition consulted available at <http://dx.doi.org/10.3931/e-rara-3226> [accessed 8 May 2016]). 'And the second angel poured out his vial upon the sea; and it became as the blood of a dead man: and every living soul died in the sea. And the third angel poured out his vial upon the rivers and fountains of waters; and they became blood.' This and other English Bible translations are those of the King James Bible, consulted at <http://www.kingjamesbibleonline.org/> [accessed 8 May 2016]. See also 'Et le premier Ange sonna de la trompette: et fut faite gresle et feu meslez de sang [...] et la tierce partie de la mer deveint sang' (Revelation 8. 7–8, f. 96r) and 'Ceux-ci ont puissance de fermer le ciel, qu'il ne pleuve és jours de leur prophetie: et ont puissance sur les eaux de les tourner en sang (Revelation 11. 6, f. 96v).
29. '*Et la mer rendit les morts qui estoyent en elle*: et la mort et enfer rendirent les morts qui estoyent en eux: *et fut fait jugement de chacun selon leurs œuvres*' (Geneva Bible, ed. cit., f. 99r, my italics).
30. III, 654–72. Critics have noted that the final two lines of this earlier passage recall Revelation 20. 13. The passage has in common with the Ocean episode the idea of corpses as the ornamentation or decoration of heaven, the use of vases, and the collection by angels of human remains.

31. Forsyth, *La Justice de Dieu. "Les Tragiques" d'Agrippa d'Aubigné et la Réforme protestante en France au XVIe siècle* (Paris: Champion, 2005), pp. 477–550; Soulié, *L'Inspiration*, pp. 527–36.
32. *Tracés, Ruptures*, pp. 217–30.
33. *Metarepresentations: A Multidisciplinary Perspective*, ed. by Dan Sperber (NY: Oxford UP, 2000). For an overview, see Sperber's Introduction to the volume, pp. 3–13. On language, see Deirdre Wilson, 'Metarepresentation in Linguistic Communication', pp. 411–48.
34. *Why We Read Fiction: theory of mind and the novel* (Ohio State University Press, 2006), p. 162. Zunshine also uses the broader concept of metarepresentations, as do the following studies. Stefan Iversen, 'States of Exception: Decoupling, Metarepresentation, and Strange Voices in Narrative Fiction', in *Strange Voices in Narrative Fiction*, ed. by Per Krogh Hansen and others (Walter de Gruyter and Co., 2011), pp. 127–46; Barbara MacMahon. 'Metarepresentation and Decoupling in *Northanger Abbey*', *English Studies*, 90 (2009), pp. 518–44, pp. 673–94; MacMachon and Lisa Hopkins, '"Come, what, a siege?": Metarepresentation in Lady Jane Cavendish and Lady Elizabeth Brackley's *The Concealed Fancies*', *Early Modern Literary Studies*, 22 (2013), pp. 1–17.
35. 'Consider the Source: The Evolution of Adaptations for Decoupling and Metarepresentation', in *Metarepresentations*, pp. 53–115.
36. Sperber et al., 'Epistemic vigilance', *Mind and Language*, 25 (2010), pp. 359–93. Jean-Marie Schaeffer, *Pourquoi la fiction?* (Paris: Seuil, 1999); trans. by Dorrit Cohn, *Why Fiction?* (University of Nebraska Press, 2010).
37. Deirdre Wilson, 'The conceptual-procedural distinction: Past, present and future', in *Procedural Meaning: Problems and Perspectives*, ed. by V. Escandell-Vidal, M. Leonetti, and A. Ahern (Emerald Group Publishing, 2011), pp. 3–31.
38. On epistemic indicators and logical connectives in epistemic vigilance, see Wilson, 'The conceptual-procedural distinction'. For a discussion of a variety of tagging mechanisms, in particular ones which are implicit or uncertain, see Kirsti Sellevold (this volume).
39. Experiments suggest that people have great difficulty processing stories that involve more than five levels of mindreading. See James Stiller and Robin Dunbar, 'Perspective-taking and memory capacity predict social network size', *Social Networks*, 29 (2007), pp. 93–104, and also P. Kinderman, R. Dunbar, and R. P. Bentall, 'Theory-of-mind deficits and causal attributions', *British Journal of Psychology*, 89 (1998), pp. 191–204.
40. Cosmides and Tooby, 'Consider', p. 105
41. *How the Mind Works* (New York: Norton, 1997).
42. 'Does Beauty Build Adapted Minds? Towards an Evolutionary Theory of Aesthetics, Fiction and the Arts', *SubStance*, 94/95, 2001, pp. 6–27 (pp. 15–16). See also 'Consider the Source', pp. 72–74, 89–93.
43. See also Paul L. Harris's argument that children across different cultures pay particularly close attention to subtle signs (such as linguistic tags) which indicate the status of invisible entities: in other words, the subject-matter of the supernatural provokes particularly close monitoring. Of course in Reformation Europe there were especially pressing reasons for attention to knowledge about the supernatural and its sources. *Trusting What You're Told: How Children Learn from Others* (Cambridge, MA: The Belknap Press of Harvard University Press, 2012), pp. 132–51.
44. pp. 217–30. 'L'entreprise poétique de *Fers* ne se confond donc pas avec la révélation prophétique' (p. 230). For the further characterisation of the prophetic and apocalyptic revelation of the following books, see pp. 230–42.
45. Sperber et al., 2010.
46. *Trusting*, pp. 78–112.
47. In his edition of the *Tragiques* (p. 659, note to l. 1476), Fanlo reads the comparison differently: Ocean is compared to us when, hearing the sound of a window or door, we see an image of a soldier about to fire. Either way, 'aussy tost' here means *as soon as (aussitôt que)*. If 'aussy tost' is not read as *aussitôt que* then the comparison makes less sense as an analogue for Ocean who misinterprets the sounds of the waves; however, even in that case, the comparison is clearly about misinterpreting sensory information, about when 'l'esprit va devant les sens' (l. 1478).
48. *Tracés*, pp. 217–30; the prophet 'is nothing but the conduit for a Voice' (p. 230).
49. Prophecy and apocalyptic are now classified as separate genres, but in the sixteenth century the genre of apocalyptic was unknown and Revelation was considered prophecy.

50. *How The Body Shapes The Mind* (Oxford University Press, 2005), p. 1.
51. See, for example, Rutvik H. Desai and others, 'A piece of the action: Modulation of sensory-motor regions by action idioms and metaphors, *NeuroImage*, 83 (2013), pp. 862–69.
52. *Le Style des gestes: corporéité et kinésie dans le récit littéraire* (Editions BHMS, 2008); trans. as *The Style of Gestures: embodiment and cognition in literary narrative* (The Johns Hopkins University Press, 2012).
53. On the continuum between conscious and pre-conscious sensorimotor understanding in literature, see *Movement in Renaissance Literature: Exploring Kinesic Intelligence*, ed. by Kathryn Banks and Timothy Chesters (Palgrave Macmillan, forthcoming); Terence Cave, *Thinking with Literature: Towards a Cognitive Criticism* (Oxford: Oxford University Press, 2016), pp. 21–24.
54. *Tragiques*, V, 1081–1092, my italics. 'Behold Tournon, Viviers, and Vienne and Valence, / Driving off with dread the presumption of Lyon, / Disturbed by a thousand corpses, which they drive away, and then / Arles which contains neither springs nor wells / Endured dying of thirst, when the passage of the blood / For ten days prohibited them from drinking from the Rhône: / *Here the third angel poured out in his turn* / *Upon the Rhône his vial and this river became blood:* / *Here the angel of the waters proclaimed. God whom we adore,* / *Who is, who was, and who shall be always:* / *Here you have practised justice for your saints* / *Pouring out blood to drink for those who have spilled it*'. Note the similar verbs in the two passages from the *Tragiques:* the inhabitants of the towns mentioned reject the bodies ('poussant', 'eslongnent') in a manner which will be recalled by Ocean's initial response ('je pousse', l. 1473; 'repoussez-les', l. 1495; 'je repousse', l. 1517); see also the use of *troubler* in the two passages.
55. f. 98r. 'And the second angel poured out his vial upon the sea; and it became as the blood of a dead man: and every living soul died in the sea. And the third angel poured out his vial upon the rivers and fountains of waters; and they became blood. And I heard the angel of the waters say, Thou art righteous, O Lord, which art, and wast, and shalt be, because thou hast judged thus. For they have shed the blood of saints and prophets, and thou hast given them blood to drink; for they are worthy.'

CHAPTER 8

'Imagine this place': Doni's utopian dream

Kirsti Sellevold

When King Utopos set up his kingdom of Utopia, his first move was to dig a wide ditch around his territory, thus separating it from the mainland and turning it into an island, a man-made island. This was of course part of a defence strategy, intended to protect his kingdom from intruders and make it more difficult to attack, as Utopia had no army. Some of the earliest translations of Thomas More's *Utopia* — the 1524 German translation, for instance — depict Utopia as an independent island, disconnected but still quite close to the mainland, whereas the woodcut map that accompanied the Latin editions,[1] made by Ambrosius Holbein, the brother of the famous painter, somewhat reduces this independence — Utopia here appears tied to the mainland with ropes.[2] This hovering between connectedness and disconnectedness could be considered a highly relevant metaphor for the way our minds, *a fortiori* our imagination, consciously (or unconsciously) decouple from the real and become immersed in fictions and dreams or, more disturbingly, illusions, hallucinations and delusions.[3] It is perhaps unlikely that Holbein had this metaphorical dimension of Utopos's defence strategy in mind when he drew his map, but More certainly structured the book as a dialectic between the imaginary and the real or between play and the serious.[4]

The Italian humanist Anton Francesco Doni and the French translator Gabriel Chappuys are important interlocutors in the ongoing dialogue about the relationship between imagination and reality initiated by More's *Utopia*. Both were instrumental in circulating *Utopia* in Western Europe: the first as editor of the Italian translation (1548), the second as translator of that version into French (1585).[5] It is however Doni's most ambitious work *I Mondi*, published in 1552 and translated into French by Chappuys in 1578 (*Les Mondes celestes, terrestres et infernaux*), which will be in focus here, as it contains a Utopia of its own. With *I Mondi*, Doni moves from being a mere disseminator of utopian texts to becoming a creative contributor to the utopian tradition. His version of Utopia — a fairly brief description of a utopian city — appears at first sight to be a modest contribution. Occupying half of a chapter whose title, 'Mondo Savio' ['The Wise World'], makes no reference to utopias at all, and buried at the heart of a much larger text, it is as if it wants to remain hidden, to pass incognito. The few critics who have commented on it usually consider it less complex and more crude than its model, a parody of it or an ironic comment on it,[6] although it has also been said to criticise the political situation in Italy at the time,[7] as indeed *Utopia* is said to do for England. The present chapter is an attempt to demonstrate how Doni creates cognitive effects that are very different from but still related to those of the original *Utopia*. As we shall see, Doni pulls out and makes explicit strands that are only implicit in *Utopia*, while leaving implicit strands that are explicit in More's text. Although Chappuys remains a disseminator, his translation of *I Mondi* will also play a role in the chapter, as it inflects Doni's text in cognitively interesting ways. Providing Doni's utopian city with a reception of its own, Chappuys's translation shows to what extent it deserves more attention than it has hitherto been given.

What seems to have escaped earlier accounts of the work is that Doni builds a thought world much more cognitively complex than More's. In *Utopia*, the clues or pragmatic factors that inform the reader of its ontological status all contribute to shaping the illusion that the island is real. It features a dialogue between real-life people, including Thomas More himself, and even the only fictional character, the Portuguese seafarer and storyteller Hythlodeus, seems to belong to the realm of the real as we are told he took part in Amerigo Vespucci's voyages to the Americas. Hythlodeus's account of his voyage to Utopia could pass for any travel account of the time, one whose truth value seems reinforced by the map of the island, the utopian alphabet, and the prefatory letters.[8] The illusory reality of the island dissolves, however, the minute the meaning of the name of Utopia, of its cities and of its rivers becomes clear. Doni's version too features a dialogue, but the historical characters are replaced here by a wise man and a madman, who not only echo Erasmus's *Praise of Folly*, but also make explicit and even push to an extreme the dialectic between the play mode and the serious mode that structures *Utopia*.[9] Furthermore, this utopia is not narrated as a travel account, but as a vision that has appeared to the wise man in a dream, in which he and the madman were taken by Jupiter and Momus (the god of satire) to a utopian city.[10] Last but not least, the wise man makes no effort explicitly to persuade the madman of its reality, he only invites him to imagine it. As opposed to More's *Utopia*, then, which elegantly although rather transparently tries to trick its readers into thinking that the island of Utopia is real,[11] Doni's utopian city is explicitly tagged as imaginary, decoupled from reality.

What kind of imaginary world does Doni stage for us, then, is it mad or is it wise? The first impression is that the prefatory narrator, 'il savio academico' (or 'wise man' of the dialogue) wants his readers to become if not deluded, at least cognitively confused, as he and 'il pazzo' (the so-called 'madman') switch roles throughout the dialogue. This would be to forget, however, that Doni also envisages that the reader might call it a Hermaphrodite world, one which fuses madness and wisdom.[12] In that light, it seems possible to argue that the aim of the dialogue is not to create confusion between the real and the unreal, but to enact a constant recalibration of these realms. I shall try to show that whenever the pull towards the imaginary becomes too strong, it is checked or cautioned by a network of subtle clues, both conceptual (*it seems to me*) and procedural (*but, nevertheless, even*),[13] whose function among other things is to mark or tag the threshold between the real and the unreal, and/or between different thought worlds, thus keeping the imagination under control.[14] As such they work in fact both ways: not only as a control, a caution against going too far, but also as a temptation to plunge into imaginary thinking. The threshold between real and unreal is thus a fragile one, unstable and constantly in need of being reassessed, a place where things might go wrong, or prove surprisingly productive.

Monitoring the boundaries between real and unreal, rational and irrational

The phenomenon the first part of the dialogue revolves around is our ability to move between real and imaginary realms, to control our imagination while giving it licence to go beyond the real. The threshold, the place where we monitor the border between these realms, is established in the very first utterance of the dialogue, which displays two contrary statements, one where the wise man acknowledges that his dream is imaginary, thus untrue, and another which goes a long way towards the opposite pole, claiming its truth:

> Ben mi pareva sogno; ben diceva io la non è cosa che possi essere, ma pure ella haveva tanto del proprio, del vivo, e del buono che la mi tratteneva con grandissimo diletto. (fol. 93 v)
>
> [*It seemed to me* indeed that it was a dream, and I said that it could not happen in reality, *but still* it was so authentic, life-like and solid that it held my attention and gave me great pleasure.][15]

The source of knowledge in question is a vision within a dream, the truth value of which is guaranteed by Jupiter who, in the second part of 'Mondo Savio', descends to earth with Momus to engage in debate with our two protagonists. The notion of 'truth' in play here, then, does not refer to an event in the real world, but to the type of truth that is conveyed by prodigies, divine messages and signs of things to come.[16] It is however not Jupiter who is the speaker here, but the wise man. His utterance stages a battle between two opposing forces: reason tells him that the dream is not true, while his emotions make him feel that it is. Which of the two forces wins, or is it at all possible to select one of them as a winner? To understand the relation between the two statements, we need to take into account the epistemic marker *mi pareva* [it seemed to me] and the procedural clues *ma* [but] and *pure* [still][17] of the utterance. Consider first *mi pareva*. The marker reveals (or metarepresents) the type of evidence the wise man relies on as a basis for the first statement. While the verb *parere* [seem] indicates that the information is the result of an inferential process derived from uncertain evidence, the reference to the speaker, *mi*, indicates agreement with the information.[18] The wise man's first reaction to his dream is thus to deny its truth value ('it could not happen in reality'), although on feeble epistemic grounds.

The pair of procedural clues, *ma* [but] and *pure* [still], which introduce the second statement, changes this situation. The role of these clues is to indicate adversative relations between statements,[19] notably that of denial of expectations where the pair activate an inference that *cuts off* a line of inference opened up by the previous statement,[20] thus attributing more argumentative or persuasive power to the second statement than to the first. Whether the inference goes through or not depends on the relation between the two statements; sometimes the assumption of the previous statement is not completely eliminated, only undermined, questioned.[21] This indeed seems to be the procedural function of the connective: rather than flatly denying the assumption of the previous statement (the dream is not true), it merely undermines it, makes it difficult to draw that conclusion. If this still leaves the argumentative power on the side of the second statement, that statement does not affirm the truth of the dream in any absolute sense either. True enough, the particle *tanto* [*so*] intensifies the dream's truth value ('so life-like'), but the grammatical structure of the statement seems rather to put it just above the threshold of being relevant ('so life-like that'): the dream is just about relevant enough to be worth the wise man's attention. The wise man has thus cleverly set up his two contradictory arguments in such a way that they do not completely exclude each other. This allows him to disconnect himself from the real and create a temporary space, signposted by the procedural clues *ma* and *pure*, where he can immerse himself in the dream as if it were true, hence speculate freely and with pleasure about it in a controlled way. In a perspective of rational versus irrational beliefs, it can be considered an everyday irrational belief, one which the wise man knows is not true but which he decides to hold all the same.[22]

What effect has this way of arguing on the wise man's interlocutor, the madman? Does he too become immersed in the dream? At this initial moment of the dialogue he has already heard fragments of the dream and is keen to hear more. The wise man's cautious, trust-inducing way of arguing, the fact that he openly and honestly displays the evidence for his claims, also primes the madman to become interested.[23] Given that he exclaims 'Talvolta vengano veri i sogni' (fol. 93 v) ['Sometimes dreams come true'], it seems indeed that the wise man's disclosure of his own (quite precarious) reliability as a source of knowledge has had the paradoxical effect of neutralising the madman's defence or epistemic vigilance mechanisms, his natural scepticism. His keenness to hear the complete narrative of the dream is also connected to pleasure. In the first place, he anticipates the prospect of pleasure for himself: 'se tu mi vuoi fare un piacer grandissimo' (fol. 93 v) ['if you want to give me great pleasure'], which at this point already shows that the two protagonists of the dialogue have switched their traditional roles.[24] But it also transpires that pleasure is a fundamental property of the new world itself:

> Mi par gran cosa veramente che si ritrovi un mondo, che ciascuno godi tutto quello che si gode in questo nostro, e che non habbino gli Huomini se non un pensiero, e tutte le passioni humani sien levate via [...]. [fol. 94 r]
>
> [*It seems to me* a great thing indeed that a world can be found where everyone has all the pleasure that we have in our world, and where people have but one opinion and are relieved of every passion.]

This pinpointing of what the novelty of the new world consists of — that pleasure can exist without passion and diversity of opinion — makes clear that the madman here acts not just as a listener; he is in fact the one who first provides information about the new world. He is the one who fills in the picture for the readers, lets them know what has been told so far. So even before the wise man has properly started to give the full account of his dream, the madman has entered into it, become immersed. The temptation to immerse completely, to take the new world as real, is, however, tempered or cautioned by a *mi par* [*it seems to me*] and by the use of the subjunctive which, in Italian, indicates possible (rather than actual) scenarios.[25] The madman thus adopts exactly the same cautious, speculative mood as his dialogue partner, openly displaying his (uncertain) evidence. As such, his immersion is as temporary as that of the wise man, and there is no risk that either of them will become lost in the dream.

To acknowledge in general that dreams can sometimes come true, and to become immersed on those grounds, is one thing, but to accept this when one is told one has been part of the dream and gone to the new world while having absolutely no memory of it, is a wholly different matter. This is, however, the situation the madman is facing when the wise man finally starts telling the full story of the dream. In a flash the madman is back in the real world, all his defences up, and no matter how many times the wise man tempers his story with the marker *mi par*, he flatly denies the case: 'So che io non ci fui, ne mi ricordo haver sognato cosa alcuna' (fol. 94 r) ['I know well that I wasn't there, nor do I remember having dreamt such a thing']. Now that the madman's natural scepticism is alerted, on guard, what strategy does the wise man use to neutralise his feeling of being manipulated, to get him back into the dream world again? Contrary to what one might have expected, he doesn't object to the madman's denial, he doesn't insist that he was there; he just asks the madman to imagine it:

> Questi Peregrini ci menarono in una gran Città, la quale era fabricata in rondo perfettissimo, a guisa d'una stella. Bisogna che tu *t'imagini la terra* in questa forma come io te la disegno in terra. Ecco che io ti segno un circolo, *fa conto che* questo cerchio sieno le muraglie, e quì nel mezzo dove io fo questo punto, sia un tempio alto, grande come è la cupola di Fiorenza quattro o sei volte. (fol. 94 r-94 v; emphasis added)

> [These pilgrims conducted us into a large city, which was built in a true circle, in the form of a star. It's necessary that you *imagine this place* just as I shall draw it for you on the ground. See here how I draw a circle for you: *now suppose that* this circle constitutes the walls, and that here in the middle where I put this dot is a tall temple four or six times taller than the cupola of Florence.]

Rather than trying to convince the madman of something he clearly is not prepared to accept, the wise man draws a circle and a dot on the ground and on this basis he urges the madman to imagine the city. The gesture that unfolds both in words and in action before the eyes of the madman is a 'stipulation of pretence',[26] the introductory gesture that marks the leap into fiction. It is precisely the type of gesture that children make when they engage in play.[27] One remarkable aspect of this gesture, so familiar that it almost passes unnoticed, is the extreme scarcity of affordances, or building blocks for the imagination. The wise man relies on a mere dot and circle to set the utopian city in motion. These minimal building blocks, furthermore, bear no resemblance whatsoever to a real city. The wise man thus makes use of knowledge learnt from an early age, widely embodied in children's games, namely that almost anything can be used as an affordance to switch on the imagination. It is true that he also draws on elements from the real world such as the cupola of Florence, but he asks the madman to blow it up to unreal dimensions, and it remains the case that his main building blocks are a dot and a circle on the ground.

This extreme scarcity of affordances for the imagination is striking in the light of a significant difference between Chappuys's translation of the chapter and Doni's original version. Chappuys's text contains a woodcut of an ideal city which is absent in the original but which matches the description of the city provided in the text.[28] The dot and the circle have expanded into the design of a proper city in the woodcut, but, importantly, this design no more depicts a real city than do the dot and circle. Instead, it is a version of Sforzinda, the Italian architect Filarete's plan for an ideal city, which was shaped as an eight-armed star.[29] There is no way of knowing why Chappuys decided to include the woodcut; perhaps he (or his printer) just had it easily to hand and thought it a fitting addition. But the fact that it is there does put constraints on the imagination. Acting almost like a film director, Chappuys spells out the textual description visually via the woodcut, thus fixing the image in a certain sense. It is as if he did not trust his readers' imaginary capacities quite as much as Doni and felt a need to furnish more building blocks than just the dot and circle. Furthermore, as the woodcut unpacks the description of the city *visually* and not verbally, it is not only an instance of the tendency towards explicitation so common in translation; it puts Doni's utopian city more firmly among the abstract city models of the Quattrocento architects.[30] At the same time, the concreteness of the woodcut creates an illusion that somehow makes the utopian city more real. If both Doni's and Chappuys's versions are imaginary versions of a utopian city, Chappuys could be said to follow more closely More's formula of creating an illusion of the real.

Despite the wise man's skilful exploitation of the power of imagination — its ability to thrive on almost nothing — his dot and circle fail to act as a springboard for the madman's imagination. It has, on the contrary, the effect of making him even more sceptical, to such an extent that he proposes they should switch identity: 'Bisognerà che noi scambiamo il nome da te a me, perche tu di cose da pazzo' (fol. 94 v) ['We should swap names, you and I, because you talk like a madman']. This is not just an explicitation of the switching of roles we saw earlier, an ingenious use of the Erasmian paradox of the *Praise of Folly*; it also suggests that the madman has come to regard the wise man's imagination as out of control; he is so immersed in his dream that he no longer distinguishes between real and unreal. Doni thus seems to challenge not just the threshold between fiction and the real (like More), but also between fiction and delusion. But has the wise man really crossed the borderline into delusion, become so immersed in his own dream that he takes it to be real? The fact that he still does not insist on the reality of the city, but only tries to persuade the madman to engage in his story, suggests that he keeps control.[31] Realising that his explicit stipulation of pretence has failed, that it has not weakened but strengthened the madman's defences, he neither denies nor confirms the madman's accusation, but starts his next move with the vocative mood, 'Ascolta' ['Listen'], to which he adds 'pure' ['nevertheless'[32]]. As we have seen, the latter is closely related to *ma* (*but*), but imposes tighter constraints on the interpretation.[33] Its procedural instruction allows the wise man, more specifically, on the one hand to concede that he indeed might be mad, and on the other to insist, in spite of this, that the madman must listen to, become immersed in, the dream. This effect is further intensified by the vocative mood. The fact that it is combined with *nevertheless*, which has emphatic qualities too, underlines to what extent this is a crucial point in the dialogue: if the wise man does not manage to get the madman immersed at this point, he never will. But the strategy finally works. Once more exposing his own precarious reliability as a source (admitting that he may be mad), the wise man again, and as paradoxically as last time, succeeds in neutralising the madman's defences, in dispelling his scepticism. For from now on the madman drops his defences for good and starts to listen properly, joining in (just as in children's play) on the wise man's account of the dream.

Who decides which is a better place?

One might quite plausibly argue that Doni with his madman and wise man plays off different aspects of the human mind against each other. Representing extreme ends on the scale of what the mind is capable of, the madman paradoxically occupies the rational or unimaginative end, someone who does not let himself easily be persuaded to detach from the real and become immersed in fictional thought worlds, whereas the wise man occupies the imaginative or (relatively) irrational end, someone who loves to engage in imaginative thinking. Yet even if we assume that Doni is in this sense superimposing the paradox of Erasmus's *Folly* on the Utopian mode of decoupling (Holbein's ropes), the two characters still do not, as we have seen, fit neatly into the categories assigned to them: the madman is only apparently rational or wise, and the wise man has turned out to be a skilful manipulator of the madman's imagination. Before we look at how this is played out in the course of the dialogue, let us pause a moment to consider the fact that it was procedural clues, not the explicit stipulation of pretence, that finally made the madman drop his defences and engage in the dream. Why do these subtle clues, these simple everyday expressions that we use so often we hardly notice them, work better on him? Why do they seem to have more rhetorical power than the explicit means of persuasion? I suggest the reason is precisely that they are *implicit* means of persuasion; they discreetly allow the madman to assess not just the competence and benevolence of the wise man, but also the content of his utterances, their argumentative or persuasive force. This ability to judge for himself whether or not to believe an utterance often has the paradoxical effect (as we already have seen) of making the hearer more, not less, inclined to believe what he hears. This might also be because procedural information works primarily on the pre-reflective level; it triggers deep cognitive mechanisms or reflexes which are more difficult to control than those activated on the reflective (metacognitive) level. For all his rationality, the madman cannot resist the drive to satisfy his curiosity, to know the story from beginning to end. The procedural clue *pure* [*nevertheless*] is hence not just a linguistic item which indicates or clarifies the relations between (or within) the utterances of the dialogue. It also triggers what seem to be complex emotional reflexes in the madman.

Several factors strengthen the assumption that the madman is open to being manipulated emotionally. The prospect of pleasure was for instance what initially got him interested in the story ('se tu mi vuoi fare un piacer grandissimo'; fol. 93 v); ['if you want to give me great pleasure'], and his first impression of the city — its star-formed shape, its transparency — also triggers an emotional reaction: 'Mi piace che arrivando uno nella terra' (fol. 94 v) ['I *like* the fact that when someone arrives in this city...']. As such his reaction echoes that of the wise man, whose experience of the dream was also that of pleasure. But whereas his was one of simple delight, the madman's is more complex or troubled. One reason is of course that his experience of the dream is not first-hand, and in that light one could imagine that his series of quite simple questions about the layout and customs of the new world[34] is driven by curiosity which, when satisfied, has the effect of intellectual pleasure. It is, however, to be noted that when he has finally passed the turning point, the 'Listen nevertheless' moment, and become immersed in the story, he is no longer interested in whether the dream is true or not, but whether he likes or dislikes what he hears. This suggests that more is in play than just intellectual pleasure.

True enough, the wise man's replies to the madman's series of questions make him (and us) imagine a world of extreme simplicity and equality, which he is attracted to at first. Even the complete equality of the citizenry (everybody adopts the same code of clothing, eats the same food, and so on) is attractive as it echoes human equality in birth and death ('Ancho questa non mi dispiace di questa equalità'; fol. 95 v) ['This equality, too, does not displease me']. The double negation, syntactical and lexical ('non mi dispiace'), indicates however a moment of hesitation. Thus, even at this early stage, he reacts with mixed emotional feelings to the main feature of utopian society. Furthermore, if he welcomes the idea that all goods may be shared ('Oh che possi egli star sempre in piedi cotesto vivere'; fol. 96 r) ['Oh, may this way of living flourish for ever'], there is one important exception: 'Quell'haver le donne in comune non mi piace' (fol. 96 r) ['I don't like this custom of holding women in common'].[35] If up to this point he could be considered as someone who takes intellectual pleasure in considering a world totally different from his own, his panurgian rejection of the sharing of women shows him up rather as jealous and frightened of being cuckolded himself.[36] The reader might so far with some plausibility have entertained the idea that Doni's madman was a sort of Erasmian fool, the kind who tells the truth, but that idea seems less convincing now. The madman here embodies the stereotypical view of a madman, someone in the grip of complex and conflicting emotions, a view which indeed seems to be confirmed by the wise man's reply: 'Anzi per esser cosa da pazzi ti harrebbe a piacere' (fol. 96 r) ['But since it's a mad idea, it ought to please you'].

What about the wise man, then? Now that the madman has been hooked by the dream, and the wise man no longer has to spend all his energy on immersing him, does he finally assume his role, personify what his name suggests? Or does Doni still, rather disquietingly, resist the Erasmian paradox, whereby the wise man should be mad, and continue to make him hover or shuttle between the two categories? Again the case is complex. On the one hand, he does act as a sort of eye-opener for the madman. His account of the agricultural practices of the new world, for instance, alerts the madman to what is wrong with these practices in the real world. On the other, he is dealing with an interlocutor who is not at all ready to take pleasure in the new world in the way he himself does. He needs to use all his skill, all the persuasive means he has at hand, to convince the madman that the utopian city is a better place than the real world. And, as we saw above, this does not exclude reproducing a stereotypical view of him. This arrogant assertion of his own authority seems, however, to be necessary in the face of a dialogue partner who not only flatly refuses to accept certain customs of the new world, but whose attention also has a tendency to slip. Take for example the madman's reply to his account of the treatment of the sick (everybody is taken to hospital): 'Oh come stava male che un ricco andassi allo Spedale.' (fol. 95 v) ['Oh, how irritating it must have been for a rich man to have to go to hospital']. This reaction shows that he has simply forgotten (or pays no attention to) the most important aspect of the new world: that everyone is equal. The wise man is in other words dealing with an unruly interlocutor, someone who is not at all prepared unreservedly to share his opinion of the new world, someone who at no point is so immersed in the dream that he buys into all aspects of utopian life.

What is the wise man's strategy, then? It is in fact exactly the same as in the first part of the dialogue: never to insist that the new world is better than the old (the real), but to cajole the madman to come to that conclusion (seemingly) all by himself, that is to say by getting him to make his own (preferably positive) judgments of the new world. And it is a strategy that for a while at least pays off. When he relates how the utopians treat the old, for instance ('che facevano l'uno all'altro, tutto quello, che ciascuno vorrebbe che fosse fatto a lui'; fol. 96 r) ['that they each did for the other what they would have liked done for themselves'], he is for the first time seen to live up to his name: 'Questa ordinatione è stata buona a uscir di bocca tua, perche è cosa savia' (fol. 96 r) ['Now that's a good rule coming from your lips, as it's a wise thought']. This might of course be (and probably is) ironic on the madman's part, but it is an indication that the madman is not just driven by emotions. That he uses both reason and emotions in his judgment of the new world is further confirmed by his comment on the next item of information, the treatment of the deformed, who are thrown in a ditch just after birth: 'La cosa mi va, ma non la lodo' (fol. 96 r) ['I accept this, but I don't praise it']. In other words, he reacts with both affect and ethical judgment to this aspect of the utopian life.

Keeping the madman's natural scepticism alert enough to judge the new world for himself while still accepting it is a difficult balance, then, and the wise man's authority is in constant risk of being defied. Exactly that happens at the point where the madman has acquired enough information about the utopian city to see its resemblance to other new or ideal worlds. As this comparison risks breaking not only the spell of the dream but also the wise man's authority (while leaving Doni himself open to a charge of plagiarism), he hesitates a moment — 'S'io non havessi paura di fastidire te e me a un tratto' (fol. 96 v) ['If I wasn't afraid of upsetting both you and myself'] — before claiming that, for every utopian law or convention the wise man proposed, he could cite an equivalent law proposed by another authority. However, the wise man dismisses this suggestion. For people who have no book-learning, he says, you don't need to cite a whole lot of pompous references; for them, 'basta che questo è sogno, questa è saviezza, questa è opinione de gli huomini, questa è pazzia' (fol. 96 v) ['it is enough that this is a dream, this is wisdom, this is human opinion, this is madness.'].

The madman's reply, 'Vero, vero, io ci sono per una gran parte' (fol. 96 v) ['True, true, I'm with you for the most part'], seems to signal that he is on the point of surrendering and is finally ready to accept the wise man's view of the new world. His next question nevertheless shows that he only accepts the wise man's dismissive view of authorities in order to again question the aspect of the utopian city he least likes: 'come facevano costoro per conto delle donne a non venire in quistioni?' (fol. 96 v) ['but I wonder how they managed not to fall out over women ?']. Despite this, the wise man's persistent arguing does in the end gradually weaken the madman's defences. He comes round to acknowledging, for instance, that the sharing of women removes jealousy — although he dislikes the fact that it implies no love and no burning desire: 'La non mi piace cotesta ordinatione, a esser privo d'uno ardente desiderio amoroso, et d'uno infervorato desio' (fol. 97 r) ['I don't like this rule of being deprived of a burning amorous desire and of fervent longing']. Faced with the argument that women's licentious behaviour has been the ruin of many an honourable family, he finally admits that the wise man's reasoning has something to it: 'L'ha ben questa tua ragione un certo che del verisimile' (fol. 97 r) ['This argument of yours has indeed some kind of plausible quality to it']. Yet he does not agree to its truth, only to its plausibility.

What this line of argument shows is that the wise man never manages completely to dispel the scepticism of the madman, who continues to hold forth about what he does and does not like. What he does succeed in doing, however, is to make him continue to imagine and question new aspects of the utopian city: in short, he makes him continue the investigation. In that sense the dialogue is not about an ideal city, but about using the imagination, where imagining and dreaming are assumed to be synonymous activities. And that in turn implies sharpening the judgment by drawing on the twin capacities of emotions and intellect which together make up the imagination. That the dialogue functions as a means of sharpening the judgment through the building of a fictional world is suggested by the madman's extremely precise yet cautious overview of the utopian society towards the end: 'La mi pare cotesta stanza, un viver da bestie in certe cose, e in certe altre da mezzi uomini, et mezzi cavalli, et altre tutte da uomini' (fol. 97 v) ['In some respects, this seems to me a way of living fit for animals, in some others for half men and half horses, and in others for complete men']. That humans with deformities are not fit to survive would correspond to the animal world; the sharing of women, to a society whose citizens are both men and animals; and finally the way the elderly are treated (do unto others as you would have them do unto you), to a fully human society.

Had our protagonists not got tired of their conversation, this verbal contest between a panurgian madman and a pantagruelian wise man could have gone on forever.[37] When the chapter moves on to its second part, we for a moment believe that the dialogue will start all over again, only this time at a higher level, between the characters supposed to guarantee the wise man's dream, namely Jupiter and Momus — for these higher-order versions of the wise man and the madman debate in exactly the same manner as their this-worldly counterparts. The celestial debate is, though, sharper than the one on earth and limited to the ontological status of the dream, whether it is true or not. Unlike the madman, Momus never thinks that dreams can sometimes be true, and the belief that he and Jupiter came down to earth, took on human form and pilgrim clothing he mocks as something like a delusion: 'et se egli si crederà, sapendosi, bisognerà crederlo in un certo modo che pare impossibile a crederlo, sapendo di saperlo certo' (fol. 99 r) [if one believes it, knowingly, one must believe it in a certain way that seems impossible to believe, knowing that one knows it for certain']. He does not seem particularly convinced either by Jupiter's claim that the dream is true since 'l'Huomo non si puo imaginar cosa che non sia stata, o non habbi sa essere' (fol. 99 v) ['man cannot imagine things that haven't been or that ought not to be']; he only gives in because it is Jupiter who says it. This higher-level debate about the truth of the story brings out even more clearly the constant need to monitor the threshold between the real and the unreal. This is also emphasised in the brief return to our two protagonists, who in this section of the narrative emerge even more strongly as themselves, the wise man more insistent on the truth of his dream, the madman more mocking than ever. The wise man's effort to bolster the truth of his dream by claiming that only his soul went to the utopian city ('io credo che l'anima mia vi fosse da vero, et che la si separasse da questo corpo' fol. 100 r); ['I think that my soul truly was there, and that it separated from my body'][38] only makes the madman think of Hermodorus (from Clazomenia), who claimed to have out-of-body-experiences all the time, with the result that, when his soul was out of his body, his wife gave him up to his enemies, who subsequently burned him. Our two protagonists thus enact not just the power of the imagination but also the risk of going too far. With his insistence on the truth of his story, the wise man is the one who exposes this most clearly, thereby not just fuelling the madman's scorn, but reawakening his worry that it is the wise man, not himself, who belongs in the madhouse: 'io dubito che bisognerà legarti, et non sarà sogno' (fol. 100 v); ['I greatly fear that you should be tied up, and then it won't be a dream'].

It is a risk with a potentially large payoff, however. For the wise man is the one who towards the end of the chapter is taken up to the higher spheres with Jupiter, the madman being left behind with Momus. He is the one who is told about how the universe and the mind are governed by a number of spirits or demons who conspire to keep the elements together, and if out of kilter do the reverse.[39] A tale of jealousy rivalling that of *The Winter's Tale* towards the end of the chapter provides an example. A young man has been ordered to accompany the wife of his master on a journey. Imagining what might happen between himself and the wife on such a long journey, he protects himself by cutting off his genitals; he puts them in a vase and asks his master to seal and guard it in his absence. On his return no protestations of his innocence have any effect on the jealous husband, who sentences him to death. Not until he is made to open the vase is the husband cured of his delusional jealousy. This tale echoes in some sense the one that the narrator relates in the preface. Having foreseen that all men would become mad by inhaling a foul-smelling vapour which would arise from the dried earth when the rain came back after a long drought, some astrologers thought they could avoid this fate by hiding in a fully insulated house. They also put out vases constructed in such a way that they would catch the vapour and seal themselves. By this means, the astrologers planned to keep their power when the vapour disappeared, and thus become a few wise men governing a mass of fools. But the vases turn out not to be so easily controlled. According to the narrator, one of the vases is Pandora's box, liable to let out all the evil in the world, another the one which Angelica made Orlando open, causing his madness.[40] Vastly outnumbered by fools, who refuse to do as they are told, the wise astrologers are forced in the end to join the crowd of fools and adopt their mad behaviour. Doni designs these two tales which strangely invert one another — in one case opening the vase cured the delusion, in the other it released it — to show how wisdom leads to folly, and folly to wisdom. Not only that: he demonstrates deep insight into the nature of delusions, the way they can take hold, and how difficult — how potentially impossible — it is to get rid of them.

Conclusion

At one level, Doni's 'Wise World' can be considered as merely a simpler variant of Erasmus's *Praise of Folly*, in which the paradox is enacted by the two characters' inversion and at times partial overlapping of roles in the course of the dialogue. In Erasmus, Folly speaks wisely and describes those who are commonly held to be most wise (philosophers, theologians, poets) as the most foolish of all men. In similar fashion, Doni's madman comes to hold the beliefs of a wise man and the wise man those of a madman, and vice versa, in an eternal round-dance. However, I would suggest that Doni engages his characters, and also us, in an equally sophisticated but different game, developed further by Chappuys, in which he exploits the inherent resources of language both to *give licence to* and to *constrain* the imagination. This is enacted by means of expressions such as *it seems to me, but, nevertheless, still*, and strategies common to children's play (stipulation of pretence). Such clues operate on the threshold between different cognitive domains or capacities, and correlate to the brain's ability correctly to tag different thought contents as true or real, as supposition, as counterfactual, as fiction, and so on, and allow humans to improvise, to play out an unlimited range of thought scenarios without acting on them; in other words, to move beyond naïve realism.[41] Yet the human mind's extraordinary capacity to move outside the constraints of the real comes at a price. As Bortolotti shows (this volume), it is often not epistemic considerations, but all kinds of biases that determine whether we hold a belief or not, and the ones we hold are often irrational.[42] We are, it seems, not always good at correctly tagging the contents of our thoughts, which again illustrates another of Bortolotti's claims, that there is considerable continuity between delusions and irrational beliefs.

As the (paradoxically) rational one of our two protagonists, the madman comes across as much more sceptical, much more difficult to lure into the dream world of the utopian city than the highly imaginative wise man. As we have seen, he is willing to be immersed, but only to a certain degree. He is the one who propels the story along, but also the one who at various points stops the wise man and questions the values of the new world, comments on things he likes and dislikes, and so on. In other words he moves in and out of the dream, which is a sign that he has tagged it 'correctly' as an imaginary object; he never gets so absorbed that he starts taking it for reality. The wise man, for his part, the imaginative one, who believes in his dream despite his better knowledge, turns out in the end to be perhaps the more complex character. As an inverted embodiment of reason, he comes across as a highly skilful exploiter of the rhetorical or persuasive powers of procedural clues, not explicitly to persuade the madman (and us) that the utopian city is true, but to stimulate his (and our) natural inclination or desire to hold irrational beliefs, beliefs we know are not true, but which we for various emotional reasons want to hold all the same.

We can, however, take a further step here. If we accept Mercier and Sperber's recent account of reason, according to which reason is essentially a form of persuasion,[43] the wise man turns out in fact to embody *both* reason and imagination, hence not to be irrational in the standard or folk sense at all. For in Doni's account he certainly embodies a reason that works as persuasion, and if he is more immersed in the dream than the madman, it is because he has been to the utopian city, has been one of them: 'E mi pareva essere un di coloro, e vi stetti un tempo parve a me' (fol. 99 r) ['It seemed to me that I was one of them, and I stayed there for a while, it seems to me']. The epistemic markers perform a chiastic embrace around his utopian experience that unequivocally tags it as a dream, ensures that it belongs to the realm of the imaginary. With his knowledge of the persuasive power of the epistemic markers, how they operate on the threshold between real and unreal, he thus knows how to keep control. Extremely skilful at exploiting the resources of these epistemic clues, he manipulates his own, the madman's and our imagination to plunge into unknown territory, while simultaneously pulling it back enough to keep control. In this sense, these expressions function like the ropes in Holbein's famous picture of Utopia, both separating the island from the mainland and holding it in place.

Notes to Chapter 8

1. From the 1517 edition and onwards. The 1516 edition had a cruder map (by an unknown painter) where Utopia had no ropes attached to the mainland.
2. Based on a detailed anatomy of the position of human teeth, the dentist Malcolm Bishop claimed that the overall design of Ambrosius Holbein's woodcut map of Utopia contains a hidden skull. See 'Ambrosius Holbein's memento mori map for Sir Thomas More's *Utopia*. The meanings of a masterpiece of early sixteenth century graphic art', *British Dental Journal*, 199.2, 107–12. Although Bishop's claim has been rejected by most commentators, it does illustrate the capacity of the human mind to imagine objects, in this case a skull, based on a selection of visual clues. As such it not only establishes an inverted link to Holbein's painting 'The Ambassadors', which illustrates another way in which our mind is able to entertain visual illusions (see Smith, this volume); it also exploits our capacity to engage cognitively with our environment. See Alva Noë, 'Is the Visual World a Grand Illusion', *Journal of Consciousness Studies*, 9 (2002), 1–12.

3. The concept of decoupling is borrowed from Leda Cosmides and John Tooby, 'Consider the Source: The Evolution of Adaptations for Decoupling and Metarepresentation', in *Metarepresentations: A Multidisciplinary Perspective*, ed. by Dan Sperber (Oxford: Oxford University Press, 2000), pp. 53–115.
4. This dialectic is evoked for example by the relation between the seemingly realistic narrative of Hythlodeus and the meaning of his name: 'teller of jokes'.
5. The third of the five early modern French translations of *Utopia*, it consisted only of Book II and was published as part of Chappuys's translation of Francesco Sansovino's *I Governi* (1561), a compilatory work on different governments. See my chapter 'The French versions of *Utopia*: Christian and cosmopolitan models', in *Thomas More's* Utopia: *Paratexts and Contexts*, ed. by Terence Cave (Manchester University Press, 2008), pp. 67–87.
6. See Paul F. Grendler, *Critics of the Italian World, 1530–1560: Anton Francesco Doni, Nicolo Franco & Ortensio Lando* (The University of Wisconsin Press, 1969), especially chapter 6, 'Utopian Alternatives', pp. 162–78.
7. See Kristin Gjerpe, 'The Italian *Utopia* of Lando, Doni and Sansovino: paradox and politics', *Thomas More's Utopia*, pp. 47–67. I wish to thank Kristin Gjerpe for making me aware of this strange spinoff from *Utopia*.
8. However, anyone with a basic knowledge of Greek — which most of More's intended readers had — easily figured out the ephemeral nature of the island. Yet some contemporary readers seemed to have read the story literally. Nina Chordas mentions for instance the example of Bishop Vasco de Quiroga, who attempted to put More's Utopia into practice in Mexico; see *Forms in Early Modern Utopia: The Ethnography of Perfection* (Burlington: Ashgate, 2010), p. 70, see also p. 24.
9. In his edition of Jean Le Blond's French translation of *Utopia* (1550) *L'Utopie* (Paris: Gallimard, 2012), p. 371, Guillaume Navaud argues that the opposition between Hythlodeus and Morus in Book I of *Utopia* is structured as a dialectic between the serious and madness, thus pointing backwards to *Praise of Folly*. In making this dialectic explicit, Doni's dialogue between a wise man and a madman endows it also with a powerful capacity for pointing forwards, for containing in embryo, as it were, its own more extreme future.
10. Only incidentally referred to in the first part of the chapter, Jupiter and Momus become real characters in the second part.
11. Of course, More did not really intend his readers to take *Utopia* for real in the sense of existing in geographical space; his trick is too obviously transparent for that. But the fact that he establishes the ontological status of the text by pragmatic factors which normally pertain only to non-fictions can neither be explained away as a joke between him and Erasmus (as some have done), nor be charged to an unethical author. What More rather seems to do here is to point to the fact that our cognitive system relates to the real in exactly the same way as it does to the imaginary. His half-concealed fiction thus triggers the uncertainty we all have about whether what we take to be real really is so. This uncertainty was a constant source of anxiety at the time: it arose in particular in the witch debates (see Maus de Rolley, this volume), and found perhaps its most graphic expression in Decartes's 'malicious demon'; see Helgeson, this volume, p. 118.
12. See *Ai Littori*, 'Se ben voi lo chiamaste mondo Hermafrodito,...' *I Mondi*, fol. 90 r. All quotations are from Gallica's 1552 edition *I Mondi del Doni* <http://gallica.bnf.fr/ark:/12148/bpt6k72373x> [accessed 12 May 2016].
13. On procedural expressions, see Chesters, this volume, p. 65.
14. More specifically, such expressions possess a capacity for epistemic vigilance; they enable hearers to assess the content and source of an utterance or text, and thus to protect themselves against (deliberate or accidental) misinformation. See Deirdre Wilson, 'The conceptual-procedural distinction: Past, present and future', in *Procedural Meaning: Problems and Perspectives*, ed. by Escandell-Vidal, Leonetti and Ahern ([Bingley: Emerald Group Publishing, 2011), pp. 3–31; Dan Sperber et al., 'Epistemic Vigilance', *Mind & Language*, 25 (2010), 359–93.
15. I am grateful to Ita Mac Carthy for checking my interpretations of the Italian text, and to both her and Terence Cave for the translations of the quotations into English.
16. See Banks, this volume, p. 132. In the second part of 'Mondo Savio', Jupiter evokes Hannibal's dream to confirm the truth of the wise man's. In so doing, he also echoes the story of Orpheus:

unable to resist looking back at the guide Jupiter has given him so that he can safely return from his encounter with the gods, Hannibal causes Jupiter's anger and the destruction of Italy. This reference also gives the wise man's dream an apocalyptic quality. As such Doni's 'Mondo Savio' could also be related to the type of apposite thinking that Chesters argues for in Sabinus's story (see this volume, pp. 65–67), which invites the reader to suspend (traditional) truth value and juxtapose the utopian city, horizontally as it were, with real cities or worlds. This happens in fact to *Utopia* itself, in Sansovino's *I Governi* (which Chappuys translated, see note 5 above), where it appears as the culminating example of some twenty existing governments. In this context it is also interesting to note that Chappuys's most important patron, Antoine Du Verdier (to whom Chappuys dedicated his translation of *I Mondi*) was considered an appositional thinker himself (in his *diverses leçons*); see Chesters (p. 67).

17. The word *pure* is highly context sensitive; here it means 'still', 'even so', though had the author written 'e pure' (instead of 'ma pure') it would have become 'and yet'. An occurrence later in the dialogue acquires the meaning of 'nevertheless'; see analysis on pp. 152–53.
18. In French this is made very clear by a comparison between *il me semble* and *il semble*, the latter of which is often followed by a subjunctive which marks uncertainty; one can also find examples where the content marks disagreement with the speaker. Cf. 'Il semble qu'on vive dans une démocratie, et voilà ce qui se passe!' See Hennig Nølke, 'La dilution linguistique des responsabilités. Essai de description polyphonique des marqueurs évidentiels *il semble que* et *il paraît que*', *Langue française : Les sources du savoir et leurs marques linguistiques*, 102.1 (1994), 84–95.
19. *Ma* (*but*) and *pure* (*still*) are thus closely related, although the former imposes fewer constraints on the interpretation than the latter, no doubt because *ma* as a conjunction is more frequently used than *pure*. *Pure* is also often emphatic and indicates more strongly concessive relations. See Astrid Nome, *Connectives in Translation: Explicitation and Relevance* (unpublished PhD thesis, University of Oslo, 2013), pp. 209–20.
20. Strictly speaking, this description only concerns *ma* (*but*); the role of the accompanying *pure* (*still*) is in this case to emphasize and confirm the function of *ma* (*but*). For this interpretation of *but*, see Alison Hall, 'Do discourse connectives encode concepts or procedures?', *Lingua*, 117 (2007) 149–74 (p. 168).
21. See Hall, p. 169.
22. As Lisa Bortolotti argues, this type of dissonant beliefs is also characteristic of delusions; see *Delusions and Other Irrational Beliefs* (Oxford: Oxford University Press, 2010), pp. 84–96 (p. 94).
23. An honest speaker who openly displays the evidence for her claim often has the effect of convincing her hearer, also in cases where the evidence is not very strong, because it allows him to evaluate the evidence for himself and to decide on that basis whether to believe it or not. By contrast, a dishonest speaker may use evidence markers to manipulate the hearer. See 'Epistemic Vigilance'.
24. In contrast with Erasmian folly, the madman is here the receiver of pleasure, not the conveyer of it. See Erasmus, *Praise of Folly*, trans. by Betty Radice, introduction and notes by A. H. T. Levi (London: Penguin Classics, 1971[1993]), p. 21.
25. This distinguishes Italian *mi par* from French *il me semble*, which (as opposed to *il semble*) never takes the subjunctive.
26. See Paul Harris, *The Work of the Imagination* (Oxford: Blackwell, 2000), in particular chapter 2, 'Pretend Play', pp. 8–29. See also Kendall Walton, *Mimesis as Make-Believe: On the Foundations of the Representational Arts* (Cambridge, Mass. and London: Harvard University Press, 1990).
27. Just as the make-believe existence of a water tap can be stipulated by making a twiddling gesture at the end of a cardboard box serving on the occasion as a bathtub, the wise man stipulates the make-believe existence of the temple by drawing the circle and dot on the ground; see Harris, *The Work of the Imagination*, pp. 9–10.
28. The woodcut has been attributed to Fra Giocondo da Verona and also to a group of anonymous draftsmen (l'Anonyme Detailleurs). See Marie-Francoise Piéjus, 'Tourner rond et filer droit: l'urbanisme utopique d'Anton Doni', *Historia, Espacio e Imaginario*, ed. by Jacqueline Covo (Septentrion Presses Universitaires 1997), 107–16.
29. See Grendler, *Critics of the Italian World, 1530–1560*, pp. 162–63.
30. Grendler, p 162.

31. A false belief based on incorrect inference about external reality, firmly held despite evidence to the contrary, is one of the defining criteria of delusion. See Bortolotti, et al., this volume, p. 38.
32. See note 17.
33. See note 19.
34. 'Era altra Città al Mondo Nuovo, di cotesta?'; fol. 94 v) ['were there not other cities in the new world?']; 'Et il restante del paese in fra queste provintie a che serviva?' (fol. 94 v) ['and the rest of the country beyond these provinces, what use did it serve?']; 'Del mangiare?' (fol. 95 r) ['What about food?'], etc.
35. The dialogue articulates here one of the most striking differences between Plato's *Republic* and More's *Utopia*, the former adopting the practice of sharing the women, the latter rejecting it. See *The Complete Works of St. Thomas More. Volume 4, Utopia*, ed. by Edward Surtz, S. J. and J. H. Hexter (New Haven and London: Yale University Press, 1974), p. xliv. The wise man's utopian city re-enacts, in other words, the *polis* of Plato's *Republic* on this point, whereas the madman echoes the rejection of the practice in *Utopia*.
36. Panurge, the main character of François Rabelais's *Tiers livre* (1546), has set his mind on marrying, but not until he can be sure that he will not be cuckolded by his future wife.
37. If Doni borrows traits from Rabelais's character Panurge for his madman (see note 36), the same could be said of his wise man, whose wisdom in many ways matches Pantagruel, the paradigmatic 'wise man' of Rabelais's comic fictions.
38. Which again shows that the type of truth in play is the one we find in the tradition of visions. See note 16.
39. The description of the spirits that govern the cosmic spheres builds on the eleventh-century demonologist Psellos's taxonomy of spirits, on whom also Ficino drew for his cosmology. On Ficino, see Giglioni, this volume. On Psellos, see T. Chesters, *Ghost Stories in Late Renaissance France: Walking by Night* (Oxford: Oxford University Press, 2011), pp. 175–85.
40. For a full analysis of Ariosto's *Orlando Furioso*, see Mac Carthy, this volume.
41. See Tooby and Cosmides, 'Consider the source'. See also Harris (*The Work of the Imagination*, p. 8) who argues that children's pretend play 'offers a way to imagine, explore and talk about possibilities inherent in reality'.
42. See *Delusions and Other Irrational Beliefs*, pp. 113–57.
43. See Hugo Mercier and Dan Sperber 'Why do humans reason? Arguments for an argumentative theory', *Behavioral and Brain Sciences* (2011), 34, pp. 57–111.

CHAPTER 9

Unstill Life: the Uses of Illusion in Hans Holbein's *The Ambassadors*

Olivia Smith

The two figures depicted in Hans Holbein the Younger's large double portrait *The Ambassadors* (1533), currently in London's National Gallery, are Jean de Dinteville and Georges de Selve.[1] Dinteville, on the left, was twenty-nine and the French ambassador to England, at the court of Henry VIII, in the year the portrait was made. Twenty-five-year-old Selve was the bishop of Lavaur.[2] They stand either side of an array of objects depicted in hyper-real still life, the paraphernalia of scientific and artistic mastery: an ad hoc cabinet set up for the sitting. Items on the top shelf — a celestial globe, a quadrant and a sundial — seem to relate to the cosmos, and items on the bottom shelf — including a lute, some flutes and a hymnbook — to earthly pursuits. Though it is Holbein's optical illusion that suggests hidden meanings most strongly, several other elements hint at a second layer to the picture as well.[3] Dinteville's white undergarment is pulled through slashes in his pink bodice, and the large green backing drape is slightly folded in the top left corner, revealing half of a crucifix. At just over two metres square, the painting was commissioned by Dinteville, who belonged to a family with a keen interest in the arts, to hang in his château at Polisy in central northern France.[4] The duo, heavy in their finery, seem rooted to the spot, but they are ambassadors: their job is to travel. There is a tension in the portrayal of Dinteville and Selve between movement and stasis that is emblematic of the painting's effects as a whole.

The painting's centre foreground is taken up by a muddled, bony mass, or at least that's the case if one views it from the front. Just as the basic art-historical facts of *The Ambassadors* are well-known, everyone nowadays knows that this bony mass is in fact an anamorphosis: if it is viewed from the correct oblique angle it appears as a skull, a death's head. For a time the skull became hidden to a greater degree than Holbein intended, as knowledge of the secret picture was lost. In 1867, the director of the National Gallery Ralph Wornum, unaware of the visual riddle being posed, described the shape as 'like the bones of some fish'.[5] The Gallery has now generated coordinates of the ideal viewing position: 120mm away from the wall surface, 1,040mm from the bottom of the picture and 790mm to the right of it.[6] A viewer standing at this exact point will see a visually corrected image, in perfect perspective where it once was warped. This painted illusion, which spills across the space between the men, below the shelves of geometrically conventional objects,

Fig. 9.1. Hans Holbein the Younger, *The Ambassadors*
(© The National Gallery, London)

was, like the globe and the quadrant, a tool of enquiry as well as a showpiece. It was intended to add a fancy quirk to the painting, to show off the artist's talent, and perhaps (as some commentators have suggested) to make a moral statement, but it also functions as a powerful device for highlighting and testing the ways in which we think. The lute in the picture is and remains a contrivance for playing music despite the fact that — vis a vis its broken string — it may represent discord. So what is the skull's function, beyond its many available symbolic meanings as a *memento mori*?[7] What kind of cognitive manoeuvre is *The Ambassadors* interested in revealing?

Investigating Movement

Whereas delusions are usually classed as beliefs,[8] illusions are perceptual experiences,[9] and the special effect that they generate is one of questioned or mis-perception. Optical illusions like the one in Holbein's painting are not based on individual pathologies but instead rely on a viewer's norms of vision, which can then undergo temporary and confected distortions. From the *trompe l'oeil* and *quadratura* of early modern churches, to the Op Art of the 1960s and 70s, they are visual cryptograms: problems to be simultaneously enjoyed and solved.[10] Illusions like these rely on a kind of agreement between creator and viewer. The viewer needs to be initiated to know what she is looking for. Tricks, games and cryptograms do not work without a respondent — they are composed with a clear communicative transaction in mind, and anticipate a specific response from their audience. The question of how the eye can apparently 'deceive' the mind is a question that has interested painters, psychologists and geometers alike, and illusionistic art has been one way of seeking an answer to this question.

Because of their relevance to several different disciplines, illusions have presented an opening for interdisciplinary discussions of cognitive effects. In the decades that followed World War II the psychologist James J. Gibson and the art historian Ernst Gombrich developed different but intertwined theories of picture perception, debating in print key issues like whether a picture can be 'true' and how much information is supplied by the viewer.[11] In their writing, both men drew on their wartime experiences to question issues of perception, finding that illusion was best investigated out of the laboratory and in the realm of live, mobile experience. During the war, Gibson was employed to help pilots fly and land aeroplanes. He discovered that much of what he had learnt about perception was useless when applied to aeroplane flight, as it was all knowledge that had been generated in the context of the academic laboratory where the subjects were sitting still, unlike his pilots who had to make sense of visual input while moving at a great (and variable) speed. At the same time, Gombrich was employed by the BBC's monitoring service, where he listened in on both friendly and enemy messages. He noticed that when the messages transmitted were incomplete he had to use a type of guesswork or inference to fill in the missing words, doing what he called 'projecting' meaning into the blanks.[12] Gibson's experience led him to believe that all perception is determined by environment and our movement through it, from which he developed his ecological account of cognition. Gombrich's time working at the listening post, spending the days focusing on language in use, led him to conclusions about how artistic communication worked and to surmise that all perception was illusionistic to a degree. The methodological circumstances that catalysed these major works on perception can tell us something: that the cognitive detail of illusion seems only to become visible when viewed in the context of action.

Despite their different theses, Gibson and Gombrich were both reacting to the realisation that illusion plays a great part in everyday life and in normal perceptual experience. For example when we watch a film we do not think we see picture after picture but rather we accept the illusion that we are seeing one continuous moving image. Likewise, we do not think we hear the film's dialogue coming from a speaker to the side of the screen, but rather we accept the illusion that it is coming from the characters' mouths. All representative art encourages us to see objects where there are really only little markings of paint, and even the most realist paintings leave places where we must guess at content.[13] Recent research in linguistics has shown that everyday communication works like this too, based on an interactive process of context-based inference.[14] Illusions give the impression of being out of the ordinary, but they are the opposite, rooted in our everyday experience. Yet though illusion has been present throughout human history and before that in nature (think of butterflies with eye-like markings on their wings, a sort of evolutionary *trompe l'oeil*), the particular feature of anamorphosis seems to have developed in the early modern period.

Although it is possible to see much older paintings as anamorphic (such as early cave paintings which are painted to compensate for the curvature of cave walls), Leonardo da Vinci's strangely elongated 'eye' (1485) is one of the earliest formal examples of the technique.[15] Normal perspective works on the basis of establishing one specific viewpoint, and anamorphosis involves establishing a second, equally fixed viewpoint.[16] Early modern painters used the mathematical laws of perspective to warp an object in a controlled way so that it was guaranteed to be corrected when viewed from an alternative position (or with the use of a glass cylinder or mirror). Not only is the anamorphic image hidden but also, in an example like *The Ambassadors,* its mathematical underpinning works to move the viewer like a chess piece into a certain pre-decided yet unexpected part of the perspectival grid. In this movement the hand of the artist is strongly felt in a way that can be as unsettling as it is ingenious, as the viewer experiences her view being controlled. In the seventeenth century, the mathematician and artist Jean-François Nicéron worked out the mathematical equations necessary for creating anamorphic images, publishing them in *La perspective curieuse ou Magie artificielle des effets merveilleux* (1638). Nicéron was working at the forefront of research into optics and geometry, in the same circles as René Descartes and Marin Mersenne, and his book crystallised the early modern taste for visual tricks and play.[17] Nicéron called the anamorphic effects 'magie' and this echoed the view of Giambattista Della Porta, whose 1589 *Magiae naturalis* included a book on 'catoptrics' (the branch of optics dealing with reflections).[18] Between the late fifteenth and the mid-seventeenth centuries a new genre or affordance had developed in art and Nicéron retrospectively characterised it.[19] The production of anamorphic illusions is such a technically precise and particular art that it has not changed much since the early modern period, and the equations generated by Nicéron and others have not become obsolete.

Like optical illusions in general, anamorphoses highlight the way that we search for meaning by slowing down that process and putting its features on show. In the early modern anamorphic diagrams we see sight lines that look like puppet strings: lengths of string pulled taut connecting the eye of the beholder and the image. The puppet-like nature of early-modern perspectival lines was dramatized by The Brothers Quay in their 1991 animation film *De artificiali perspectiva, or Anamorphosis,* for which Ernst Gombrich was art consultant, and in which we see figures undergoing anamorphic transformations on a miniature stage set.[20] The Quays called anamorphosis 'a most powerful device for controlling understanding', labelling it the 'art of delaying access to deeper meaning'. They were reacting to the way that anamorphic images lead the viewer on a contrived journey through various states of comprehension, damping and then releasing their perceptual cognition.[21]

It is significant that the Quays, who are famous for their work with puppets, chose the topic of anamorphosis for a short film, as it is a technique that results in the body being moved by an unseen hand, involving the use of a mechanism that is both hidden and on show. Their method of film itself — that of stop-motion animation — is a type of illusion in which the appearance of continuous movement is produced by photographing models and objects at slightly different positions and then fitting the frames together, as in a flipbook. The puppeteer is perfectly placed to perform experiments with perception and movement, as can also be seen in the work of Stephen Mottram, whose *Animata* involves a variety of models. Using ping-pong balls on puppet strings, Mottram investigates the minimal prompts an audience will require to 'see' human movement.[22] Though we do not forget that Mottram holds the puppet strings, we do, for a moment, 'see' in the bare silhouette he presents a man walking down the road. Mottram's show flickers between entertainment and experiment: we enjoy the fiction while also engaging with its behind-the-scenes rationale. In theoretical neurobiology, recent research uses illusions to investigate the way the brain anticipates motion. Mark Changizi has explained how the brain experiences a 'neural lag', making sense of images one-tenth of a second after light hits the retina. Changizi has suggested that the brain may compensate for this lag by generating images based on a prediction of one-tenth of a second into the future, and that illusions occur when the brain guesses the future wrong.[23] Holbein's *Ambassadors* is there in the pre-history of these more recent investigations, an early modern contribution to illusionistic thinking. As a large painting combining elements of portraiture, still life and anamorphosis, it is also a study of the complexities of perception and movement.

The early moderns knew of a relationship between illusion and movement beyond what we find in the work of contemporary mathematicians. By the time Shakespeare was writing, the act of looking sideways at visual puzzles had entered the repertoire of early modern *dénouement*, so that when he included it as an analogy in *Richard II* he knew that he would have the recognition of his audience. Bushy, a servant, makes a speech to persuade the Queen that her grief is unfounded and imaginary:

> Each substance of a grief hath twenty shadows,
> Which shows like grief itself but is not so.
> For sorrow's eye, glazèd with blinding tears,
> Divides one thing entire to many objects —
> Like perspectives, which rightly gazed upon
> Show nothing but confusion; eyed awry
> Distinguish form: so your sweet majesty,
> Looking awry upon your lord's departure,
> Find shapes of grief more than himself to wail;
> Which, looked on as it is, is nought but shadows
> Of what is not. Then, thrice-gracious Queen,
> More than your lord's departure weep not: more is not seen,
> Or if it be, 'tis with false sorrow's eye,
> Which for things true weeps things imaginary.[24]

Bushy's metaphor melds a technical idea of illusion with a pathological one. While he understands the technique of perspectival anamorphoses like *The Ambassadors*, he also knows that there was a contemporary sense of illusions as something more akin to delusions, as in Thomas More's example of a man who was 'moved to kyll him selfe by illusion of the Devill which he reckoned for a revelacion', and he combines the two to bewilder the Queen.[25] His metaphor twists backwards on itself as he refers accurately to the technicalities of a hidden image, but then casts the 'awry' position as the one that brings about misperceptions as he tries to persuade the queen that the 'hidden picture' she sees is just a mirage. In this quotation it is not only the appearance of an anamorphic metaphor that is exciting but the way that Shakespeare intuits a connection between movement and perception.[26] The Queen is not looking awry at a still picture but rather she is looking awry on the king's *departure*. As the recent insights of puppeteers and scientists demonstrate, the illusion comes into being when the King moves away and the Queen processes that movement. An action and a noun, departure itself incorporates the contradictions of fixity and mobility that we find in Holbein's painting.

Hiding and Revealing

Although anamorphosis does yield veridical perception (i.e. the images produced are 'really' there and not personal delusions), Holbein's skull is certainly capable of generating a feeling of uncertainty about perception. Because it takes time to re-form the image, we are made to confront its mode of production, both psychological and material. When we look at the main portrait of *The Ambassadors* from the side what we see is an oblique image of Dinteville and Selve. When we look at the skull from the front we do not see an oblique painting of a skull, but rather the machine of anamorphosis laid bare. Past critics have emphasised how the spectator encounters the unsettling element of the painting when she moves to the side and comes face to face with the skull, yet it may well be true that the most frightening position from which one might view this painting is the 'correct' frontal one. It is from here that we first experience a flash of doubt about our capacity to understand the item that is being handed to us by the painter. Like a stage prop which must be legible to the audience but is an obvious confection close up, we are shown the unrealness of Holbein's skull from the outset. As when we view the stop-motion work of the Quays or Mottram's puppeteering, we are both behind the scenes and in the audience at once, privy to and in thrall to the trick.

The early modern period was marked by an interest in technologies of hiding and revealing. Inverted or encoded alphabets were invented for cryptographic writing and secret correspondence. Brachygraphy, or as we would now call it shorthand, was developed. Recipes for invisible ink were circulated.[27] James Daybell describes a letter from the spy Thomas Rogers which featured one message in normal ink followed by a second in ink that could only be read when warmed with a candle.[28] Citrus juice was a popular invisible ink that showed its message when it was heated, as the acid in the juice caused the text to turn brown, only revealing its contents to a reader who was initiated into its technique. Like the mathematical recipes for anamorphosis, recipes for invisible ink were passed around as secrets and magic, and Della Porta's book (mentioned above) featured discussions of both these hiding technologies.[29] Before attending to any textual features, the recipient or interceptor of a letter in lemon juice had to move the whole material object into a particular set of conditions, bringing about a visual change. Secret writing technologies toy with the communicative force of the written letter: the hidden writing is certainly present, but upon receiving it there is a moment where the recipient has to think twice about how they will make the message visible and the meaning accessible. Like *The Ambassadors*, hidden texts seem superficially to have just two settings: revealed or hidden, yet as the recipes and instructions that accompany them attest, it is the process of seeking meaning that they highlight as much as the moment of revelation.

Purely practical applications of hiding technologies are different from artistic applications. The way that a letter written in invisible ink hides and then reveals its content is not quite the same as the way in which Holbein's skull seemingly flits in and out of existence. With the former we want to crack the code to get at the contents, but we will probably not want the writing to disappear again. With the latter we can see the anamorphic image and then walk in the vicinity of the painting with the knowledge that we could make it appear once more: we can, and will want to, repeat the effect. But practical technologies *are* on a continuum with creative ones: it is simply that words or paints become the tools for both the message and the disguising medium. This material-literary impulse — essential to *The Ambassadors* — to explicitly hide something, was already there in the early Anglo-Saxon riddles of the Exeter book, where shields and fish described themselves obliquely to make the listener slowly deduce their identities.[30] At its most complex — for example in the medieval *Pearl* poem and throughout the traditions of allegory and lyric poetry — this kind of writing evades complete apprehension to provoke slow reflective interpretation. William Carlos Williams described poetry as a kind of machine and anamorphosis has similar qualities.[31] It is a particular kind of device that capitalises on our enjoyment of delayed comprehension.

As well as hiding and revealing, texts sometimes get their readers to emphatically shift from one perspective to another, producing a sort of anamorphic effect. John

Donne's first satire does this by switching between pronouns. The plot of the poem is that a scholar is accosted by a 'motley humorist' who convinces him to leave his book-filled study and go for a walk around town.[32] In the first section, the scholar addresses the humourist — who is trying to persuade him — as 'thou'. It is only once the pair have changed location that the voice moves to describing the humourist in the third person, as 'he'. This is the section of the poem where the shift occurs:

> I shut my chamber door, and 'Come, let's go.'
> But sooner may a cheap whore, that hath been
> Worn by as many several men in sin,
> As are black feathers or musk-colour hose,
> Name her child's right true father 'mongst all those;
> Sooner may one guess who shall bear away
> Th'Infant of London, heir t'an India;
> And sooner may a gulling weather-spy
> By drawing forth heav'ns' scheme tell certainly
> What fashioned hats or ruffs or suits next year
> Our supple-witted, antic youths will wear,
> Than thou when thou depart'st from hence canst show
> Whither, why, when, or with whom thou wouldst go.
> But how shall I be pardoned my offence,
> That thus have sinned against my conscience?
> Now we are in the street: he first of all,
> Improvidently proud, creeps to the wall,
> And so imprisoned, and hemmed in by me
> Sells for a little state his liberty[33]

A time lag between the scholar shutting his chamber door and arriving on the street is cleverly drawn out with the rhetorical figure of *adynaton* or *impossibilia* (the 'sooner than...' formulation implying high unlikeliness), and then suddenly 'we', the 'we' of the poem's two characters, are outside. After this point, the humourist is addressed as 'he'. The change in pronoun brings about a realignment of perspective for the reader that takes extra work to acclimatise to, with 'we' — of 'Now we are in the street' — creating a moment of uncertainty, acting as a pivot point between the 'we' of thou and I and the 'we' of me and him. As with *The Ambassadors*, a physical shift occurs and a new perspective on the poem opens up. The implied movement between the pronouns and of exiting the lodging between 'Come: let's go' and arrival on the street is filled here by temporal impossibilities. But, outside the realm of writing, what fills the equivalent gap in which we think through the variant perspectives of Holbein's masterpiece? How best to characterise its particular brand of special effect?

Enacting the Spectacle

Jurgis Baltrušaitis, the author of *Anamorphic Art* (1955) saw a very coherent intention behind the special effects associated with the skull — that of the stage play. He writes that Holbein 'conceived of his *Vexierbild* in terms of a theatre, with a change of scene and décor as in a dramatic spectacle.'[33] He reminds us that the painting was designed to be hung in a very specific place in Dinteville's house, the Château de Polisy — probably in a 'vast room, opposite one door and near another, each corresponding to one of the two viewing-points.' *The Ambassadors* is read here as part of a site-specific performance:

> Let us imagine a room with an entrance in the middle of one side, and two side-entrances opposite, with the picture placed between the two side-doors, in the axis [...] *The Mystery of the Two Ambassadors* is in two Acts. *Act One* is played when the spectator enters by the main door and finds himself a certain distance away from the two nobles, who appear at the back as on a stage. He is amazed by their stance, the display of luxury, the intense realism of the picture. He notes a single disturbing factor: the strange object at the ambassadors' feet. Our visitor advances in order to have a closer look. The scene becomes even more realistic as he approaches, but the strange object becomes increasingly enigmatic. Disconcerted, he withdraws by the right-hand door, the only one open, and this is *Act Two*. As he enters the next room, he turns his head to throw a final glance at the picture, and everything becomes clear: the visual contraction causes the rest of the scene to disappear completely and the hidden figure to be revealed. Instead of human splendour, he sees a skull. The personages and all their scientific paraphernalia vanish, and in their place rises the symbol of the End. The play is over.[34]

Unlike a typical stage play where the actors move while the audience watches, Baltrušaitis imagines the viewer (who he calls the 'visitor') shifting around the theatre-space of the vast room while the picture puts on the performance, producing the spectacle from its stationary spot. In addition to any prompt for movement that the original architecture would have issued, the painting itself suggests how and where to move by the way that the skull's shadow falls in a different direction from the other subjects of the double portrait, denoting a shift in time and place. The viewer travels the floor in a series of steps as if she herself is the moving picture in a flipbook thumbed by the skull.

The phenomenon of the mobile viewer reminds us that there are other conventions of representing death that are less static than the still life *memento mori*. Although this skull is part of the same tradition in which the ambassadors' other objects are painted, it also, in its ability to reposition its interlocutor, seems to invoke the theatricality implied by the *totentanz* or dance of death. This was a genre that Holbein had been interested in for decades by the time he came to paint *The Ambassadors*, and his own book of *totentanz* scenes was published in 1538.[35] Instead of taking the form of a lively circular dance, the book features forty-one images in which death visits different types of people, intruding into their customary settings. In each, we see death entering and surprising his victim, appearing jarringly in their world to usher them to his. We can see the continuation of Holbein's interest in the idea of death interrupting normal business in *The Ambassadors*.

Conceiving of *The Ambassadors* as a play is just another way of describing the effect of those perspectival lines that were plotted by Nicéron and reiterated by the Quays. The viewer acts out a set of movements that have been directed and rehearsed by the painter. This part of the painting encourages the viewer to contemplate the skull, but the force of the perspective trick makes it seem more as if the skull is contemplating the viewer, holding her poised at arm's length in a reversal of the Yorick pose so familiar from *Hamlet*. Ellen Spolsky and Guillemette Bolens have written about the way we respond to physical movements as they are depicted in art and literature, explaining how the body recognises, reads and infers meaning from other people's gestures.[36] Their approach assumes cognition to be something done by the whole body (rather than just the brain-based mind). Bolens explains how this 'kinesic intelligence' works through the example of Jean Baptiste Siméon Chardin's painting of a child playing with a spinning top: we use our experience of spinning a top to understand the position of the boy's hands immediately after launching it.[37] But how does this theory work when the bodily movement to be understood — undertaken, as per Baltrušaitis — is encrypted into the painting using perspective rather than simply depicted?

Holbein's challenge is a very physical one, but one that involves historical space outside the picture frame. After focusing on the poses of the ambassadors, our kinesic intelligence does not straightforwardly respond to an action depicted on the canvas, but rather to the curious sidestep around the external room (first the Château de Polisy and later the National Gallery) that so many other viewers must have undertaken in the past. Through this process the viewer is indexed to both a specific historical location, and an exact position in relation to the painting. Although a painting like *The Ambassadors* can be moved, and indeed it has been, the way that it demarcates a larger space than that which the canvas occupies gives it an affinity with more permanent, room-sized installations (a category in which *trompe l'oeil* and *quadratura*, mentioned above, also belong). Salvador Dalí's 'Face of Mae West' in the Dalí Theatre and Museum in Figueres is a room-sized three-dimensional anamorphic installation that can only be perceived from one point, on a platform up a ladder, while looking through a curved glass window. The viewing platform itself becomes a special perspectival place — the only one from which the whole room makes sense — and for a moment each viewer is important, framed by a lavish curtain and watched by other visitors. The Mae West illusion was installed by Dali himself between 1974–76 and has never moved. Though the comparative banality of the National Gallery setting serves to mask some of the particularity of viewing the Holbein, you can still access a sense of being part of an ongoing physical enactment of the spectacle. The interpretative process is dramatized and socialised. The action of the spectator around the Holbein painting is like a ghostly kinesic implicature.

In the case of the Dalí example, it is the fact that we have wandered through the Mae West room first (and can see other people doing so from the viewing platform) that makes the special perspective interesting — we recognise the furniture and admire its transformation. While most discussions of Holbein's anamorphosis emphasise the either/or nature of the painting's two viewpoints and discuss their incommensurability, it is worth remembering that *The Ambassadors* too has this kind of perspectival no-space factored in: space around the painting in which the viewer might be standing or walking, aware of all of the painting's contents yet seeing none of them perfectly. There is always a room or a wider viewing context; even in Nicéron's instructive diagrams the presence of the artist and his tools reminds us that this will be an environment in which other things happen than the production of an illusion. Baltrušaitis's theory of *The Ambassadors* as stage play, in which he imagines the spectator turning her back on the painting to walk away for the exact time it takes to reset the 'scene' (with the architecture cueing her to turn back to the painting at exactly the right moment), excludes the truth that a moving, walking spectator will inevitably get into positions where she sees the painting imperfectly, seeing neither a complete skull nor a properly focussed duo of ambassadors but rather a hint of both in the wider context of the panting's situation. Though his description gives the sense of a fully embodied conception of the viewing experience, he is actually still trading in what Gibson would call 'aperture vision' (that of a single eye at a fixed point of observation with a constricted field of view). It is compelling to think of the painting as a stage play with a perfectly repeatable *deus ex machina*, but in doing so we may overlook the ways in which the messier thinking-space between 'acts' contributes to the painting's power. Moving beyond the idea of the stage play we might look again at critics who have attributed a more general ludic quality to the painting's style.

Playfulness

In *Renaissance Self-Fashioning* Stephen Greenblatt wrote that the skull was, like the many inconsistencies and omissions in Thomas More's *Utopia*, the 'object of the artist's profound, playful attention'. He elaborates on what this playfulness could mean as follows:

> The arts of mapmaking, calculation, and measurement that figure so prominently in 'The Ambassadors' and *Utopia* have important practical functions in everyday life, but they are present here as recreation, the elegant play of distinguished and serious men. This play is not conceived by humanists as an escape from the serious, but as a mode of civility, an enhancement of specifically human powers. As such, the globes and compasses, along with the lute and flutes, sit without contradiction next to the book of merchant's arithmetic, on the one hand, and the book of divine worship, on the other, just as the mock alphabet and maps of *Utopia* are bound up — literally and figuratively — with a searching inquiry into the sources of human misery and the possibilities of human government. The distorted skull in Holbein's painting, for all the grimness of its imagery, is itself an invitation to the viewer to play, while the reader of *Utopia* is invited to enter a carefully demarcated playground that possesses nonetheless a riddling relation to the outside world.[38]

The theme becomes a key for understanding *Utopia* and the way in which More was consistently interested in visual blind spots and literary structures which challenged the stability of reality, such as the dialogue between Vincent and Antony in More's *Dialogue of Comfort Against Tribulacion* in which one persistently questions whether the other is dreaming or not.[39] More's many literary inversions are linked, for Greenblatt, to his life as a constantly reinvented member of Henry VIII's court whose great adaptability manifested itself as self-estrangement and self-fiction. The idea of the *Ambassadors*' strength coming from its playfulness is suggestive, and Greenblatt aligns this feature with a political 'civility'. His phrasing indicates that he may have taken his concept of play from Johan Huizinga, the Dutch philologist and historian of the medieval and early modern periods who argued in *Homo ludens* that early modern play was meaningful and not simply trivial, as colloquial usage of the term might imply. *Homo ludens*, which was first published in German in 1944 and English in 1949, puts forward the theory that play is the major force in culture. Huizinga collapsed the apparent dichotomy between ritual and play by arguing that the two have many common elements and are often indistinguishable, and that what separates them in our typology is only a conventional understanding that one is profound and the other is not:[40]

> Let us consider for a moment the following argument. The child plays in complete — we can well say, in sacred — earnest. But it plays and knows that it plays. The sportsman, too, plays with all the fervour of a man enraptured, but he still knows that he is playing. The actor on the stage is wholly absorbed in his playing, but is all the time conscious of 'the play'. The same holds good of the violinist, though he may soar to realms beyond this world. The play-character, therefore, may attach to the sublimest forms of action. Can we now then extend the line to ritual and say that the priest performing the rites of sacrifice is only playing?[41]

The humanistic understanding of play we inherit from New Historicism argues that if we are to attribute playfulness to *The Ambassadors* then this does not make it light-hearted or trivial — quite the opposite. The term 'play' points to serious thinking of one sort or another.

Huizinga's *Homo ludens* anticipates findings from recent research in cognitive psychology, which in turn extend (and add experimental evidence to) these earlier insights from studies of early modern literature and culture. In *The Work of the Imagination*, Paul Harris has challenged the dominant narrative on play in his discipline, which takes imaginary play to be the product of a kind of irrational thinking that happens in early childhood yet is eventually overturned by rational, adult thought.[42] Through his research with young children, Harris has found that rather than being a separate immature phase, playing instead develops crucial cognitive capacities that are integral to our mature selves. One of his most striking findings is that play requires a set of conceptual and causal knowledge about the real world. So, instead of children's imaginary play taking place during a pre-rational developmental stage, it seems that children are only able to undertake certain types of make-believe *after* they have understood how the real world works, usually at some point during their second year. Play becomes a sign of maturity rather than immaturity, only emerging in late infancy — it often involves distortions or inversions, but only as a way of thinking through possibilities inherent in reality. The idea that Huizinga had of play being 'different' from ordinary life is sharpened by Harris who states that play can only diverge from normal life where it is based on it, and that divergences have to be understood in relation to our robust intuitive understanding of the way the real world works. It is, to use his phrase, 'causally coherent'.[43] And the reality that children base pretend stipulations on is not limited to the world they have encountered at first hand: in a subsequent book Harris has shown that children accept testimony about the world from others, even when that testimony contains information that does not correspond to what they can see.[44] It turns out that the psychological hallmark of playfulness is not naivety but know-how: the maturity to cope with a process of simultaneous showing and revealing — that same process we see at work in *The Ambassadors* and with simple and extended conceits.

Harris is a child psychologist, but his thesis about play has huge implications for adult psychology, because it suggests how adults deal with situations involving pretence. As Harris says, the first feature of common pretence is that 'either play partner can bring make-believe entities into a temporary, public existence via a simple fiat or stipulation'.[45] One of Harris's examples is of two people pretending to bathe a teddy in a cardboard box and of one twiddling make-believe taps to indicate the situation to a child playmate, who may then (having got the idea) turn the 'taps' on and off as they wish. In Harris's findings about play (viz. that no matter how many contortions, fictions and heterodoxies are introduced the causal fabric of reality remains intact) we almost have a definition of the kind of experiments that a writer like Thomas More was making. As a fictional journey modelled on the narrative of a real one, as a utopia hidden in what might appear to be a travel book, accompanied by a map of nowhere that is effective because it looks like a real map, More uses norms of the travel writing genre to engage his readers in a set of fantastical stipulations. If Holbein's skull is an object of the artist's 'profound, playful attention', it is so in the sense that the painter offers it to the viewer with the expectation that she will interact with it. The viewer is not at all tricked (in the sense of the eye deceiving the mind) but rather invited to participate in a complex game — a game played, as Huizinga would have it, in sacred earnest.

The example above from Harris's work highlights the way in which the play-invitee holds several ideas of the play-object in mind.[46] The child sees the box as both a box and a bath without indulging in any errors of perception. Though fiats and stipulations bring make-believe entities into existence, they do not completely cancel out the original, more prosaic entities that have been reimagined. This theory could also explain the unsettling effect, mentioned above, of *The Ambassadors'* frontal view, in which the out-of-kilter skull does not resolve itself into a coherent alternative representational object. We laugh at that nineteenth-century idea from the uninitiated curator of the anamorphic painting representing 'the bones of some fish', but his grapple for meaning is not entirely cancelled out by the later revelation of the painting's perspectival trick. From the front, even when we know how *The Ambassadors* works, we still see an incomprehensible covering of paint. The painting plays by stipulating a complicated visual scene in the first place, but also by introducing clever glitches into the process by which its stipulations can be taken up.

Gibson argued that, because of the fact we move around in our environment (rather than simply pose to engage in aperture vision, like a test-subject in a laboratory or one of the perfect viewers in a perspective manual), any painting or picture will always be understood doubly. Like Harris's player who flicks between the box and the bath, Gibson's perceiver will flick between the scene and the surface — the scene with its representational depiction and the surface as a 'plaster wall, or a sheet of canvas, a panel, a screen, or a piece of paper' — able to see both. When asked 'what do you see?' the perceiver could always just as well answer that she sees a wall or a canvas as some water lilies or a battlefield.[47] He explains that

> We distinguish between the surface *of* the picture and the surfaces *in* the picture. In paintings such as those of the Impressionists, we can see the difference between the illumination *of* the picture and the illumination *in* the picture. The two sets of surfaces are not comparable, and the two kinds of illumination are not commensurable.[48]

Gibson's idea introduces another kind of incommensurability to discussions of *The Ambassadors*, one that juxtaposes the material, multi-dimensional status of the painting with its interior contents — the difference between what we see in our natural 'path' of vision (as we move) and what we see at a 'point' of vision (the perfect, stationary eye of the early modern perspective manual). His insight about this duality of vision points to a way in which we might further understand the kind of game this painting plays. Anamorphosis effects a pressure point at the meeting of scene and surface, seeming to present a second frontal view, the painting's interior themes confusing our perception of its external dimensions. In response to Gibson's assertion above, that the two sets of surfaces are not comparable, Holbein might have replied that there *is* an exploitable amount of seepage between them, and that therein the delight of his *Ambassadors* lies.[49] By making viewers decode the ambiguous paint of the skull and physically puzzle over the multiple inbuilt viewing positions, Holbein complicates their grasp of both the represented picture and the picture-as-object.

Memento Mori / Vivere

Let us revisit that question from the opening paragraphs of this chapter: what is the skull's function, beyond its many available symbolic meanings as a *memento mori*? It is no coincidence that Gibson and Gombrich had their career-defining realizations about perception and illusion while working in World War II, focusing on landing planes and decoding messages that meant the difference between life and death for hundreds and thousands of people. The very mechanics of illusion, which involves a kind of sleuthing, embodied acrobatics, only works — against the scientific objectivity implied by the laboratory or those diagrams of perspective manuals with their artificial eyes — when it is combined with a real living, moving viewer. The skull is a *memento mori* not just because it is a skull and skulls are a reminder that death waits inside us all, but because it is embedded in a complicated artwork that emphasizes the necessity of the viewer's participation, and which functions as a sort of call and response, checking for vital signs even as it raises the spectre of their removal. Embedded in the larger context of the painting, hovering just below the many items on the shelves, the skull is a mutating still life that proves life is not still. The other objects in the scene seem to know this: Dinteville's hat sits at an angle almost parallel to the anamorphosis, ready to slide off into that other plane, suggesting that he too knows how to manoeuvre, hide, bewilder and reveal. When we consider the painting in light of its cognitive force, the question of exactly what the skull alone signifies becomes less relevant, because the entire composition so clearly works as a unified device. Theories which attribute an either/or setting to the painting's visuals miss the point that *The Ambassadors* in its entirety functions as a meditation on movement, communication and physical mortality. It encapsulates all the dark ironies of the *totentanz*, depicting — through the response it elicits from the viewer — the animation of life even as it invokes the theme of death.

Notes to Chapter 9

1. Hans Holbein the Younger, *The Ambassadors* (1533) in the National Gallery (Acc. no. NG1314). I acknowledge the support of a Wellcome Trust Fellowship [grant no. WT103171MA] which enabled me to finish work on this chapter and the editing of the book after the end of my Balzan fellowship.
2. Mary F. S. Hervey was the first person to identify the ambassadors, in her book *Holbein's 'Ambassadors', the Picture and the Men* (London: George Bell and Sons, 1900).
3. The painting, and particularly its anamorphic element, has fascinated critics of different kinds over the twentieth century. Two influential accounts from different paradigms came from the psychoanalyst Jacques Lacan who used it to develop his idea of the gaze in *The Four Fundamental Concepts of Psycho-analysis*, ed. by Jacques-Alain Miller (Harmondsworth: Penguin, 1994), and Stephen Greenblatt who read the skull as emblematic of a process of estrangement in *Renaissance Self-Fashioning: From More to Shakespeare* (Chicago: University of Chicago Press, 1980).
4. See Elizabeth A. R. Brown, 'The Dinteville Family and the Allegory of Moses and Aaron before Pharaoh', *Metropolitan Museum Journal*, 34 (1999), 73–101.
5. Ralph Wornum, *Some Account of the Life and Work of Hans Holbein, Painter, of Augsburg* (London: Chapman and Hall, 1867), p. 276.
6. *Holbein's Ambassadors: Making and Meaning*, ed. by Susan Foister, Ashok Roy, and Martin Wyld (London: National Gallery Publications, 1997), p. 53. Foister et al. describe an alternative way of viewing the skull by 'holding a glass cylinder at a slight diagonal at a distance of a few metres in front of the picture' (pp. 53–54). However, they add that it is uncertain whether sixteenth-century viewers would have known about this method (which became more widespread in the use of seventeenth-century anamorphic pictures).
7. Using the theory of distributed cognition, Gail Kern Pastor has challenged the notion that early modern skulls, as they appear in famous settings like *Hamlet* and *The Ambassadors*, represent the seat of all thought and meaning making. She argues that far from being the abandoned chambers of one person's thought as per the cerebral understanding of cognition, *memento mori* skulls function as just another object (albeit one with very particular cultural values) that the mind can flow and reach into. See Pastor, 'Thinking with Skulls in Holbein, *Hamlet*, Vesalius, and Fuller', *The Shakespearean International Yearbook*, 11 (2011), 41–60: 'The skull — instead of being a sign of undifferentiated absence — becomes a sign of the mind pouring itself into symbolic containers and doing its own characteristic work of extension' (p. 48).
8. See Bortolotti, this volume.
9. I have used 'perceptual experience' instead of 'perception' because in some cases perception may be reserved for only the veridical whereas sometimes illusions can be false. I am grateful to Chris Cowie for a discussion of this distinction and other philosophical aspects of illusion.
10. *Quadratura* (a type of trompe l'oeil) is illusionistic ceiling painting, used to create the appearance of large architectural spaces or domes.
11. See for example the exchange of letters from Ernst Gombrich, James J. Gibson and Rudolf Arnheim in *Leonardo*, 4 (1971), 195–203.
12. Gombrich relates this in *Art and Illusion: A Study in the Psychology of Pictorial Representation* (London: Phaidon Press, 1960), p. 171. Gibson led a series of aviation experiments during WWII in which he explored the validity of using 'motion pictures' (rather than still ones) in the training and selection of pilots. His experiments were published as James J. Gibson, *Motion Picture Testing and Research*, AAF Aviation Psychology Research Report No. 7 (Washington

DC: U.S. Government Printing Office, 1947). These experiments informed Gibson's argument in *The Perception of the Visual World* (London: George Allen & Unwin, 1950), for example pp. 129–30.

13. The example Gombrich gives is of Jan Van Eyck's Ghent altarpiece, which is minutely detailed, but still leaves us to fill in the picture of the angel playing the organ, who is only hinted at in the painting by a few dashes of red to indicate the very edge of its clothes and hair (*Art and Illusion*, p. 177). Gombrich calls the process by which we do this 'intellectual inference', and in many ways his theory anticipates the ideas that Relevance Theorists (see note 14) will later have about inference in spoken communication and, by extension, literature.
14. Relevance Theory argues that communication is always underspecified, and that listeners will look for meaning in an utterance, and then, using the implicatures it conveys, they will draw out the speaker's intention using inferential processes dependent on context. For the classic account of Relevance Theory, see Dan Sperber and Deirdre Wilson, *Relevance: Communication and Cognition* (Oxford: Blackwell, 1986, revised ed. 1995) and more recently the work of Robyn Carston, *Thoughts and Utterances: The Pragmatics of Explicit Communication* (Oxford: Wiley-Blackwell, 2002).
15. Leonardo da Vinci, *Study of Eye, With Juvenile Face*, Codex Atlanticus, folio 98r, Veneranda Bibliotheca Ambrosiana.
16. Art historian Hanneke Grootenboer explains the anamorphic effect: 'We should remember that anamorphic art gives the impression of radically breaking with linear perspectival conventions, even as it is created strictly according to perspectival rules. Unlike perspective's initial promise to enable the creation of lifelike or illusionist pictures, anamorphic art uses perspective's own weapons against it in order to pursue its opposite: rather than showing images, it hides them.' Grootenboer, *The Rhetoric of Perspective: Realism and Illusionism in Seventeenth-Century Dutch Still-Life Painting* (Chicago: University of Chicago Press, 2005), p. 98.
17. Jean François Nicéron, *La perspective curieuse ou Magie artificielle des effets merveilleux* (Paris: Pierre Billaine, 1638). Nicéron's book was republished in 1652 with added treatises on optics by Mersenne. See Stuart Clark, *Vanities of the Eye: Vision in Early Modern European Culture* (Oxford: Oxford University Press, 2007).
18. Giambattista Della Porta, *Magiae naturalis, Sive de miraculis rerum naturalium* (Naples: Horatius Salvianus, 1589). This was the second, enlarged edition of the book.
19. See Terence Cave, *Thinking With Literature: Towards a Cognitive Criticism* (Oxford: Oxford University Press, 2016), pp. 54–59, for genre as a type of affordance, in an extension and updating of Gibson's terminology.
20. *De artificiali perspectiva, or Anamorphosis*, dir. The Brothers Quay (1991) in *Brothers Quay 1979–2003: The Short Films* (London: British Film Institute, 2006).
21. I am grateful to Marina Warner for her discussion of the work of the Quay brothers at the workshop 'Weak Implicatures, Strong Effects' held at St John's College, Oxford on 7 June 2013.
22. Mottram performed his demonstration with ping-pong balls as part of the above workshop. See <http://www.stephenmottram.com> [accessed 2 May 2016].
23. Mark Changizi, *The Vision Revolution: How the Latest Research Overturns Everything We Thought We Knew About Human Vision* (Dallas, Texas: Benbella books, 2009). The brain jumps to conclusions in a way that is similar to how the deluded brain reasons wrongly, as discussed by Ita Mac Carthy in this volume.
24. Shakespeare, *Richard II*, II.ii.14–27.
25. Thomas More, *A Dialoge of Comfort Against Tribulacion* (London: Richard Tottell, 1553), chapter 16. See Maus de Rolley, this volume, for a discussion of a kind of illusion different from the one discussed here.
26. Another perspectival trick appears in *Cymbeline*, I.iii, where Imogen considers her husband Posthumus's departure. Pisano relates the spectacle of Posthumus's departure on a ship for Imogen who then imagines having been there, seeming to conceptualise Posthumus's receding shape in perspective terms: 'I would have broke mine eye-strings; cracked them, but / To look upon him till the diminution / Of space had pointed him sharp as my needle' (I.iii.17–19). Thanks to Terence Cave for drawing my attention to this example.

27. See James Daybell, *The Material Letter in Early Modern England: Manuscript Letters and the Culture and Practices of Letter-Writing 1512–1635* (Basingstoke and New York: Palgrave Macmillan, 2012), pp. 166–67.
28. Daybell, *The Material Letter*, p. 158.
29. Adrian Johns, 'Ink', in *Materials and Expertise in Early Modern Europe: Between Market and Laboratory*, ed. by Ursula Klein and Emma Spary (Chicago and London: University of Chicago Press, 2009), p. 105.
30. *Anglo-Saxon Riddles of the Exeter Book*, trans. by Paull F. Baum (London: Cambridge University Press, 1963).
31. Introduction to *The Wedge*, in *Selected Essays of William Carlos Williams* (New York: New Directions, 1969), p. 256.
32. John Donne, Satyre 1, *The Complete Poems of John Donne*, ed. by Robin Robbins (Abingdon and New York: Routledge, 2013), pp. 366–75.
33. Donne, Satyre 1, lines 52–70.
33. Jurgis Baltrušaitis, *Anamorphic Art*, trans. by W. J. Strachan (New York: Harry N. Abrams 1977), p. 104.
34. Baltrušaitis, *Anamorphic Art*, p. 105.
35. Hans Holbein the Younger, *Les simulachres et historiées faces de la mort, autant élégamment pourtraictes, que artificiellement imaginées* (Lyon: Melchior and Gaspar Treschel, 1538).
36. Guillemette Bolens, *Style of Gestures: Embodiment and Cognition in Literary Narrative* (Baltimore: Johns Hopkins University Press, 2012), and Ellen Spolsky, *Satisfying Skepticism: Embodied Knowledge in the Early Modern World* (Aldershot: Ashgate, 2001).
37. Bolens, *Style of Gestures*, pp. 3–5.
38. Greenblatt, *Renaissance Self-Fashioning*, p. 24.
39. Greenblatt, p. 25. For a new, in-depth discussion of mutually doubting interlocutors and the cognitive effects of Utopian literature see Kirsti Sellevold's chapter in this volume.
40. This is Huizinga's definition of play: '[P]lay is a voluntary activity or occupation executed within certain fixed limits of time and place, according to rules freely accepted but absolutely binding, having its aim in itself and accompanied by a feeling of tension, joy and the consciousness that it is 'different' from 'ordinary life.' Johan Huizinga, *Homo ludens: A Study of the Play Element in Culture* (London: Maurice Temple Smith Ltd., 1970), p. 28.
41. Huizinga, *Homo ludens*, p. 18.
42. The work being done by Harris follows the investigations of Kendall Walton whose *Mimesis as Make-Believe: On the Foundations of the Representational Arts* (Cambridge, Mass. and London: Harvard University Press, 1990) used a description of the way in which children's toys function as props from which fictional worlds are conjured (which in turn contain knowledge that is in a sense 'true') to explain the effects of representational art.
43. Paul L. Harris, *The Work of the Imagination* (Oxford: Blackwell, 2000), p. 58.
44. Paul L. Harris, *Trusting What You're Told: How Children Learn from Others* (Cambridge, Mass. And London: The Belknap Press of Harvard University Press, 2012).
45. Harris, *The Work of the Imagination*, p. 10.
46. Usually in Harris's vignettes the person initiating the play is the researcher while the person taking up the invitation is the child test subject.
47. James. J. Gibson, *The Ecological Approach to Visual Perception* (New Jersey: Lawrence Erlbaum Associates, Inc., 1979) p. 281.
48. Gibson, p. 282.
49. Notes on the Gallery's restoration of the painting in the 1990s seem to belie some of this seepage between the two Gibsonian types of surface in the painting. The Gallery's technical bulletin confirms that one of the most delicate and fraught areas that the team worked on was the anamorphic skull. Its blank patches were seemingly more worrying, and more contested than others elsewhere: 'restoration of the skull was left until the end of the work, and was the subject of much research and debate.' Martin Wyld, 'The Restoration History of Holbein's *The Ambassadors*', *National Gallery Technical Bulletin*, 19 (1998), 4–25. [http://www.nationalgallery.org.uk/technical-bulletin/wyld1998].

INDEX

aberration 3
affordances 6–9, 13 n. 15, 54, 151–52, 166–67
afterlife *see* ghosts
alien abduction belief 8, 14 n. 18, 41–43, 45, 46–47, 48, 49 n. 21
Alighieri, Dante, *Divine Comedy* 7, 11, 55
allegories 4–5, 169
anamorphosis 163, 166–70, 172, 175, 176, 177 nn. 3 & 6 & 10, 178 n. 16, 179 n. 49
ancestor-worship 55
animacy 57, 60
animal spirits 73, 74, 77, 79, 86 n. 40
animals, minds and dreams 4, 112, 120, 122 nn. 7 & 8
anthropology, cognitive *see* Boyer, Pascal; Cosmides, Leda
anti-Freudians 25
aperture vision 173, 175
Apocalypse *see* Revelation
apparitions 28–29, 53, 64, 76, 78, 79
  see also ghosts
appetites and desires 96, 97
apposite thinking 65–67, 160 n. 16
Aquinas, Thomas 73
Ariosto, Ludovico, *Orlando furioso* 5, 9–10, 11, 34 n. 32, 158
  Olimpia's delusion 22–23
  and Orlando syndrome 24–32
  and Othello syndrome 18–20
  and reverse Othello syndrome 15–18, 20–24
Aristotelianism 87 n. 52, 92, 119, 122 n. 8
Aristotle:
  cognitive theory 73, 76–77, 78–79, 80, 87 n. 52
  theory of species 88 n. 63
  treatise on dreams 91
astrologers 158
Augustine, St. 64, 74, 75, 78
authorial tagging 10–11
automatic beliefs 7–8
awareness:
  degrees of 60, 90, 93, 95, 99, 105, 106
  during sleep paralysis (ASP) 42–43

Baillet, Adrien 111, 120, 123 n. 24
Baltrušaitis, Jurgis 170–71, 172, 173
beliefs:
  and affordances 6–9
  demarcation from clinical delusions 38–39, 45–48
  see also delusions; dreams and dreaming; fictional beliefs; illusions; limited counter-intuitive violation; play
Belleforest, François, *Histoires prodigieuses* 67, 132–33
Bible:
  Christ's resurrection 64
  figurative reading of 8
  Joel 130
  Paul the Apostle 81–82, 83
  and prodigy literature 133–34, 141
  Revelation 46, 125, 133–34, 136, 137, 138, 140–41, 143 nn. 28 & 30, 144 n. 49
  sola scriptura 93
black bile 76, 77, 78
Blakemore, Diane 113
Boaistuau, Pierre, *Histoires prodigieuses* 67, 132–33
Boccaccio, Giovanni 29–30
body as microcosm concept 79, 87 n. 50
  see also soul
Bolens, Guillemette 139, 172
Bortolotti, Lisa 27, 28, 31, 35 n. 40
Boyer, Pascal:
  limited counter-intuitive violation 7–8, 9, 13 n. 16, 57–58, 57, 59, 61
  theory of magical concepts 56–59, 60, 62
brachygraphy 169
brain:
  computational model of 135
  mapping of 74, 79, 85 n. 15
British Psychological Society 19
Brothers Quay 167, 169, 171
Butler, Peter V., B.X. reverse Othello syndrome case study 17–18, 20, 21, 24, 25–26, 27, 28, 31

Calvin, Jean 64
Calvinism 125, 131, 133, 142 n. 14
Canon episcopi 73, 78, 81–83
Capgras delusion 38
Cardano, Girolamo 2, 91, 92, 97, 100, 103, 104, 105–06, 107
Cartesianism *see* Descartes, René
Cassirer, Ernst 80
Catholicism:
  French Wars of Religion 125, 130, 131, 132
  and Purgatory 53, 55, 66
catoptrics 166
cell doctrine 74, 77
Cervantes, *Don Quixote* 34 n. 27
change blindness 3

Changizi, Mark 167
Chappuys, Gabriel 147, 148, 152, 158, 160 n. 16
Chardin, Jean Baptiste Siméon 172
Charles V, Holy Roman Emperor 24
Charles VIII, King of France 23–24
Chesney, Elizabeth 35 n. 33
children:
  and play 136, 151, 153, 158, 162 n. 41, 174–75, 179 n. 42
  and theory of mind 7, 112, 138, 144 n. 43
chivalric romance 21, 22–23, 24, 25–26, 34 n. 27
Christ, Jesus 64
Clancy, Susan A. 41–42, 43, 46–47
Clark, Billy 69 n. 22
Clark, Stuart:
  'The scientific state of demonology' 71
  Thinking with Demons 6–7, 8, 72
  Vanities of the Eye 6–7, 72, 78–79
clinical case-studies:
  alien abduction belief 41–42, 42–43
  B.X. reverse Othello syndrome 7–18, 20, 21, 24, 25–26, 27, 28, 31
  self-enhancing beliefs 44–45, 45–46
  thought insertion 39–40
Codex Exoniensis, see *Exeter Book*
cognitive anthropology see Boyer, Pascal; Cosmides, Leda; Tooby, John
cognitive inflexibility 3–4
cognitive linguistics 79–81
cognitive narratology 60
cognitive perspective 1–2
cognitive philosophy and psychology 3, 15, 17, 18, 22, 23, 30, 31, 32, 37, 174
Colie, Rosalie 6
common sense 73, 74
communication:
  communicative principle of relevance 62–63, 69 n. 22
  and illusions 165, 166, 177
  and metarepresentational structures 134
  see also epistemic vigilance; Relevance Theory
conceptual expressions 113, 122 n. 13, 123 n. 16, 148–49
consciousness see dreams and dreaming
corpse concept 60–61
Cosmides, Leda 134–36, 137, 138
counter-intuitive violation see limited counter-intuitive violation
Crichton, Paul 24, 25
cryptograms 165, 169
culture:
  and delusion definition 38, 39, 43, 44, 46
  and dreams 89, 90–91, 92
  early modern European 7, 8–9
  and ghosts 53, 55, 60
  and illusions 44
  and metaphors 80–81

  and play 174
  see also religious beliefs
Cyprian, St. 77

Dalí, Salvador 172
Dante see Alighieri, Dante
d'Aubigné, Agrippa, *Les Tragiques* 2, 10–11
  extract from Ocean episode 126–29
  scope and limits of sources of knowledge 125, 130–34
  source tagging and metarepresentational structures 134–37, 141
Daybell, James 169
death 163, 171, 176–77
deception 3, 24–25, 71, 74, 76
decoupling 6, 60, 135, 147, 148, 153
  see also source tagging
default reasoning 57, 58, 59, 60
Della Porta, Giambattista 166, 169
delusions:
  alien abduction belief 8, 14 n. 18, 41–43, 45, 46–47, 48, 49 n. 21
  Capgras 38
  as coping strategy 5–27, 45–46, 47–48
  cultural factors 38, 39, 43, 44, 46
  and deception 3, 24–25
  definitions of 3–4, 37–39, 43, 46, 89, 162 n. 31
  delusio 25
  demarcation from clinical delusions 22, 32 n. 8, 34 n. 26, 38–39, 45–48
  Doni, *I Mondi* 157–58
  erotomania 26, 28, 34 n. 24, 38, 50 n. 38
  everyday 22, 34 n. 26
  Italian words for 15
  and jealousy 18–19, 24–25, 28, 157–58
  More, *A Dialogue of Comfort Against Tribulation* 168
  Orlando syndrome 24–32
  Othello syndrome 18–20, 24–25, 28, 33 n. 20
  pathological 16–17, 18–19, 31, 36 n. 51
  of persecution 38
  reverse Othello syndrome 15–18, 20–24, 25, 27, 28, 31, 50 n. 38
  self-enhancing beliefs 39, 44–45, 45–46, 47–48
  thought insertion 39–41, 46, 49 n. 12, 50 n. 40
  two-factor 21, 33 n. 23
Democritus 102, 104
demonology 3, 71–83
  Canon episcopi 73, 78, 81–83
  Clark's theories 6–7, 72, 78–79
  and culture changes 8–9
  Descartes, evil demon hypothesis 8–9, 118, 160 n. 11
  devil as juggler 72, 75, 85 n. 29
  early modern treatises 71–73
  Kramer's theories 73–75, 78
  Le Loyer 67
  and metaphorisation of the mind 78–83
  More 68 n. 8

Sabinus 66–67
Weyer's theories 76–78, 88 n. 75, 93–94
  see also witches
Dennett, Daniel 26
Descartes, René 1, 2, 11, 84 n. 4
  dream argument 9, 90, 111, 112–21, 121 n. 1,
    123 n. 25
  evil demon hypothesis 8–9, 118, 160 n. 11
  and memory 123 n. 23
  mindreading 112
  slave/captive simile 71, 118, 119, 120, 123 n. 22
devilry see demonology
diabolic agency see demonology
Diagnostic and Statistical Manual of Mental Disorders, see
    DSM–5
Dinteville, Jean de 163, 168, 171, 176
discernment 4, 92, 96, 99–100, 104–05, 106
distancing 135
distributed cognition 8, 177 n. 7
divination 50 n. 40, 92, 93–98, 98–101, 102, 103, 104,
    106–07
divine contemplation 114
divine intervention 21, 45–46, 50 n. 40, 107, 130
dogs' dreams 112
Domenico Leoni 27
Doni, Anton Francesco, *I Mondi* 5, 7, 11–12, 147–59,
    160 n. 16
  boundaries between real and unreal 149–53
  comparison with More's *Utopia* 147–48
Donne, John, *Satire* 1: 169–70
Dorat, Jean 131
dreams and dreaming:
  animals 4, 112, 122 nn. 7 & 8
  antidotes to delusion 92, 94, 98–101, 108 n. 7
  Ariosto, *Orlando furioso* 5, 16, 28–31
  Butler's B.X. case-study 31
  Cardano 91, 92, 97, 100, 103, 104, 105–06, 107
  as a cosmological function 102–04
  d'Aubigné, *Les Tragiques* 10–11, 131, 134, 137
  Democritus 102, 104
  Descartes 9, 111–21
  digestive 91, 97
  and divination 50 n. 40, 92, 93–98, 98–100, 102,
    103–04, 106–07
  Doni, *I Mondi* 5, 12, 148, 149–53
  dream narratives 4–5, 11
  drowsiness, delusion and discernment 104–07
  early modern European views on 9, 89–91
  Ficino 91, 92, 93, 94, 96–97, 97–98, 99–100, 101,
    106
  and freedom 3, 4, 93, 101, 106, 107, 118
  Freud 95
  Galen 96
  hemispheric specialization 30
  Hippocrates 94–95, 96, 98
  Iamblichus 91, 93, 94, 98–99, 99–101, 103, 106
  interpretation of 4, 90–93

lucid 105, 118, 119
Plato 95, 96, 98
Porphyry 93, 98, 99, 100
prophetic 4, 16, 90, 91, 93, 94, 98–101, 103, 106, 121
Sanchéz 91–92, 95, 103–04, 105
and the soul 94–95, 99, 101, 102, 103, 105
Synesius 90, 91, 98, 100, 102–03, 104, 105, 106–07
see also alien abduction belief
DSM–5: 16–17, 18, 19, 32 n. 8, 33 n. 17, 43
Du Pont, René 66
Du Verdier, Antoine 67, 160 n. 16
Durling, Robert M. 32 n. 2

ebony trees 56, 57
ecstasy 83, 104, 105, 130, 142 n. 10
ego 36 n. 50, 41
embodied cognition 30, 36 n. 47, 125, 138–39, 140, 141
epilepsy 33 n. 20, 35 n. 44
epistemic innocence 26, 35 n. 40
epistemic modality 135
epistemic vigilance 12, 29, 31, 35 n. 46, 135, 138, 150,
    160 n. 14, 161 n. 23
Erasmus, *Praise of Folly* 2, 7, 11, 23, 35 n. 38, 148, 152,
    153, 154, 158, 160 n. 9
erotomania 26, 28, 34 n. 24, 38, 50 n. 38
see also love-madness
essays 2
Estienne, Henri 131
ethnography, comparative 55
Everson, Jane 21
evidentiality 135
Exeter Book 169
extended cognition 8, 177 n. 7

faculties of the mind 73, 74, 75, 76–77, 84 n. 12,
    85 n. 15, 97
  see also imagination; senses
Fanlo, Jean-Raymond 131, 134, 137, 138, 139, 144 n. 47
fantasy see imagination
Ficino, Marsilio:
  and dreams 91, 92, 93, 94, 96–97, 97–98, 99–100,
    101, 106
  and spirits 55, 162 n. 39
  theory of imagination 76, 77
fictional beliefs 5, 8, 9–12
  Doni, *I Mondi* 147–59
  Erasmus, *Praise of Folly* 148, 153, 158
  More, *Utopia* 147, 148, 152, 160 nn. 8 & 11 & 13
  scope and limits of 125, 130–31, 137–41
  source tagging and metarepresentational structures
    125, 134–37, 141, 149
fidelity, delusions of 17, 18, 19, 20, 22, 24–25, 28
figurative and literal boundaries 73, 80–81, 83, 88 n. 60
Fodor, Jerry 84 n. 12
Foister, Susan 177 n. 6
Forsyth, Elliott 133
Frankfurt, Harry 123 nn. 23 & 25

freedom and dreams 3, 4, 93, 101, 106, 107, 118
French Wars of Religion 125, 130, 131, 132
Freud, Sigmund 36 n. 50, 95, 118

Galen 96
Galenism 92
Gall, Franz Joseph 84 n. 12
Gallagher, Shaun 139
Gerrans, Philip 4
ghosts 53–67
  Boyer's account of magical concepts 7, 8, 56–59, 60, 62
  concept of 53–54, 56, 59, 60, 61, 62
  early modern European views on 53, 55–56
  Ovid, *Metamorphoses X* 54–55, 60, 62
  and Relevance Theory 58–59, 62–63
  Sabinus, *Fabularum Ovidii interpretatio* 12, 63–67
  vain embrace 61–62
Gibson, James J. 165, 166, 173, 175–76, 177 n. 12
Giglioni, Guido 36 n. 47, 50 n. 40
God:
  Boyer's account of magical concepts 56
  and demonic possession 75, 76, 78, 86 n. 42
  and Descartes' theories 112, 114, 116
  divine intervention 21, 45–46, 50 n. 40, 93, 98, 100, 103, 107, 130
  and miracles 72
  see also religious beliefs
Gombrich, Ernst 165–66, 167, 176, 178 n. 13
Goschler, Juliana 87 n. 57
Goulart, Simon 67, 131
Greek medical theory 74
Greenblatt, Stephen, *Renaissance Self-Fashioning* 173–74, 177 n. 3
Grootenboer, Hanneke 178 n. 16
Guicciardini, Francesco 23–24
Guyanacape 55

hallucinations 31, 71, 147
  hypnopompic 42–43
  see also dreams and dreaming; thought insertion
Harbus, Antonina 80, 87 n. 59
Harris, Paul L. 5, 138, 144 n. 43, 161 n. 27, 162 n. 41, 174–75, 179 nn. 42 & 46
hemispheric specialization 30, 36 n. 49
Hepper, Erica G. 45
hiding and revealing 168–70
Hippocrates 94–95, 96, 98
historical context, d'Aubigné, *Les Tragiques* 125, 130, 131–32, 134, 140–41
Hobbes, Thomas 120
Holbein, Ambrosius 147, 153, 159, 159 n. 2
Holbein, Hans, *The Ambassadors* 159 n. 2, 163–65, 164
  death theme 176–77
  hiding and revealing 168–69
  and movement 166, 168
  and play 173–74, 175, 176

restoration of 179 n. 49
  as theatre 170–73
Homer:
  Iliad 61
  Odyssey 106
  as prophetic poet 131, 142 n. 14
hopes and fears:
  and delusions 2, 17, 20
  and dreams 30, 90, 106–07
horizontal faculty of psychology 84 n. 12
Huizinga, Johan, *Homo ludens* 5, 9, 174, 175, 179 n. 40
humanism 11, 55, 174
  see also Doni, Anton Francesco; Weyer, Johann
humours 21, 74, 75, 76, 77, 78, 86 n. 42, 88 n. 75
hypnopompic hallucinations 42–43

Iamblichus:
  and dreams 91, 93, 94, 98–99, 99–101, 103, 106
  and imagination 76
idola 102, 104
illusions 2–3
  anamorphic 163, 166–70, 172, 175, 176, 177 nn. 3 & 6 &10, 178 n. 16, 179 n. 49
  demonic 9, 71–73, 75, 76, 77, 78, 79, 80, 81–83, 86 nn. 41 & 42, 88 n. 75
  hiding and revealing 168–70
  illudere and *illusio* 3
  momento mori 176–77
  and movement 165–68, 175–76
  optical 163–77
  and play 3, 173–76
  positive 44–45, 47
  as theatre 170–73
  see also fictional beliefs
imagination 10, 13 n. 11
  Aristotle's theory of faculties 76–77
  Canon episcopi 82
  and dreams 90, 91, 92–93, 95–96, 97, 98, 100, 101, 102, 103, 105, 106, 107
  and fictional belief 11–12
  idola 102, 104
  imaginatio 90, 97, 99
  Kramer's theory of demonic illusion 73–74, 75
  Montaigne 9
  phantasia 90, 95, 97, 99, 102
  and play 5–6, 144 n. 43, 161 n. 27, 174–75, 179 nn. 42 & 46
  and reality 147, 148–49, 151, 152, 153–58, 159
  Weyer's theories of demonic illusion 76, 93–94
  see also delusions; perceptual experiences
imposture and prestige 71–72, 73, 74–75, 85 n. 29
Inca culture 55
infidelity *see* fidelity, delusions of
intellect 76, 90, 96, 97, 98, 103, 105, 156
  divine 100, 101
intellectual inference 178 n. 13
intelligence, kinesic 172

intuitions 53, 54, 55, 56, 57, 60, 64
invisible ink 169
irrationality:
    and delusions 3, 4, 7, 37, 38, 45–48
    and play 1, 174
    and rationality 8, 148, 149–53, 153–58, 159
Italian Wars 23–24

Jack and Jill communicative principle of relevance example 63, 69 n. 22
Japan:
    festivals of the dead 55
    positive illusions 44
Jaspers, Karl 3, 16
jealousy 18–19, 24–25, 28, 157–58
Jesus Christ 64
Johnson, Mark 5, 79–80, 87 n. 59
Jones, Matthew L. 123 n. 23
Jossa, Stefano 34 n. 32
judgment 22, 31, 38, 41, 112, 117, 155, 156
justification by faith alone *see* sola fide

Kaiser, Walter 6
kinesic intelligence 172
knowledge:
    dreams and foreknowledge 90, 92, 94, 95–96, 97, 98–99, 100, 101–02, 105, 106–07, 108 n. 7
    fiction as a source of 137–41
    scope and limits of 125, 130–34
    sensory 36 n. 47, 138–39, 140
Kramer, Heinrich 72–73, 73–75, 76, 78, 79, 81, 82, 83, 85 nn. 19 & 29, 88 n. 73

La Pléiade 130
Lacan, Jacques 177 n. 3
Lakoff, George 5, 79–80, 87 n. 59
Latin 80, 82
laws of proportionality between cognitive and vital processes 96–97
Le Loyer, Pierre 67
Lecointe, Jean 142 n. 14
Leonardo da Vinci 166
Leong, Gregory B. 18
Lercheimer, Augustin 66
levitation 41, 72
limited counter-intuitive violation 7–8, 9, 13 n. 16, 57–58, 57, 59, 61
linguistics:
    and illusions 166
    and metaphors for the mind 79, 80, 87 n. 57
    and Theory of Relevance 62–63, 65
    see also conceptual expressions; metarepresentational structures; procedural expressions; source tagging
literal and figurative boundaries 73, 80–81, 83, 88 n. 60
love-madness 22, 27, 34 n. 24, 35 n. 45
    see also erotomania

lovers' ramblings 83
lycanthropy 82
    see also witches

madness *see* love-madness
magical concepts, Boyer's theory of 7, 8, 56–59, 60, 62
    see also ghosts
McKay, Ryan 26, 38
McNally, Richard J. 41–42, 46–47
medical students' positive illusions 44–45
medical writers, sixteenth century 27–28
melancholy 77, 78, 79, 86 n. 41
    love 26, 27, 34 n. 24, 35 n. 42
    women and 76
memento mori 165, 171, 176–77, 177 n. 7
memory:
    autobiographical 44
    and dreams 105, 116, 123 n. 23
    kinaesthetic 139
    Kramer and internal illusions 73, 74, 75, 82
men, and demonic delusions 76, 83
Mercier, Hugo 159
metamorphosis:
    of the devil 71–72, 78
    of witches 82
metaphors:
    anamorphic 168
    Ariosto, *Orlando furioso* 24
    and dreams 5, 11, 103, 147
    reification 80
    Shakespeare, *Othello* 33 n. 20
    spatial 78–81, 82, 87 nn. 57 & 59, 88 n. 50
    wandering mind 11, 81–83
metarepresentational structures 125, 134–37, 141, 149
Mexía, Pedro 67
mind:
    errant 11, 81–83
    and imagination 76–78
    metaphorical 78–81
    rational and irrational 153–58
    theory of 61, 84 n. 12, 112, 134, 136
    topographical 73–75
mindreading 112, 120, 134, 144 n. 39
    see also Theory of Mind
miracles 72
modalizing expressions *see* procedural expressions
Montaigne, Michel de:
    Essais 2, 12 n. 3, 67, 112, 114, 122 n. 9
    'On the Power of the Imagination' 9
More, Thomas:
    A Dialog of Comfort Against Tribulation 168, 173
    Utopia 2, 11, 147, 148, 152, 159 n. 2, 160 nn. 4 & 8 & 9 & 11, 162 n. 35, 173, 175
Moss, Ann 6
Mottram, Stephen 167, 169
movement and illusions 165–68, 175–76

myths:
  Doni, *I Mondi* 12
  Greco-Roman 3, 54–55, 61–62, 63, 64, 66–67, 130
  pagan 67

nature, and demonology 72
Navaud, Guillaume 160 n. 9
Neoplatonism 7, 29, 55, 76, 121, 121 n. 1
neurobiology 167
New Historicism *see* Greenblatt, Stephen
Nicéron, Jean-François 166–67, 171, 172–73
Nuttall, A. D. 20, 21

object constancy 112, 122 nn. 6 & 7
Oedipus complex 25
Op Art 165
opinions 76, 118, 123 n. 25
optical illusions 3, 163, 165–66
  see also anamorphosis
Orlando syndrome 24–32
  see also reverse Othello syndrome
Othello syndrome 18–20, 24–25, 28, 33 n. 20
  see also reverse Othello syndrome
Ovid:
  Metamorphoses X 54–55, 60, 62
  Remedia Amoris 27
  see also Sabinus, Georg

Pandora's box 158
Paster, Gail Kern 177 n. 7
Paul the Apostle 81–82, 83
Pearl (poem) 169
perceptual experiences 2–3, 165, 166, 167, 175–76, 177 n. 9
person concept 59, 60, 61–62, 64, 65
perspective, mathematical laws of 166
persuasion 153, 155, 159
Pinker, Steven 136
Plato:
  cave myth 3
  dreams 95, 96, 98
  Republic 96, 162 n. 35
  see also Neoplatonism
Platonism 92, 93, 96, 98, 100, 101, 104, 106
play:
  child's 136, 151, 153, 158, 162 n. 41, 174–75, 179 n. 42
  Huizinga's definition of 179 n. 40
  illudere and *illusio* 3, 35 n. 37
  and illusions 3, 173–76
  imaginative 1, 5–6, 144 n. 43, 147, 148, 161 n. 27, 174–75, 179 nn. 42 & 46
  and rituals 174
pleasure 150, 154, 155, 161 n. 24
Pléiade, La 130
Plutarch 67, 132
pneuma 102, 103, 104
  see also spirit

poetic fiction 130–31, 133, 137, 138, 140, 141
Porphyry 93, 98, 99, 100
positive illusions *see* self-enhancing beliefs
Post Traumatic Stress Disorder (PTSD) 42, 46–47
prejudices 39
prestige and imposture 71–72, 73, 74–75, 85 n. 29
pretence *see* stipulated pretence
procedural expressions 6, 9, 10, 13 n. 9, 14 n. 19, 122 n. 13, 123 nn. 16 & 17
  d'Aubigné, *Les Tragiques* 136
  Descartes, *Meditations On First Philosophy* 113–14, 120
  Doni, *I Mondi* 148–49, 149–50, 153–54, 158, 159
  Sabinus, *Fabularum Ovidii interpretatio* 65, 66, 67
prodigy literature 67, 125, 132–33, 134, 141, 143 n. 20, 149
prophecies:
  d'Aubigné, *Les Tragiques* 10, 11, 125, 130–31, 137, 138–39, 141
  and dreams 4, 9, 16, 31, 90, 91, 92, 93, 94, 98–101, 103, 106, 121
  and fiction 5, 138
  genre of 144 n. 49
  Protestant Reformation 53, 55, 66, 68 n. 1, 93–94
  French Wars of Religion 125, 130, 131, 132
Psellos 162 n. 39
Pseudo-Augustine 78
puppetry 167, 169
Purgatory 53, 55, 66

quadratura 165, 172, 177 n. 10
Quay Brothers 167, 169, 171
Quixotic reasoning 34 n. 27

Rabelais, François, *The Life of Gargantua and of Pantagruel* 11, 12, 14 n. 23, 79, 162 n. 36, 162 n. 37
racist beliefs 39
Ramachandran, Vilayanur S. 23, 30, 36 n. 49, 36 n. 50
Rapid Eye Movement (REM) 42
rationality:
  definition of 89, 92
  and irrationality 8, 148, 149–53, 153–58, 159
reality:
  and dreams 89, 90, 92–93, 94, 96, 97, 98, 99, 100, 101, 102–03, 104, 105, 106, 107, 115, 173
  and imagination 147, 148–49, 152–53
  see also Quixotic reasoning; senses
reality testing 17, 28, 30, 31
reason *see* rationality
reflections 166
Reformation *see* Protestant Reformation
Regino of Prüm 81
Reisch, Gregor 77
Relevance Theory 54, 56, 58 59, 62–63, 65, 69 n. 22, 178 nn. 13 & 14
religious beliefs 4, 7, 8, 13 n. 16

Catholicism 53, 55, 66, 68 n. 1
French Wars of Religion 125, 130, 131, 132
Protestant Reformation 53, 55, 66, 68 n. 1, 93–94
and Relevance Theory 56
self-enhancing 45–46
see also divine contemplation; divine intervention; God
Rémy, Nicolas 66
Renaissance:
art 7
faculties of the mind 74
humanism 67
see also Synesius
Revelation 46, 125, 133–34, 136, 137, 138, 140–41, 143 nn. 28 & 30, 144 n. 49
reverse Othello syndrome 15–18, 20–24, 25–26, 27, 28, 31, 50 n. 38
see also Orlando syndrome; Othello syndrome
rituals 174
Rodis-Lewis, Geneviève 121 n. 1
Rogers, Thomas 169
Romero, George A. 61
Ronsard, Pierre de 131
Roth, Ilona 5

Sabinus, Georg, *Fabularum Ovidii interpretatio* 12, 63–67, 160 n. 16
Saccone, Eduardo 32 n. 2
Sanchéz, Francisco 91–92, 95, 103–04, 105
Sawday, Jonathan 87 n. 50
scalar expressions *see* procedural expressions
scepticism 12, 151, 152, 153, 155–56, 158–59
Schaeffer, Jean-Marie 5
schizophrenia 6, 39, 41, 48
see also thought insertion
secularism 8, 9, 13 n. 16
Sedikides, Constantine 45
self-enhancing beliefs 39, 44–45, 45–46, 47–48
Selve, George de 132, 163, 168
sense of coherence 47–48
senses:
and dreams 91, 94, 95, 96, 97, 98, 102, 103, 115, 116
and illusions 71, 74, 75, 77–78, 79, 81, 82, 86 n. 42
sensory perception 72, 73, 74, 76, 79, 80
sensorimotor resonance 2, 125, 138–40
sexual impotence 72
Shakespeare, William:
Cymbeline 178 n. 26
Hamlet 53, 172
Othello 3, 18, 19–20, 21, 24–25, 28, 31, 33 n. 20, 35 n. 44
Richard II 167–68
As You Like It 23
shared pretence *see* stipulated pretence
Short, William 82
shorthand 169
situatedness *see* embodied cognition

six non-naturals 96
skulls 159 n. 2, 177 n. 7
see also Holbein, Hans, *The Ambassadors*
sleep and wakefulness 115–17
sleep deprivation 109 n. 56
sola fide 93
sola scriptura 93
soul:
and Aristotelianism 122 n. 8
and the devil 75
and dreams 90, 94–95, 96, 97, 98, 99, 100, 101, 102, 103, 105, 107
and ghosts 55, 60
out of body experiences 157
Soulié, Marguerite 130, 133
source tagging 6, 60, 134–37, 137–38, 159
see also decoupling; procedural expressions
Sperber, Dan 56, 58–59, 62–63, 113, 135, 159
spirit 83, 102, 103, 104
spirits *see* demonology; ghosts
spiritualist churches 46
Spolsky, Ellen 172
Sponde, Jean de 131
Stephens, Walter 55, 83
stipulated pretence 10, 11, 12, 14 n. 20, 151, 152, 153, 158, 162 n. 41, 174–75
superstitious beliefs 39
Synesius 90, 91, 98, 100, 102–03, 104, 105, 106–07

tagging *see* authorial tagging; source tagging
Taylor, Shelley E. 44
tempestarii 78
Theory of Mind 61, 84 n. 12, 112, 134, 136
Thomas, Keith 68 n. 1
thought insertion 39–41, 46, 49 n. 12, 50 n. 40
Tooby, John 134–36, 137, 138
totentanz 171, 177
trompe l'oeil 165, 166, 172, 177 n. 10

Uduk people 57
unrealistic optimism 44

vain embrace trope 61
Valladier, André 64
vapours 76, 77, 78, 79, 86 n. 42, 158
Vergil *see* Virgil
veridical dreams *see* prophecies
Vesalius 74, 77, 86 n. 40
Virgil:
Aeneid 61–62, 68 n. 18, 130, 131
Georgics 27
visions 2, 10–11, 28–29, 72, 78, 81, 97, 98, 102, 105, 106
d'Aubigné, *Les Tragiques* 125, 130, 131, 132, 133, 134, 135, 136, 137, 140, 141
Descartes 115, 116
divine 93, 94, 95, 99, 100, 101

Doni, *I Mondi* 148, 149
and ghosts 55
see also dreams and dreaming; prophecies

Wakefield, Jerome C. 36 n. 51
Walton, Kendall 5, 179 n. 42
wandering mind 11, 81–82
Weaver, Elissa B. 32 n. 7, 35 n. 45
wellbeing 38, 46, 47–48
Wells, Marion A. 34 n. 24
werewolves 72
Weyer, Johann 72–73, 76–78, 79, 82, 83, 86 nn. 40 & 41 & 42, 88 n. 75, 93–94
Williams, William Carlos 169

Wilson, Deirdre 58–59, 62–63, 113, 122 n. 13
Wind, Edgar 13 n. 15
witches 4, 49 n. 21, 66, 72, 75, 76, 81, 160 n. 11
    Kramer's theory of demonic illusion 73, 75, 83
    lycanthropy 82
    male 76
    tempestarii 78
    and wandering mind 82–83
    Weyer's theory of demonic illusion 76, 78, 86 nn. 41 & 42 & 45, 93–94
writing, cryptographic 169

zombie concept 61, 62
Zunshine, Lisa 134, 136

www.ingramcontent.com/pod-product-compliance
Lightning Source LLC
LaVergne TN
LVHW061251060426
835507LV00017B/2018